A HISTORY OF ELIZABETHAN DRAMA

VOLUME 4

SHAKESPEARE

AND ELIZABETHAN POETRY

D1428487

A HISTORY OF ELIZABETHAN DRAMA
BY M. C. BRADBROOK

Volumes in the Series

These six books give a continuous history of Elizabethan drama; three are general books and three are on Shakespeare. The first two, *Themes and Conventions of Elizabethan Tragedy* and *The Growth and Structure of Elizabethan Comedy*, deal with the genres of tragedy and comedy, establishing the different kinds of drama as they developed between 1576 and 1642, with a close study of leading playwrights. The third, *The Rise of the Common Player*, deals with the social history of the playhouses and the actors, their relations with court and city. All three books were the first of their kind.

The study of Shakespeare in *Shakespeare and Elizabethan Poetry* is limited to the sixteenth century, and explores the connexion with the general poetic developments of that time. *Shakespeare the Craftsman* concentrates upon the crucial years at the turn of the century, when the drama established a lead over all other poetic genres, and when Shakespeare's own development was at its most intensive; the period culminates in *Hamlet*. *The Living Monument* deals with the Jacobean Shakespeare, his tragedies and final plays, against a background of the general development of theatrical art, including the court masque.

These books present a coherent account of the greatest period of English dramatic history, on a scale larger than any other history at present available: the emphasis throughout is on poetry seen in its social context. The series will be especially useful to students of English literature, drama or social history.

All these volumes are available in paperback from Cambridge University Press, either as a cased set or individually: some of them may also be purchased in hard covers – Volumes 1 and 6 from Cambridge University Press, and Volumes 2 and 3 from Chatto and Windus.

SHAKESPEARE
AND ELIZABETHAN POETRY

*A Study of his earlier work in
relation to the poetry of the time*

M. C. BRADBROOK

*Professor Emerita of English
in the University of Cambridge
and Fellow of Girton College*

CAMBRIDGE UNIVERSITY PRESS

CAMBRIDGE

LONDON · NEW YORK · MELBOURNE

CAMBRIDGE UNIVERSITY PRESS
Cambridge, New York, Melbourne, Madrid, Cape Town,
Singapore, São Paulo, Delhi, Tokyo, Mexico City

Cambridge University Press
The Edinburgh Building, Cambridge CB2 8RU, UK

Published in the United States of America by Cambridge University Press, New York

www.cambridge.org
Information on this title: www.cambridge.org/9780521295284

First published by Chatto & Windus Ltd 1951
Reprinted 1961, 1965
First published by Cambridge University Press in paperback 1979
Re-issued 2011

A catalogue record for this publication is available from the British Library

ISBN 978-0-521-29528-4 Paperback

Contents

Plates

Preface

IN the following pages I have attempted to survey a vast field, which I could not possibly hope to cover, and to touch on a vast number of issues, political, religious and artistic on which I have few qualifications to speak. I have ventured because it seemed that there was an urgent need for something of the old-fashioned Victorian attempt to give a comprehensive account of a great subject, although the growth and growing specialization of modern research means that such a task can be attempted only by the foolhardy. Shakespeare's plays and poems and their relation to the poetry and life of his age is a subject which can claim to interest many who are not literary specialists. I hope that what I have written may give them some picture, however rough and crude, of the general tendency of critical thought on these subjects, and that the specialists may find enough to annotate, amend or simply to cross out, to repay them for reading a good deal that is familiar, in a more qualified and scholarly form, from the works of others or from their own.

My indebtedness is wide in matters of detail: I have been a constant but I hope neither an unconscious nor an unacknow-ledging debtor. Some of the writers who have helped me most are those from whom I found myself dissenting. Part of this book was thought out in the nineteen-thirties; some of my conclusions have been reached independently of work published since from which I may seem to borrow. The war years and other duties have intervened; but the work as it now stands was written in the summer of 1949. In places I have endorsed earlier works of my own and in others I have contra-dicted them, without troubling the reader with references or explanations. Had the times permitted a more leisurely and well-digested study I should have preferred to give more time to the subject, which indeed provides material enough for several re-incarnations; but if a subject cannot be pursued unremittingly—and this, under modern conditions, is scarcely possible—it becomes stale. I have therefore preferred something in the nature of an interim report; something also in the nature of a kite-balloon. If I have helped to pull the question together for reconsideration by others better qualified than myself, there could be no clearer justification either for my platitudes or my howlers.

CHAPTER I

INTRODUCTION—MEDIEVAL AND MODERN

The Medieval synthesis—allegory and symbolism in Medieval and Renaissance thought—the transition in England

THERE is a good deal of uncertainty about the date which may be most fittingly selected to celebrate the start of Modern Times. The English historian tends to put a stop to the Middle Ages at 1485, with the accession of the first Tudor, Henry VII. The literary historian might date it from the sack of Constantinople, the American historian from the voyage of Columbus: the Russian historian would push it forward to the reign of Peter the Great at the end of the seventeenth century, which is when his modern history officially begins.

The Middle Ages began to die in England, perhaps, with the end of Richard II's reign, in 1399, and did not finally expire till the accession of Charles II in 1660. These two hundred and fifty years which saw the Reformation, the Great English Vowel Change, the rise of modern science and of the modern state, saw the slow decline of what might be called the medieval world picture. I do not think Dr. Tillyard would disagree[1] if I were to say that there is *no* Elizabethan world picture. There are at least two pictures superimposed upon each other, one fading, the other emerging. Hence the peculiar complexity and the fascination of that age.

The medieval world was a unity. The cosmography was known: the territory of human knowledge was known—it was not a world in which discovery in the modern sense was possible. Even Francis Bacon could take all knowledge for his province, not to be developed so much as to be mastered. The great international Civil Service provided by the Church might be split with the kind of quarrels not unknown between

1

various departments of the modern Civil Service, but it ran diplomacy, the local health services, the old-age pension scheme, and to a large extent it controlled the Treasury. There was one really international language, Latin, and to a much more limited extent an international code of manners for the profession of arms. Perhaps the unity is far less—and certainly it is far less simple—than it looks from the vantage-point of Modern Times: but compared with anything that has been known since, it is enviable.

The dominance of the Church in the intellectual life of the Middle Ages meant that all knowledge was subsumed under Theology, Queen of the Sciences. History reflected the purpose of God, Science demonstrated His creative plan, and the world of man and nature formed a whole, dominated by its Final Cause. Allegory could relate the grandest truths in the humblest terms, symbolism could see in the meanest forms the embodiment of eternal power and love. The seven deadly sins put on flesh and walked the streets of Langland's London, whilst Christ appeared in the outward lineaments of a good workman, Piers the Plowman.

Because the unity of this system is so different from anything that can now be achieved, we tend to think of it as stable and fixed and agreed upon. But it was not. Theology was in certain fields tentative; heretics were often treated with human tact if they were not likely to stir up public disturbance; there was such local autonomy that the Church in Iceland, for instance, not only retained a married clergy but conducted its own canonizations![2]

Medieval Theology may appear at first sight heavily argumentative. The haggling and logic-chopping of the schools is distasteful and seems perverse. But these men had no other means of exploring the world than by ratiocination: their brains were their only capital. The establishment of reason as formal cause was bound to lead to those laborious and elaborate methods which medieval disputation provided. Such habits penetrated and established themselves in regions of life other than the purely religious. Probably the most powerful and persistent of the medieval achievements can be seen in our modern legal system, which was so largely shaped in these centuries and partly shaped by clerks trained in theological discipline. The system emerged as the result of hundreds of years' work; and it did not emerge as a set code, but a living organism. The magnificent inheritance of the English Common Law—untidy, tribal, flexible, capable of growth and mutation—was the product of earlier times, transmitted through the hands of the supposedly codified, inflexible and Byzantine Middle Ages. Even Byzantium itself, that garrison outpost of Christianity, is now thought by historians far less petrified in its customs and thought than previous generations had supposed.

To an age like ours, the Middle Ages are particularly fascinating. Their integration of thought and life appeals to us because it is so different from what we know: on the other hand, recent experiences of violence, bestiality and tyranny have enabled us to understand the dark side of the picture better than our fathers or grandfathers could do. To them, the murder of hostages, the systematic torture of those guilty of no more criminal offence than being born of an accursed race, and the fear of a complete submergence of civilized life, were old unhappy far-off things.

The violence of the Middle Ages—which explains why tolerance operated only in so limited a field—is complementary to its strictness of rational control. This is something quite as alien to us as to our fathers. The physical filth and dirt and the personal vengeances of Dante's Hell are not stronger than the discipline which ranks them all in intellectually regulated degrees of damnation. There is an absolute cleavage between human values and eternal values, which is most poignantly illustrated when Dante encounters his friend and master Brunetto Latini on the circle of the burning sand. Dante's love for Brunetto, still so true and strong, does not lead him to question the fate of the sinner, or even to lament it.

The medieval conception of theological issues is in general too legal for modern minds. The Atonement became a

judicial transaction, Christ paying the fine which Divine
Justice demanded of man. Mercy and Justice were opposites,
not complementary.

Theology took some colouring from forensic methods as
well as from legal concepts: Abaillard's *Sic et Non* set a model
for disputation which was that of the legal debate. In such a
work as Langland's *Piers the Plowman*, shapeless and confused
as it has long appeared, a pattern can be discerned if it is seen
as a mixed work, theological-sociological, but with the
emphasis on the theology. It embodies much scholastic dispute
transmuted into literary form[3] and its method is often that of
debate, or question and answer. The significance of this
poem—and of the fourteenth-century mystic writers who lie
behind it—consists in the fact that it contains, as in a matrix,
all the difficulties and problems which confronted the writer—
religious, social and personal. These are all worked out
together. As well as being concerned with society, Langland,
like the mystics, is concerned with the problem of the individual, with what would now be called his psychology. He
had not the scientific terminology of a modern writer, but he
had both skill and understanding in the exploration of the
inner life. And once such exploration has begun, the picture
of the universe is bound to lose something of its firm out-
line. For each individual has his private view of the common
world, and this, the introspective religious is not slow to
discover.

Therefore, though Langland approaches the problem of
man in general as a single problem—that of the *condition
humaine*—he does not find the unity for which he sought and
which he presupposed: his anguish lies precisely in that he
does not find it. The later fourteenth century sensed impend-
ing change; Langland knew that there was a storm, social and
religious, in the offing.

If Dante is taken as the representative Medieval Man,
Langland may be considered the representative of medieval
England; but he lived two generations later than Dante, and
had no longer full security of belief. Yet the exploration of

the inner life was still conducted under the guidance of certitudes such as no modern mind can assume.

Ille.   We have lit upon the gentle, sensitive mind,
        And lost the old nonchalance of the hand;
        Whether we have chosen chisel, pen or brush,
        We are but critics or but half create,
        Timid, entangled, empty and abashed,
        Lacking the countenance of our friends.

Hic.   And yet
        The chief imagination of Christendom,
        Dante Alighieri, so utterly found himself,
        That he has made that hollow face of his
        More plain to the mind's eye than any face
        But that of Christ.

Ille.   . . . He set his chisel to the hardest stone.
        Being mocked by Guido for his lecherous life,
        Derided and deriding, driven out
        To climb that stair and eat that bitter bread,
        He found the unpersuadable justice, he found
        The most exalted lady loved by a man.[4]

Both Dante and Langland had a vision of the eternal things which dominated their vision of the world, though in Langland's case it did not unify it. And Langland is the last medieval poet in England. By the end of the century, lyrics of the Passion show the gradual transformation of the Son of God into the Son of Mary, the gradual increase of emphasis upon the human pain, the physical weakness, the personal appeal from one Man to another instead of the transcendant offer of All for nothing. This change can be more strikingly seen in the pictorial art of the period, as Professor Huitzinga[5] clearly established. Indeed the later medieval Flemish pictures of the sufferings of Christ are too clearly born of the world of human violence—the world of the Jacquerie—to be tolerable to our modern taste. We cannot look at them without a sense that there must have been a perverted gloating over the sufferings—that insensibility could not have been so great as to make this kind of representational art necessary. Yet the common habits of the day were such as to render it quite possible.[6]

An excellent example of transition is provided in Froissart's account of the Burghers of Calais. The speech of Eustace de St. Pierre, the first of the volunteers, who says eloquently that he hopes God will show mercy to him if he is willing to die for his friends, is surpassed by that of the second volunteer who simply rises and says, 'I will keep company with my gossip Eustace'. Their reception by the angry King Edward who looked 'felly' on them, and ordered their instant execution, the appeal of the Queen 'for the honour of the Virgin Mary and the love of me', is what might be expected from the medieval codes of war and of religion: the response of the King—'Ah, Dame, I would ye had been as now in some other place', belongs to no code save that prevailing at all times between husbands and wives. Froissart in his version of the story shows a lively sense of the dramatic possibilities of contrast which conquers a diplomatic sense of decorum, of what it is 'proper' to make a king say. Edward's grandson and successor, Richard of Bordeaux, is the first English King of whom we possess an authentic personal likeness, a portrait in the modern sense, as distinct from a formal kingly effigy. The two facts are perhaps not unrelated.

II

The medieval student began his study of Theology, the Queen of the Sciences, by learning to read and comment upon the scriptures and the fathers. The Bible was the great set book of the medieval university, and its study provided the basis of the student's training. Any habits which he formed in such reading became the common literary habits of the time[7] and have therefore a general literary significance for the understanding of the medieval world.

The most striking feature of *divina lectura* is its use of allegory to explain and correlate the work into a whole. Every passage had a fourfold interpretation—its literal, moral, anagogical and tropical meaning. Indeed, sevenfold meanings had been propounded. The method was necessary if unity were to be achieved. The history of the Jews afforded plenty of unedifying stories, the New Testament provided in *Revelations* one of the most fruitful allegories; by this means the episode of David and Bethsabe could be made 'doctrinal',[8] and Jewish apocalyptic literature given a topical significance.

The allegorical method spread to every type of literature, and to other departments of life than the literary. *Ovid Moralisé*, the compilation of a thirteenth-century monk, permitted piety to extract useful instruction from the scandalous tales of the *Metamorphoses*. Natural science, art, even clothes and colours, numbers and hours of the day took on a special significance. The whole world became one vast allegory of God's writing, interlocking and coherant.[9] In detail, there might be disputes. But the whole world system was governed by three assumptions: it was allegorical, it was hierarchical and it was mutable.

Nature was allegorical down to the least detail. Biblical meanings were provided by the popular bestiaries for the scapegoat, the birds of Noah's ark, the Agnus Dei and the Dove. Classical fables of the Phoenix and the Unicorn typified the Resurrection or Incarnation. Legends about animals were given appropriate meaning:[10] plants and stones had their own significances: the stars, the seasons, the colours of the world, jewels, metals, parts of the human body, the signs of the zodiac were all carriers of heavy moral significance.

Nature was also hierarchical. The lion, king of beasts, and the eagle, king of birds, were given characteristics which no real lion or eagle could be expected to possess.[11] A familiarity with dogs did not prevent the student from ascribing the habits of Aesop's dogs to the whole canine creation. As animals were ranked in a fixed order of nobility, so there were base and noble metals; there were higher and lower degrees throughout all creation. And all these hierarchies were or could be interrelated.[12] The whole depended, in the image which Professor Lovejoy has made familiar once again, on the great chain of being descending from God.

Man, as he was organized in society, imitated the ordered and harmonious world of Nature in degree. Heraldry, which began as a necessity of the battlefield, utilized the marvels of the bestiaries. The lion of England, Richard II's badges of the hart, the sunburst and the broompod, appear linked to his devotional piety in the elaborately symbolic beauty of the Wilton Diptych.[13]   In the later part of the Middle Ages every part of a cathedral, as well as the vestments of the clergy, had ideally its symbolical meaning. The different parts of a knight's armour had their significance. Secular history was composed of characters like the Nine Worthies and the Seven Champions of Christendom.

Yet the whole universe, ordered and significant as it was down to its smallest part, was subject to mutability and in a constant state of flux and decay. The parts were for ever dying and being renewed: stability resided only in the relationship and correspondences existing between the various elements, and not in the elements themselves. There was a permanent connexion for example, between the twelve signs of the zodiac, and the twelve divisions of the human body, though all human bodies were in an incipient state of dissolution: between the Microcosm and the Macrocosm: between the human body, the Body Politic and the Church, which was the Body of Christ.

The complete synthesis of course never existed. But it was always held to be possible; and presumably to exist in the mind of the Creator. There was no great demand for consistency. As the Marxists believe that the course of history is economically determined in its basic design, but allow for the play of subsidiary factors in the shaping of particular situations, so the medieval philosopher or artist would allow a variety of interpretations, or even two or three mutually incompatible interpretations, to exist side by side. If his 'authorities' differed he would not have been disconcerted, but would have tried in some way to reconcile or justify them all.

Nor did the 'inner' meaning supersede the 'outer' meaning. All meanings were true, on their different levels.[14] The essential point was that Nature, being the Art of God, was both Many and One, and that all the meanings of a symbol were necessary to an understanding of the fact in its universal implications. Nevertheless, the assumption of correspondences could lead into the parody of deductive logic with which Francisco Sizzi tried to controvert Galileo on the existence of the satellites of Jupiter.

'There are seven windows in the head, two nostrils, two eyes, two ears, and a mouth: so in the heavens there are two favourable stars, two impropitious, and Mercury alone undecided or indifferent. From which, and many other similar phenomena of nature, such as the seven metals, etc., which it were tedious to enumerate, we gather that the number of the planets is necessarily seven'.[15]

As a method of conducting scientific inquiry, the allegorical and hierarchical method was slow to be superseded. It was not always barren. Kepler believed that the universe figured the Trinity, the Sun representing the First Person, the Fixed Stars the Second, and the Planets the Third, whilst the layout of the universe corresponded with the five regular solids. 'It was in quest of the verification of this wholly fanciful hypothesis that Kepler discovered the third law of planetary motion'.[16] Even Francis Bacon, though he is inclined to throw out final causes as the explanation of why animals are made as they are, ('well enquired and collected in metaphysic, but in physic they are impertinent'), yet retains three of the fourfold ways of reading the Scriptures.[17]

III

It was in Italy, and particularly in the Platonic Academy at Florence, that a new and secular doctrine of the world grew up, to nourish the great artists and poets of the Renaissance. The art of the new age relied on a blending of the natural with the traditional. Botticelli's symbolism was old, his anatomical studies were new. In those Hymns to Heavenly Love and Beauty, the Primavera and the Birth of Venus, the design is based on the iconography of Annunciation and the Baptism,[18] and the allegorical meaning may have been of an elevated Platonic kind; but if the end was to delight the eye and thereby lift the mind to virtue, the delight of the eye had become in itself a goodly thing.

Botticelli's master Ficino was also the master of Pico della Mirandola, who may be set in contrast with Dante, as the type and example of Renaissance Man contrasted with Medieval Man. Born about a hundred years later than Dante, Pico found that the Arabian and Chaldee writings and the Kabbala provided a surer means to the study of divinity than the traditional works of the fathers. Whilst he was still medievalist enough to take all knowledge for his province, and offer to dispute, under nine hundred questions, of all things known, he was, like Faustus in the legend, a believer in magic as the shortest route to all knowledge, human and divine.[19] This young prodigy, who astounded France and Italy with the breadth of his learning, ended his short life a convert and a penitent, prepared to walk barefoot through the world preaching; but even in his conversion there could have been no return to the earlier world. Dante had known the unity of all knowledge; the systematic theology of St. Thomas Aquinas held together his whole universe, and Aristotle was undisputed master of those who know.[20] The Platonists believed that the Ancients had left a body of secret knowledge —not moral precepts or ethic doctrine but knowledge of the secrets of nature. This secret wisdom was transmitted through their mythology.[21] Hence the stories of old gods became keys to a holy mystery, which was not to be revealed unto the vulgar. But there were no fixed codes of interpretation. Ficino, the master of Botticelli and of Pico, is explicit about this:

Just as the Christian theologians find four senses in the sacred word, the literal and moral, the anagogical and the allegorical, and follow up the one in one passage and the other mainly in another, so have the Platonists four modes of multiplying the Gods and spirits and they apply a different mode of multiplication in different places as it is fitting. I too in my commentaries am used to interpret and distinguish the deities differently as the context requires.[22]

Knowledge was not fixed; neither was the nature and destiny of mankind. Above all, in his ability to detach himself from the base world below him, man grew in the *capacity* of the soul. In himself, according to Pico, man has 'the germ of every form of life' so that 'whatsoever seeds man cultivates, these seeds will grow to maturity and bear in him their own fruit'.

The magic knowledge of the ancients, and the capacity to determine his own future, gave to the New Man a dangerous freedom, which Marlowe depicted in his tragedy of *Faust*. This power of self-determination received its most splendid formulation in Pico's treatise, *On the Dignity of Man*. Here God, addressing His creature, says:

The nature of all other things is limited and constrained within the bounds of laws prescribed by me: thou, coerced by no necessity, shalt ordain for thyself the limits of thy nature, in accordance with thy own free will, in whose hand I have placed thee. I have set thee at the world's centre, that thou mayest from thence observe more easily what is in the world. I have made thee neither of heaven nor of earth, neither mortal nor immortal, so that thou mayest with greater freedom of choice and with more honour, as though the maker and moulder of thyself, fashion thyself in whatsoever form thou shalt prefer. Thou shalt have the power to degenerate into the lower forms of life, which are animal; thou shalt have the power, out of thy soul's judgment, to be reborn into the higher forms of life, which are divine.[23]

It was in his dynamic capacity for growth and change that man exceeded even those creatures superior to him in the order of creation, the angels in their various hierarchies. The dangerous gift of choice had been planted in him from the beginning. Such a speech, in Dante, could have come only from the lips of a heathen like Ulysses.

In his attempt to formulate a synthesis of the ancients, the fathers and the great heretical schools of Arabia and the East, Pico stood alone. He saw all these as symbolic and finite reflections of truths which could never be distinctly formulated; but instead of rejecting most of them, he embraced most of them, and was hence with difficulty rescued from the charge of heresy. Indeed the belief in the plurality of worlds for which that later Platonist, Sidney's friend, Bruno, went to the stake, was less fundamentally dangerous than Pico's. He was not advocating any mere system of tolerance: each moment of history and each individual human being was a new start, established new relations with and within the total order of things. The freedom of the individual man establishes a general principle of indeterminacy.[24]

The unity of Dante's world did not involve any rejections. The pattern which Dante imposes on his experience is a hierarchic one, but the basis of his experience is cold fact. It would now be generally agreed, I believe, that he begins with life in the raw. In the great synthesis of the *Vita Nuova* and the *Divina Commedia*, Dante, holding fast to the choice which had been for him at once inevitable ('Ego dominus tuus,' Love had said, the Lord of terrible aspect), and the supreme exercise of choice, had found that through the successive phases of his love for Beatrice he had reached a knowledge of the eternal things. He learnt to walk the circles of Hell and climb the stairs of Purgatory and gaze upon the great white rose of the redeemed multitudes through the seed that was sowed by his meeting with a little girl when he was nine years old.

For the Platonists, Beauty was a rare and fleeting visitant of the earth. The child or the common multitude could have no glimpse of the Heavenly Venus, as they could have no knowledge of the secret wisdom of the ancients. Life had become more exciting, more indetermined, only for the few. The new Platonic Science was essentially aristocratic in its conception.

Unity of belief was no longer an acceptable ideal for the explorer of the new age. He must in fact become many-sided, and learn to live in separate and divided worlds, or to reject the lowest, without any hope of establishing a bridge from the lowest to the highest. What most notably remained was the desire for some formality, some synthesis, some unity of *living*. The courtier or many-sided man was perhaps attempting to salvage, in one of a few self-conscious and selected beings, the power to see life steadily and see it whole. The continuity of the older hierarchical view had been broken. Light was now diffused from above: man, proud man, trusting firmly in his godlike reason,[25] had to raise himself above a world which was not simply fallen, but essentially base. Pico della Mirandola's interpretation of the fable of Circe will illustrate the distinction:

There was sometime (in Aenea) a woman called Circe, which by enchantment, as Virgil makes mention, used with a drink to turn as many men as received it into divers likenesses and figures of sundry beasts, some into lions, some into bears, some into swine, some into wolves, which afterwards walked ever tame about her house and waited on her in such use or service as she list to put unto them. In likewise the flesh changeth us from the figure of reasonable men into the likeness of unreasonable beasts, and that diversely after the convenience and similitude between our sensual affections and the brutish properties of sundry beasts—as the proud-hearted man into a lion, the irous into a bear, the lecherous into a goat, the drunken glutton into a swine, the ravenous extortioner into a wolf, the false deceiver into a fox, the mocking jester into an ape. From which beastly shape may we never be restored again to our own likeness unto the time we have again cast up the drink of the bodily affections by which we were into those figures enchanted.[26]

Here are not only the transformed monsters of *The Faerie Queene*, but the animal shapes of Jonson's *Volpone*, Middleton's *Changeling* and perhaps of Milton's *Comus*. The universe has become, so to speak, a one-way-traffic system. Because they were so particularly conscious of the Flesh, the men of the Renaissance were more stern than their immediate predecessors. The need to illuminate, control and irradiate became imperative. The poets of the fourteenth century might discover in the figure of a girl the force which moved the sun and the other stars, or in the figure of an ordinary English labouring man the lineaments of Christ. Those who tasted the sceptical thought of the 'new philosophy' or enjoyed the sheer physical riches of the new courtly mode of life, and the sensuous riches which the arts provided for great men, felt an overwhelming need to master the flesh before Circe's cup transformed them.

IV

During the fifteenth century England was held back in the realm of the arts by the political uncertainties of the times. But though the emergence of poetry and drama from the pit of the fifteenth century was slow—and it is really only the most hopeful of literary historians who pretend that these 'seed-times' are full of neglected beauties—and though the start made under Henry VIII was checked by other religious and political difficulties during the mid-Tudor period, the reign of Elizabeth was not a continuation of the later Middle Ages. Some modes of thought survived and our new interest in the Middle Ages makes it natural for us to rediscover them with pleasure. But the differences are as important as the likenesses, since they make up the rich and fecund welter of Elizabethan life, thought, and language.

For example the hierarchical structure of the Tudor State was something which no medievalist would have tolerated, though the principle of hierarchy itself would be familiar. The image of the hive—the singing masons building roofs of gold—which is used so tellingly by Shakespeare in *Henry V* is an old image applied to a new purpose. Hooker, the historian of the Elizabethan church settlement, may set forth a conception of the order of things which is anti-Machiavellian, but it is pro-Marsilio,[27] and Marsilio could not be selected as exactly typical of medieval thought upon the functions of church and state.   Religious and political issues had not yet been separated, as scientific and moral issues had not yet been distinguished: the physician Cardanus wrote a book of consolation, cast the horoscope of Edward VI (which turned out all wrong) and of Jesus Christ (to test the efficacy of horoscopes, as he said: but he was nearly prosecuted for blasphemy). Elizabeth and her father created a new nobility, who employed old distinctions, such as those of heraldry, to new ends.   The businesslike insignia of the medieval fighting unit—revived in the modern divisional signs of the British Army—were used as part of the personal battle for Elizabeth's favour and the very substantial fruits of that favour[28] for which a courtier like Ralegh might hope.   He started as a poor Devonshire gentleman, but produced sixteen quarterings to his arms. Such a coat looked well in a tourney, but would not have served for identification in war.

In the realm of thought, the allegorical and symbolic modes which had represented the older picture of the universe were retained, but in a fragmentary and diversified form.[29]   The great impersonal symbols of the Church were applied to smaller things: Elizabeth borrowed from the cult of the Virgin,[30] but the cult of the Virgin had not grown up without reference to the system of which it formed a part.   As the Tudor gentlemen had built their fine new houses from the stones of the monasteries, so the Tudor writers built from the debris of the older traditions.   Ramus's combination of rhetoric and logic in his dialectic method was new, it was needed, and it made possible some of the greater triumphs of Elizabethan literature: but the notion of *argument* in the Ramist sense— that the relations which linked the whole hierarchic interlocking scheme of things entire could be established from *any* point of vantage—that you could start from anywhere— introduced a principle of instability.

An indication of the new standards is provided by the different way in which during the sixteenth century it was possible to be funny.   The medieval idea of being funny usually meant a straight burlesque: a feast of fools, Mak the Shepherd parodying the finding of the Christ Child in the Wakefield nativity play, Mère Sotte and her courts of injustice. This method survived in the Christmas games of Elizabeth's court but it was not the only way of being funny. The simple parody of an *accepted* institution which can be parodied only because it is not fundamentally to be questioned existed side by side with the much more sophisticated parody implicit in Shakespeare's 'My mistress' eyes are nothing like the sun'. The dark lady is not beautiful, but the poets, who describe their mistresses as being more beautiful than in truth they are, show a pitiful lack of wit and invention. This kind of parody depends on playing with an older, but not altogether discarded, mode of thought.

The mystical theory of numbers could in the thirteenth century produce an orthodox poem like *The Lily and its Five Leaves:*

> Ful feir flour is the lilie
> wid fif levis hire sal hulie:
> fif to beren hire is ful imunde,
> for that is hire propre cunde.
> that first betokenit charite
> to louen thin louer more than thee,
> vid word vid herte vid al thi mist,
> for that is treve loue arist. . . .[31]

The sacred significance of the lily's leaves is witness to the sacred symbolism behind all nature. This same use of sacred number is widely used by Dante to interpret the events of his life, and in particular the story of his love for Beatrice, which is ruled by re-occurrence of the sacred figures three and nine.

This medieval theory persisted throughout the fifteenth and sixteenth centuries: Elizabethan poetry can offer examples of the use of sacred numbers which are exactly parallel to the use made of them by the thirteenth-century poet and by Dante (for instance, there is the lengthy encomium on three and nine at the end of Drayton's *Endimion and Phoebe*). But on the other hand the tradition could be used in jest: it did not survive unquestioned. Donne, *Upon the Primrose*, is not writing in the manner of his predecessor, when he in his turn comments upon the five-leaved flower:

> Live, Primrose, then and thrive
> With thy true number, five;
> And women, whom this flower doth represent,
> With this mysterious number be content;
> Ten is the farthest number: if half ten
> Belong unto each woman, then
> Each woman may take half us men;
> Or if this will not serve their turn, since all
> Numbers are odd or even and they fall,
> First, into this, five, women may take us all.[32]

This is, however, no simple parody. Donne is using various symbols, a logical structure and an elaborate series of alternatives to intensify, while he laughs at, the power of women over men. The final effect is a kind of delighted suspension of the judgment in paradox.

It was not till late in the reign of Elizabeth that the Platonism of Ficino and Pico finally reached this country. It found root in the circle of Sir Philip Sidney, the work of Lodowick Bryskett and Matthew Roydon, Spenser and Drayton, Chapman and Henry Reynolds. Henry Reynolds's *Mythomystes* is probably the most thoroughgoing piece of Platonism in English. Nature is presented as the Hieroglyph of God, and Poetry as the only true key to the secrets of the ancients.

The Platonic view received its most splendid statement in Spenser's *Hymns*. But it remained comparatively uncongenial. For beside this view of Nature, there had grown up, at times entwined with it, a rival view of Nature as the great rich fecund unsystematic Cornucopia of God—one which might be called the Epicurean or Lucretian view, and to this the poets turned.

The history of thought behind the poetry of the fifteen-eighties and fifteen-nineties in England is largely one of a combat between the Platonic view and this newer Epicurean view, which eventually conquered. The story is partly told in Chapter IV.

CHAPTER II

THE ARTIFICE OF ETERNITY: THE COURTLY
POETRY OF THE SIXTEENTH CENTURY

*Queen Elizabeth and Court Poetry—Sidney and the
Petrarchan Sonnet—Spenser and festal poetry—'The
Phoenix and the Turtle'*

THE Court poetry of the early Elizabethans cannot be
understood without a sense of the life that was behind it,
and of which it formed a part. It is more than occasional
poetry in the modern sense; rather is it like a libretto, designed
expressly to be set to music, and specially framed at all points
to that end. In 'the music of men's lives', as Shakespeare
termed it, the arts were a determining power; but they in
turn were modified by their purpose. The moral significance
of painting, the echoing of themes between painting and
poetry, and the close relation of both to the pageantry of
court life, made up a kind of triple harmony in which each
part was fitted to the other as the verse, the picture and the
motto were fitted together in an emblem.

For some of the characters the world was indeed a stage.
Queen Elizabeth, the centre of all the poetry, the pageantry
and tributary arts, was worshipped under many different titles.
Spenser gave her two main roles and as many as five subsidiary
ones in *The Faerie Queene*.[1] The supreme Ruler of Church and
State formed a centre round which all other life moves. The
alternatives were inexhaustible. She appeared as Astraea,
the Virgin Goddess of Justice, who brings back the Golden
Age to earth, and is therefore also Goddess of the Spring:
as Cynthia or Diana, the Goddess of chastity and ruler of the
sea: in the zodiac she reigned as Virgo: finally she could
attract the epithets of the Virgin Mary: she was Rosa Electa,
Virgo Beata, crowned with the stars and with the globe under

her feet.[2]   The State Virgin was in turn mocked (and blasphemed, her adorers would have said) by the Catholic underground movement.

Her ladies, those lesser stars, were celebrated in like manner. The language of scripture itself might be adapted to their praise, as in this naïve versifying of the *Song of Songs:*

> Fair is my love that feeds among the lilies,
> The lilies growing in love's pleasant garden,
>   Where Cupid's mount that well-beloved hill is,
> And where that little god himself is warden.
>   See where my love sits in the beds of spices
> Beset all round with camphor, myrrh and roses,
>   And interlaced with curious devices,
> Which her from all the world apart encloses.[3]

There were indeed many medieval parallels to this use of the sacred page in worship of an earthly love.   The sonneteers of the court who adopted, even while they mocked at, the common forms of Petrarchan description, were in theory as Platonic in their devotion as the worshippers of Elizabeth were expected to be.   But with increasing skill and practice, their powers of description deepened, the 'Muses that sing love's sensual empery' intruded, and the quality of the writing changed.[4]

At the same time courtly poetry itself provided models for more philosophic poets, who in turn wrote Coronets of Sonnets for their mistress Philosophy, wresting the conventional language of love to transcendental themes.   In *Ovid's Banquet of Sense*, Chapman evoked a scene of extreme sensual delight only to reject the expected conclusions and to present his Ovid and Julia as models of Platonic chastity, who could extract all the delights of the senses without succumbing to their lure.

> Gentle and noble are their tempers framed
> That can be quicken'd with perfumes and sounds,
> And they are cripple-minded, gout-wit lamed,
> That lie like fire-fit blocks, dead without wounds,
> Stirred up with nought but hell-descending gain . . .

Sweet sounds and odours are the heaven on earth
Where virtues live. . . .

(*xxxv–xxxvi.* [5])

The courtly poets, like all other poets of the time, were presented with a bewildering variety of symbols from which they must make their choice. In addition to all the grand public imagery of Elizabeth as a goddess, there was the familiar imagery of her private circle, based partly on heraldry and partly on nicknames.[6] It is this kind of code perhaps which is behind the beast fables of Spenser, such as the February and March *Eclogues, Mother Hubbard's Tale* and *Muiopotmos.*[7] The great pageantry of Spenser's verse provides the fullest triumph of courtly style: but the Queen was also celebrated by Ralegh's *Cynthia,* Barnfield's *Cynthia,* Chapman's *Hymns,* John Davies the lawyer's *Hymn to Astraea.* At the very end of his career, the greatest of her poets also looks back, and in the magnificent vision of Elizabeth which closes the play of *Henry VIII,* Shakespeare recalls, not merely a great queen, but a world and a way of life which had centred in her. This play sums up his recollections of Elizabethan poetry and the lessons which it had for the young poet, his earlier self. The drama opens with a speech of lament and farewell from Buckingham: that Buckingham, whose father appears as the first of the lamenting ghosts in *The Mirror for Magistrates,* the great storehouse of early Elizabethan tragic story.[8] The fall of Buckingham, told by himself, would set the mind of the attentive spectator back to that earlier age and prepare his mind for the theme of the play, which is the old one of fortune's mutability. Then, when the sad procession of Buckingham, Katherine and Wolsey is over, comes the vision of a new life, the restoration of a golden age. In the birth of Elizabeth, the Heaven-sent Infant, we witness the Descent of Astraea. All the full splendours of Vergil's greatest *Eclogue*[9] are invoked in the images of fertility, the patriotic and religious implications that deck the appearance of this wondrous creature. 'Iam redit et virgo, redeunt Saturnia regna. . . .'

She shall be . . . .
A Patterne to all Princes liuing with her,
And all that shall succeed: *Saba* was neuer
More couetous of Wisdome and faire Vertue
Then this pure Soule shall be.   All Princely Graces
That mould up such a mighty Piece as this is,
With all the Vertues that attend the good,
Shall still be doubled on her.
Truth shall nurse her,
Holy and Heauenly thoughts still Counsell her:
She shall be lou'd and fear'd.   Her owne shall blesse her:
Her Foes shake like a field of beaten Corne,
And hang their heads with sorrow.
Good growes with her.
In her dayes, Euery Man shall eate in safety,
Under his owne Vine what he plants: and sing
The merry Songs of Peace to all his Neighbours.
God shall be truly knowne and those about her
From her shall read the perfect way of Honour
And by those claim their greatnesse, not by Blood
                                                  (5. 5. 23–39.)

This passage presents the peculiar stability and sense of coher-
ence which emerged from the welter of attributes ascribed
to Elizabeth.   She was no lay figure on which compliments
could be draped.   The precarious but irresistible potency
which resides in a person used as a symbol enabled the remains
of old medieval traditions, and the accretions of new learning,
to hold together.

In our time we have seen this personal power in the state
mightily abused, but for that very reason we are not likely to
underrate it as a force of unity and a spring of devotion.
Shakespeare was not a court poet, and in his earlier writing
courtly life and the great political themes were treated
separately, the one in his comedies, the other in his histories.
There can be no doubt however that he learnt much from
courtly poetry, and here, looking back from a vantage-point
of distance, he pays his tribute.   The Golden Age was by then
in the past.   *Terras Astraea reliquit.*[10]

II

Not the whole of Elizabeth's reign could be celebrated as a poetic Golden Age. The early years were barren except for the few scattered song-books, the snowdrops of the time. The shadow of religious and political controversies did not lift quickly. But spring came suddenly in the fourth quarter of the century. Sidney, Spenser, Ralegh, Lyly all enriched the eighties with their lyrics. The difference between this generation and the earlier one of Gascoigne and Turberville is overwhelming. But their poetic achievement was in one kind: it is closely connected with the arts of courtship and the art of living: it is personal in its setting, but also, in the best sense, artificial. Personal relations were not the real subject, though often the ostensible one. Poets were concerned with education, civilization, with a mode of behaviour and a pattern half-moral, half-aesthetic. The Petrarchan tradition enabled the poet to control, manipulate and deal with his subject-matter. His difficult job of learning to be a perfect courtier called for strict discipline, for the ideal was ethical as well as gracious; and Sidney was a graver character than Castiglione's Courtier, upon whom he modelled himself. Nevertheless, Castiglione's great passage in praise of love provided the whole age with its creed.[11]

In Sidney the Elizabethan gentleman recognized his model: in life and in literature Sidney provided the age with that heroism, gaiety, strength and sobriety which it demanded of the perfect courtier, the many-sided man. His literary work is therefore of particular significance both in itself, and for what it represented.

Sidney himself repudiates Petrarch and the conceits of his school:

> You that poor Petrarch's long-deceased woes
> With new-borne sighs and disguised wit do sing:
> You take wrong wayes: those far-fet helps be such
> As do bewray a want of inward tuch
>
> *(Astrophel and Stella, xv.)*

His friends dutifully repeated his repudiation whilst he, and they, made free use of the conceits they affect to despise.[12] Before writing Sidney down a hypocrite, it should be recognized that he was not merely appropriating those conceits, but using them as *arguments* in the Ramist sense—means of establishing relationships between different and divided worlds. The need was to connect, to make all life 'harmonious'— always the highest term of praise. Petrarchan love was both something more than a disguise for the natural feelings and something more than a storehouse of images. The need to control and prune the natural feelings was recognized, and the strongest of the instincts offered the boldest challenge. If Mephistopheles had intruded into the Petrarchan world, as he did into the Forest and Cavern scene of Goethe, turning a holy thought into a dirty joke, the courtier would not have been shocked, but merely irritated. The devil would be guilty of no more than a social solecism. The world of amatory intrigue was not relevant to what was being discussed: the fact that it was there did not prejudice the situation. The Petrarchans provided a standard which was an absolute, therefore inhuman one; it was not priggish, because not ignorant or condemnatory of Nature; but it was none the less aristocratic and heroically competitive.

To respond to Beauty yet to retain the power of surmounting Circe's charm was the mark of true nobility. Marlowe puts the creed into the mouth of his Tamburlaine, meditating on the sufferings which Beauty can inflict in the form of Desire:

I thus conceiuing and subduing both
That which hath stoopt the tempest of the Gods,
Euen from the fiery spangled vaile of heauen,
To feel the louely warmth of shepherds flames,
And martch in cottages of strowed weeds,
Shall giue the world to note, for all my birth
That Vertue solely is the sum of glorie,
And fashions men with true nobility
(*Tamburlaine*, Pt. I 5.2 [18].)

This same Platonic Love was celebrated in their several

fashions by Botticelli and Spenser under the figure of the
Heavenly Venus.

It is an ancient and two-edged method of combating the
devil to use his own weapons. The Magnificence which was
the supreme virtue of a Prince or Ruler must be utilized for
the development of self-knowledge, self-control and the four
imperial virtues. His mind's natural response to Beauty was
a first step in the development of the Magnificent or Magnanimous man, calling out all his best qualities. Hence, cultivation
of the arts and the clear embodiment of the heavenly Idea of
Beauty in the most persuasive physical terms became his duty.
The ruler or the courtier, appearing in the tourney as some
notable historic personage, writing a poem in which he described the tourney, presenting the poem to his lady accompanied by some suitable jewel or device[14]—in all these ways,
might educate himself in virtuous and gentle discipline. The
end of art was life, or action. The means were as varied as
could be devised: the greater their variety, the greater their
efficacy. All embodiments of the Idea must be transitory and
fleeting, as all were imperfect. The world was still unstable
and ruled by Mutabilitie, the terrifying Titaness, elder than
the gods.[15]

Moreover even the greatest man could never achieve in life
the noble vision which he saw in his mind's eye. Accidents,
the temporal rubs and hindrances of the world, would always
intervene.[16] But the transmutation of the impermanent and
fleeting into the permanent and eternal is the purpose of art.
'Those are pearls that were his eyes.' The more difficult the
climb from flesh to Idea, the greater the need that art should
assist and immortalize. The more impermanent the earthly
beauty which the courtly poet worshipped, the more passionate his hope that in his verse such beauty might for ever live.
Thus both the Platonic and Epicurean poets reached the same
conclusion. Spenser's *Visions* and Shakespeare's *Sonnets* are
alike in transposing that beauty which lives no longer than a
flower into 'the artifice of eternity'.

Such a search for the permanence of art could in fact spring

only from the depth of immediate need. Sidney's artificial
world is constructed upon genuine feeling. The imaginary
grief of Stella for some imaginary tale of love is delicately
mocked (in accents which Shakespeare may have remembered
in *Twelfth Night*)[17] and turned to a plea for pity.

> Stella oft sees the very face of woe
> Painted in my beclowded stormie face,
> But cannot skill to pitie my disgrace,
> Not though thereof the cause herself she knows:
> Yet hearing late a fable which did show
> Of louers neuer knowne, a grieuous case,
> Pitie therof gate in her breast such place,
> That, from that sea deriu'd, teares spring did flow.
> Alas, if Fancie, drawne by imaged things
> Though false, yet with free scope, more grace doth breed
> Than seruants wracke, where new doubts honor brings;
> Then thinke, my deare, that you in me doe read
> Of louers' ruine some sad tragedie.
> I am not I: pitie the tale of me
>   (*Astrophel and Stella*, xlv.)

If this seems to forecast Richard II requiring his queen to tell
'the lamentable tale of me', it should be offset against those
passages in which Sidney renounces all artifice.

> Because I breathe not loue to euery one,
> Nor do not use sette colours for to weare,
> Nor nourish special locks of vowed haire,
> Nor giue each speech a full point of a grone,
> The Courtly nymphs, acquainted with the mone
> Of them which in their lips loue's standard beare:
> What he! (say they of me): now, I dare sweare
> He cannot loue: no, no, let him alone
>   (liv.)

At the same time this renunciation of artifice is itself one of the
recognized gambits: Berowne, swearing by russet yeas and
honest kersey noes, and Benedick are equally skilled in 'dis-
claiming'. Like the Petrarchan phrase in which Petrarch's
methods are abjured, or the borrowed line which asserts

independence of all borrowing, passages of mock-simplicity demand recognition before their full subtlety can be extracted. On occasion however Sidney does indulge in the genuinely colloquial phrase, the lively scene and well-turned repartee which suggests a fairly direct transcript of experience. Such familiar ease as that of the Second Song was not to be heard on the stage of his day, nor for some years after his death.

> O sweet kisse! but ah! she's waking;
> Lowring beautie chastens me:
> Now will I for feare hence flee;
> Foole, more foole, for no more taking.

Banter and even the parody of one's own feelings were of course a well-known feature of courtly poetry. Chaucer in his *Triple Rondel* and Dunbar, *When he list to feign*, denounce the cruel fair with an obvious enjoyment of their own predicament. So Sidney can begin with a dramatic outcry more spirited than convincing:

> Fly, fly, my friends; I have my death's wound, fly:
> See there that boy, that murthering boy, I say,
> Who, like a theefe hid in darke bush doth ly. . . .
> (xx.)

The palinode or rejection of earthly love was also an ancient conclusion to a love poem. 'Leave me, O loue which reachest but to dust' looks back at least to the end of *Troilus and Criseyde*. Yet in Sidney's poems, filled as they are with the outward signs of a courtly passion (the tiltyard scene, the jealous address to her little dog and pet sparrow) artifice still embodies a personal melancholy:

> With how sad steps, O Moon, thou climbst the skies,
> How silently and with how wanne a face. . . .
> (xxxi.)

frank gaiety:

> Gone is the Winter of my miserie!
> My Spring appeares! O see what here doth grow . . .
> I, I, O I may say that she is mine!
> (lxix.)

and sometimes self-effacing and painful devotion. The courtly life was one of splendour, emblematic and never unstudied; yet it was for his personal qualities that Sidney won the admiration of the age. He may show reason kneeling to love,[18] yet love was a liberal education, which put before him as a standard the need for the highest excellence, to be attained with 'sprezzatura', natural ease. The young spitfire who warned Robert Molyneux that at the sign of any further interference with his correspondence 'I will thrust my dagger into you'[19] was famous for his interest in the new schools of rhetoric, as well as in the graver issues of politics and religion. His *Arcadia* won its contemporary reputation not only as courtly romance but also as a store-house of philosophical and rhetorical learning: it was quoted in such textbooks as those of Abraham Fraunce. It was typical of Sidney that he should interest himself in Ramus, the Huguenot teacher who replaced the older logic of the schools by a shorter and simplified system aimed at practical oratory, and designed for use in the pulpit or the court of law. A useful but comprehensive knowledge was the courtly ideal: Ralegh was soldier, sailor, historian and philosopher as well as poet and courtier: Sidney was a soldier and statesman, who could never have felt, with Castiglione, that conversation was in itself sufficient employment for courtiers. He stole off to the wars, even if he took a copy of the *Cortegiano* in his pocket. The brief reconciliation between the arts of living and of writing of which he was the living example did not long persist after his death.

III

Spenser was an incomparably greater poet, but he did not write such good sonnets as Sir Philip Sidney. This is symptomatic of the difference between them. Sidney was a court poet in the full sense: he himself was a living part of the life he celebrated. Spenser, though a greater poet, described it from the outside. His great festal poems are written for the world or a patron: they have neither the intimacy nor the 'sprezzatura' of the poem that is an adjunct to living.

Perhaps the best way to approach Spenser's poetry is through that of the modern poet who best understood him and learnt most from him, W. B. Yeats. Yeats's sense of the beauty of ceremony, his use of people as symbols, the object of passionate but impersonal and even inhuman devotion, and his placing of these people in a particular setting were all learnt from the Elizabethans. His vision of the changes wrought by time and his assertion of the eternal being of beauty is Neo-Platonic:[20]

> Things out of perfection sail,
> And all their swelling canvas wear,
> Nor shall the self-begotten fail
> Though fantastic men suppose
> Building yard and stormy shore,
> Winding sheet and swaddling clothes.
> *(Old Tom Again.)*

> All lives that has lived;
> So much is certain;
> Old sages were not deceived:
> Somewhere beyond the curtain
> Of distorting days
> Lives that lonely thing
> That shone before these eyes
> Targeted, trod like Spring
> *(Quarrel in old Age.)*

The Golden City of Byzantium is the refuge of those who can no longer live in the country of the young, where

> The salmon falls, the mackerel-crowded seas,
> Fish, flesh, or fowl commend all summer long
> Whatever is begotten, born and dies. . . .
> *(Sailing to Byzantium.)*

That fecund country was also celebrated by Spenser in his ripest and most splendid verse, the *Epithalamion*, Calidore's

Vision of the Graces, and some of the 'pageants' of *The Faerie Queene*. He too sought on occasion the refuge of his own Byzantium, his Platonic world of eternal Beauty, being driven out perhaps from the gracious and kindly world of youth. From the November *Eclogue*, that pastoral lament with its sudden transmutation of grief into rejoicing, to the Quartet of his *Hymns*, Spenser was haunted by the cruelty and bitterness wrought by time and change, and driven by the need to find some security. Most of his early poems are laments for the transience, vanity and misery of the world.

Yet this intensely personal theme is embodied in poems of a strictly formal kind, many of which are based on French or Italian originals. Spenser was a professional poet, a craftsman who was not afraid to demonstrate his skill upon conventional material. His relationship to Sidney was one of admiration and gratitude. In the great series of emblems which Spenser composed and translated, he celebrates the metamorphosis of Sidney. After a prolonged lament upon the ruins and cruelties of time, fate and change, come a number of visions, among which is this:

> Whilst thus, I looked, lo, adown the Lee
> I saw an harp strung all with silver twine
> And made of gold and costly yvorie
> Swimming, that whilome seemed to have been
> The harp on which Dan Orpheus was seen
> Wylde beasts and forests after him to lead,
> But was the harpe of Philisides now dead.
> At length out of the river it was reared,
> And bare above the clouds to be divin'd,
> Whilst all the way, most heavenly noyse was heard
> Of the strings stirred with the warbling wind,
> That wrought both joy and sorrow in my mind:
> So now in Heaven a signe it doth appear,
> The harp well known beside the Northern Bear.

The power of Orpheus to awake sentience is ironically invoked in the opening lines (as it is in *Henry VIII* in the song 'Orpheus with his lute' where the power of the sweet singer who

ventured into hell to recover his Eurydice is offered as matter
of consolation to an exiled princess, forsaken and harried by
'wolves'). But Spenser's emblem is one of a series and in
itself it has little force except in the image of the trembling
strings. By his rhythm rather than his images Spenser conveys
the power and moving life of his poetry: in one line he could
set up the pulse of the wedding march:

> Then came the Bride, the lovely Medua came[21]

and in his great processional poems, *Prothalamion* and *Epithalamion*, the emblematic descriptions are from the country of
Byzantium, whilst the delicate dancing movement of 'staff
and band' belongs to the country of the young.

> With that I saw two Swannes of goodly hue
> Come softly swimming down along the Lee;
> Two fairer Birds I yet did never see;
> The snow, which doth the top of Pindus strew,
> Nor Jove himself, when he a Swan would be,
> For love of Leda, whiter did appear;
> Yet Leda was (they say) as white as he,
> Yet not so white as these, nor nothing neare;
> So purely white they were,
> That even the gentle streame, the which them beare,
> Seemed foule to them, and bad his billowes spare
> To wet their silken feathers, least they might
> Soyle their faire plume with water not so faire,
> And mar their beauties bright,
> That shone as heaven's light
> Against their brydale day, which was not long:
> Sweet Themmes! runn softly, till I end my Song.

Besides being perhaps heraldic (the swan had been a badge
of the House of Lancaster and the Somersets were descended
from the Beauforts) the swans were Venus's birds, emblems of
purity, and royal fowl. The use of the story of Leda, inset
like a tapestry picture, amplifies the splendour of the occasion
by bringing down a God into the scene.[22] Yet the swans are
also real swans, their feathers sprinkled but not damped by

the current. The modern reader may find it difficult to accept both the swans and the ladies; the fact that there might well have been real swans on the Lee as the procession came down to Temple stairs allows both to appear in the same picture, as they might have done in a painting of the scene. Whiteness belongs directly to the brides as well, and is of course a symbolic use of the colour:[23] the winding rhythm directly suggests the winding procession.

In his ceremonial poems, such as the November and April *Eclogues*, the four *Hymns*, *Prothalamion* and *Epithalamion*, and in certain of the episodes of the *Faerie Queene* Spenser achieved the transmutation which all the poets of his age were seeking, the conquest of Mutabilitie. The great classical myths become, like the figures on Keats's Grecian Urn, types with all the grandeur of the timeless and all the warmth of immediate experience. One of the loveliest and earliest of such scenes is Arachne's tapestry depicting the rape of Europa in *Muiopotmos*:

> She seem'd still back unto the land to look
> And her playfellows' aide to call, and feare
> The dashing of the waues, that vp she tooke
> Her daintie feete, and garments gather'd neare. . . .
> Before the Bull she pictur'd winged Love
> With his young brother Sport, light fluttering
> Upon the waues, as each had been a dove:
> The one his bow and shafts, the other Spring
> A burning Teade about his head did move
> As in their Sires new love both triumphing,
> And manie Nymphes about them flocking round,
> And manie Tritons which their hornes did sound.

Spenser's world is not a world of human relationships, in the sense of private relationships. The feelings of the characters are reduced to terms of how they looked. His sonnet sequence, *Amoretti*, is witty yet slight compared with Sidney's, but in *Epithalamion* the public triumph carries implications which are both delicate and assured. Spenser's method is glancing and peripheral in these matters. His knights and ladies spend their time looking for each other or fighting for each other, but when they meet, their wooing is dismissed with brevity. When Britomart recognizes Artegall, she flutters most convincingly:

> Soon as she heard the name of Artegall
> Her hart did leap and all her hart strings tremble,
> For sudden joy and secret fear withall;
> And all her vital powres with motions nimble
> To succour it themselves gan there assemble
> That by the swift recourse of flushing blood
> Right plain appeared, though she it would dissemble
> And feigned still her former angry mood,
> Thinking to hide the depth by troubling of the flood.
>
> (*The Faerie Queene*, 4, 6, xxix.)

yet the account of their courtship is almost comic in its anticlimax (4, 6, xli). The emblematic nature of the figures in *The Faerie Queene* is emphasized by the minor characters, who are often as flat as a series of playing cards: the sensations, the passions and the life of the age gave them a depth they do not now possess. I do not mean that the historical allegory was all-important, but that the power to interpret such 'pageants' in a variety of ways simultaneously has now very largely disappeared. It was an inheritance from the older allegorical modes of thought, though it differed from them.

IV

In the one poem which he wrote in a courtly kind, *The Phoenix and the Turtle* (1601), Shakespeare contributed to the most extraordinary literary miscellany which even the Elizabethan age produced. *Love's Martyr or Rosalin's Complaint, Allegorically Shadowing the Truth of Love in the Constant Fate of the Phoenix and the Turtle* includes a Life of King Arthur: an ABC (like the medieval ABCs to the Virgin) written by the Turtle in praise of the Phoenix, a herbal-lapidary-bestiary, and a series of anagrammatic poems, also apparently by the Turtle.

The Phoenix and the Turtle are united by Nature, who appears in this poem to play much the role that she does in Chaucer's *Parlement of Foules*. [24] The Phoenix herself symbolizes the whole of Nature's work, since she is 'Nature's fairest creature'—this is made plain in the herbal-lapidary-bestiary—and there is an anatomy of the Phoenix which interprets her in terms of precious stones, animals and of the planets, whose moral significances are elsewhere made plain, so that she becomes 'a little world' in a special sense.

> *Eyes.*   Under this mirror are her princely eyes,
> Two carbuncles, two rich imperial lights,
> That o'er the day and night do sovereignize,
> And their dim tapers to their rest she frights:
> Her eyes excel the moone and glorious sunne,
> And when she riseth, all their force is done.

This is the Idea of a woman: [25] yet it is also a real person. Ben Jonson says in his contributory poem:

> After all, let no man
> Receive it for a fable,
> If a bird so amiable
> Do turn into a Woman
> Or (by our Turtle's Augur)
> That Nature's fairest Creature
> Prove of his Mistress' feature
> But a bare Type and Figure.

The union of natures which is Platonic Love, Shakespeare, like Spenser, sees as a relationship between one immortal and another immortal, in which their mutual relationship, the third term, is the dominant, and not the persons themselves.

> But they, which love indeede, looke otherwise,
> With pure regard and spotless true intent,
> Drawing out of the object of their eyes
> A more refined form. . . .

And then conforming it unto the light
Which in itself it hath remaining still
Of that first Sunne, yet sparkling in his sight,
Thereof he fashions in his higher skill
An heavenly beauty.

(An Hymne in Honour of Beautie:)

So they loved, as love in twaine
Had the essence but in one,
Two distincts, division none,
Number there in love was slaine.

Hearts remote, yet not asunder,
Distance and no space was seene,
Twixt this Turtle and his Queene;
But in them it were a wonder.

So between them Love did shine,
That the Turtle saw his right,
Flaming in the Phoenix sight;
Either was the other's mine.

This great poem, Shakespeare's one work in the Platonic mode, might alone be taken as the justification of courtly poetry.[26] Its concentration and simplicity show what can be achieved when the great artist finds the proper occasion to make full use of a great tradition.

CHAPTER III

THE WEB OF BEING—ELIZABETHAN POETIC AND THE POPULAR STAGES

The nature of poetry in courtly doctrine—the nature of style—the drama and the theory of Decorum—popular species of drama—Shakespeare's views

IT may seem almost sacriligious to quote Ben Jonson's epitaph 'On My First Sonne' for any reason than its portrait of sorrow.

> Rest in soft peace, and, ask'd, say here doth lye
> *Ben Jonson* his best piece of *poetrie*.
> For whose sake, henceforth, all his vowes be such,
> As what he loues may never like too much.[1]

Ben Jonson is not using the metaphor in the way in which it might have been used later, purely for its poignancy, measuring the beauty of the child against what he had loved next best in the world. He is speaking as a *maker*, one who saw in poetry a second creation.

Put in lowest terms, poetry was a craft like that of the musician or an accomplishment like that of horsemanship. As such it could be learnt, used, if necessary put aside. Put in highest terms, poetry was inspired, representing eternal truths which might be breathed into the poet by supernatural powers.

The courtly poets held both theories, as it suited them, and of the two professed courtiers who have left statements of their theory, Puttenham, the older, inclined to the first view and Sidney to the second. The work of these two, scholarly but not scholars, may be taken as representing with moderation the Elizabethan view of the nature and purpose of poetry.

Under images of the natural world, the poet presented an interior world. Of an objective, contingent fact in the modern scientific sense the Elizabethan poet had not much conception, if any. There was the world of appearance, of to-day and to-morrow, always differing slightly for every man and always imperfectly understood; and there was poetry, 'a higher and more philosophical thing than history', as Aristotle had said, in which permanent truths were so embodied that they subdued the imagination, convinced the reason, and inspired the will. Poetry was more potent than any other art in the 'excitation to virtue and deflection from her contrary',[2] for by means of its 'delightful persuasion' it gave appropriate and adequate embodiment to Ideas in a complete and therefore irresistible form. Such was Platonic theory: Puttenham takes a more practical view. For him, poetry was a skill pertaining to utterance;[3] he takes it for granted that the ends are useful ones, such as praise of the gods, celebration of princes, songs for weddings, funerals and birthdays, and the courting of a man's mistresses, whom he expects to exist in the plural. Emblems are poetry for Puttenham, and he devotes much time to novelties such as poems in the shape of lozenges or fusées, anagrams and acrostics. What the poet describes 'true and lively' is the life that is set before him.

For Sidney on the other hand the poet was the gardener of Nature, improving her by his art, but always with the aim of working upon the auditory.

Nature neuer set forth the earth in so rich tapestry as divers Poets haue done, neither with plesant riuers, fruitful trees, sweet smelling flowers, nor whatsoeuer els may make the too much loued earth more louely. Her world is brasen, the poets only deliuer a golden. . . . Which deliuering forth also is not wholly imaginatiue, as we are wont to say by them that build castles in the Ayre: but so farre substantially it worketh, not only to make a *Cyrus*, which had been a particular excellencie, as Nature might haue done, but to bestow a *Cyrus* on the worlde, to make many *Cyrus's*, if they wil learn aright why and how that Maker made him.[4]

The Golden World of poetry might be a tragic world, but it was clearer, simpler, more unified than Nature—like the medieval world whose image lay in the past, half-forgotten.

At the very end of his work, Puttenham, who was an older man than Sidney but outlived him, takes up this question, and considers the relations of the natural and the artificial in poetry. Puttenham had not Sidney's power of argument, and he was somewhat suspicious of the Italianate and new-fangled theory of the Platonists. He insists therefore that the art of the poet, though it improves Nature, is natural to him as Man—man being set over all other creatures to improve them.[5]

> In another respect arte is an aide and coadiutor to nature . . . but an alterer. . . . The Gardner by his arte will not only make a herbe, or flowr or fruite come forth in his season without impediment, but will also embellish the same in virtue, shape, odour and taste, that nature herself would neuer haue done, as to make a single gillyfloure, or marigold, or daisie, double. . . . Finally in another respect arte is as it were contrary to nature. . . . But what else is language and utterance and discourse and persuasion and argument in man . . . little less naturall than his very sensuall actions . . . euen as nature, working herself by her own peculiar vertue and proper instinct, and not by example and meditation. . . .

It was the memory of some such passage which justified the philosophic gardeners of Shakespeare's *Richard II,* and indeed may have supplied the image of England as the King's garden which runs through that particularly self-conscious and literary play.

Shakespeare seems again to be echoing Puttenham in *The Winter's Tale,* though here the argument is not used in defence of poetry as such, but as a general principle. Perdita says:

> The fayrest flowres o' th' season
> Are our Carnations and streak'd Gilly-vors
> (Which some call Natures bastards) . . . and I care not
> To get slips of them . . . for I have heard it said
> There is an Arte, that in their pideness shares
> With great Creating Nature.
>
> > (5. 3. 81ff.)

Polixenes defends the artificial improvement of Nature as 'An Art that Nature makes' which is precisely Puttenham's point.

He does not, however, succeed in convincing Perdita that such improving of nature, even to a natural end, is any better than painting the face to get a husband.

The Magnificent or Magnanimous Man had thought of poetry as a means of educating himself, bringing out the best that he could do, and, perhaps, more truly presenting than the circumstances of life would ever allow, what his highest nature might be. The poets who conferred immortality on their patrons were not thought of as providing a kind of Whispering Glades. What they celebrated were the patron's virtues, which were already immortal.[6]

The aim of the poet might however be less exalted; and in this case the very strength and charm of his work might constitute its evil. This was the argument of those who attacked poetry; its abuse was a national danger.[7] The poet might aim at fashioning a gentleman in all noble discipline, or converting guilty creatures sitting at a play; he might instruct the magistrate; he might persuade or flatter a mistress. Yet the lady might be persuaded to be naught, the audience tickled with an immoral jest, the rival discountenanced by a dry mock, a privy nip, or a fleering frump.

Sir John Harington, in the preface to his *Orlando Furioso*, provides a gay parody of the moral view of poetry and subverts the detractors who might otherwise object to his amorous verses:

> Remember, when you read of the old lecherous Friar, that a Fornicator is a thing that God hateth: when you read of *Alcina*, think how Joseph fled from his enticing mistress: when you light on Anselmo's tale, learn to loathe beastly covetousness: when on Richardetto's, know that sweet meat hath sour sauce: when on my host's tale (if you will follow my counsel) turn over the leaf and let it alone.[8]

He adds that he is afraid his readers are already looking up these passages and cursing him for omitting an index to the smutty stories.

II

The poet's means and method varied in accordance with the variety of purpose which he might propose. He worked according to law and his law was that of Decorum, or the right adaptation of means to ends. His object being settled, he was able to take a workmanlike attitude towards the task in hand, as even Sidney observed.

The end of all earthly learning being vertuous action, those skills most serve to bring that forth that have a most just title to be princes over all the rest.[9]

The chosen subject was the first and principal means towards his end, the conversion of the reader's whole mind. This involved 'the use of the imagination in the service of reason to move the will'.[10] The problem of finding fitting means was however chiefly a problem of style. The three styles or modes of writing—high, middle and low—which the Renaissance inherited from the Middle Ages would be appropriate not so much to given subjects as to given intentions.[11] An heroic purpose would require a lofty subject and a high style— elaborate, richly ornamented with figures and images: the same matter, with base comparisons, tumbling metres, and the appropriate figures, might be used to a very different end. Whatever else may be said of Shakespeare's *Troilus and Cressida*, he has taken a lofty and heroic story and treated it in a manner that cannot be called entirely lofty or heroical.

The choice of subject was however the poet's first step towards the shadowing forth of his Idea.[12] The rhetorical garment was the means of its incarnation. 'Style is a garment' only as the body is the garment of the soul: the apparel proclaims the man and does not disguise him. It cannot be stripped off, leaving the real meaning underneath. For the Elizabethan, the naked man was not natural man: he was a poor, bare, forked animal and fit clothing made him an individual. Moreover in addition to the style which he may adapt as best suited to his purpose, every writer has his own idiom, which he must modify to some extent, but which cannot be basically changed. It is not a matter of figures and ornaments, but of tone and manner.

Stile is a constant and continual phrase and tenour of speaking and writing, extending to the whole tale or processe of the poem or historie, and not properly to any peece or member of the tale, but is, of words, speeches and sentences together, a certain contrived forme and qualitie, many times naturall to the writer, many times his peculiar by election and arte, as such either he keepeth by skill, or holdeth on by ignorance, and will not or peradventure cannot alter into any other . . . therefore there be that have called stile the image of man, *mentis character*.[13]

The rhetorical tradition, whilst it regarded artifice as natural, did not preclude individuality; and the deliberate quality of much Elizabethan writing was not incompatible with a highly personal style, which sometimes, as in the writing of Marlowe, amounts almost to a sign manual.

In the nineties there was indeed a revolt against the artificial style as such. Daniel, in his appeal to 'Custome that is before all Law, Nature that is aboue all Arte', though he was the friend of Sidney, Greville and the Countess of Pembroke, seems to have taken up a position incompatible with that of the *Apology* or even of Puttenham. He will not allow verse to be governed 'with all the Rules of idle Rhetorique . . . otherwise than custome and present obseruation will allow'. Yet he goes on to say that 'all excellencie being sold us at the hard price of labour, it followes, where we bestow the most thereof, we buy the best successe'. His opposition to rhetoric does not amount to advocacy of the spontaneous overflow of powerful feelings.

When Shakespeare began to write, the popular theatre was outside the pale of courtly criticism. Lodge, the son of a very respectable grocer of London, might have written his *Defense of Plays*, but it amounted only to the answering of abuse with counter-abuse. Indeed the theatre never reached the level of providing matter for the theorists. The learned critics in tragedy had produced a *Gorboduc* and might rise to a *Mustapha* or even to *The Conspiracy and Tragedy of Biron;* satirical comedy was the only kind which Sidney and Lodge recommended and which Chapman and Jonson were later to practise. Yet the immense force and popularity of stage plays, even at court, cannot be contested. The Courtly theory might be applied indirectly, or it might serve in the manner of a warning or 'mirror' for dramatists. Such was its prestige, however, that no rival theory was possible. Hence the experimental manner of the Elizabethan theatre, coloured but not guided by the views of poets of a higher style than that of the common stages. Puttenham's 'merry matters (not unhonest) being used for man's solace and recreation' were to give Shakespeare his opportunity.

There was none the less one aspect of formal criticism which did profoundly influence the common stages, and that was the doctrine of decorum as applied to the particular *species* or kinds of drama. Polonius's catalogue of the players' repertory, though a trifle overdone, was based on distinctions which every company would have recognized. In choosing a subject the poet had already limited himself but in electing to treat his subject in a Comical, Pastoral or Historical manner he limited and enriched himself at once. The different species of poetry were appropriate to different areas of experience, different aspects of life, and they provided the 'decorous', 'decent' or fitting means of embodying them. Having chosen to write, say, a Revenge tragedy, a poet would find that a certain amount of his rough work had been done for him, if he cared to make use of the tradition. Certain themes and certain sets of images, certain situations and characters, forms of ornament and bits of stage business lay in stock. the dramatists, unlike the courtly poets, built up their own species largely from practical experience of what would please: the Petrarchan tradition stretched over some two hundred years and was well defined: Revenge tragedy existed as a species only in the practice of the common stages. Puttenham gives an account of the species, and of the decorum proper to each, which is clearly a theoretic recipe. But when Ben Jonson describes varieties of modern poetry in his *Discoveries* he defines them experimentally, as a practising poet would do, from the feel of the verse on his tongue.[14]

Among the tragic species of the popular stages the most distinct was that of the Revenge play.[15] It had a more or less fixed story, with plot, characters and stage situations so well defined that they might be parodied, or used as an ingredient to make a separate sub-plot. Shakespeare used the old story of *Hamlet* for his first mature tragedy, and it was not merely the story which he borrowed from the tradition. Kyd had created a setting, the dark intriguing circles of Hispano-Italian diplomacy, with poisonings, stabbings and secret murders of all kinds, where despair and cunning on one hand, tyranny and utter ruthlessness on the other, made up the balance of contending forces. It was 'black tragedy' in every sense: the stage was hung with black, the night scenes of churchyards, ghosts and treacherous revels, with murder carried out by torchlight, were reinforced by a body of images which constituted the poetic side of the tradition. These were largely drawn from the Vergilian journey to the underworld: darkness, hell-flames and Stygian depths coloured the atmosphere, in which tortured figures such as those of Ixion and Tantalus, or ghosts from a medieval hell, such as usurers choked with melting gold, were displayed to point the moral of the story. The moral was always that of crime and punishment—the inevitability of heavenly justice, of the vengeance which fell upon wickedness and vice. The stern ethical doctrine of these plays had as garment of style the imagery of torment and of night.[16] The first appearance of this style in Shakespeare is in Clarence's Dream in *Richard III*.

Many of these things had derived from earlier Elizabethan writings. But towards the end of the sixteenth century, the nature of Revenge tragedy changed. It had been crossed with the new satiric comedy[17] and a more complex species had resulted.

The old story was retained but the tone and imagery were

new. A bitter sardonic note had crept in: a new set of images, less dignified and more 'diminishing', reinforced the satire: the minor characters were often fools, or knaves, or both. Social satire replaced ethics: a critical attitude towards society appeared as part of the melancholy of the heroic avenger. The images of a Vergilian Hell, of Tantalus and Ixion, gave way to more realistic ones of disease, decay, rottenness and lust among the characters themselves. In the New Revenge Tragedy of Marston, Tourneur and Webster the great were humiliated in the corruption of power by tyranny, and of beauty by lust, and of both by the grave.

O Lucian, thy ridiculous Purgatory! to find Alexander the Great cobbling shoes, Pompey tagging laces and Julius Caesar making hair buttons! Hannibal selling blacking and Augustus crying garlic! Charlemagne selling lists by the dozen and King Pepin crying apples in an old cart drawn with one horse![18]

In Lucian's Tenth *Dialogue of the Dead*, the poet asks to see Helen of Troy and is told 'This skull is Helen'. Here is the germ of the graveyard scene in *Hamlet*, where not only the skull but Lucian's accent of wry mocking horror reappears:

Heere hung those lipps, that I have kist I know not how ofte . . . Now get you to my Ladies Chamber, and tell her, let her paint an inch thicke, to this fauour she must come. . . . Dost thou think *Alexander* look't o' this fashion i' th' earth? . . . And smelt so? Puh.

Death had lost its dignity, vice had become squalid as well as terrifying. The new mode was the most popular form of tragedy in the early seventeenth century. How far the species provided a general level of accepted commonplace can be tested by looking at the very poor sub-plot in the Revenge manner, which Dekker thrusts into the first part of *The Honest Whore*.

The Honest Whore is largely a realistic picture of London life, depending for its value on pathos and knockabout comedy in equal instalments. Into this melodrama Dekker drops an Italianate Revenge action, with frustrated hero, murderous tyrant, and murdered lady all complete. In the central scene

Hippolito the hero, who corresponds to Hamlet, meditates at a table set out with a book, a skull, a picture of his dead mistress, and a taper to signify the shortness of man's life.

> Here tis read
> False colours last after the true be dead.
> Of all the roses grafted on her cheeks,
> Of all the graces dancing in her eyes. . . .
> Look, a painted board
> Circumscribes all. . . .
>   What's here?
> Perhaps this shrewd pate was mine enemie's:
> 'Las! say it were: I need not feare him now.
> For all his braves, his contumelious breath,
> His frowns, though dagger-pointed, all his plots,
> Though ne'er so mischievous, his Italian pills,
> His quarrels, and that common fence, his law,
> See, see they're all eaten out! here's not left one:
> How clean they're picked away to the bare bone. . . .
> Draw me my picture, then, thou grave neat workman,
> After this fashion, not like this: these colours,
> In time, kissing but air, will be kissed off:
> But here's a fellow: that which he lays on
> Till Doomsday alters not complexion.
> Death's the best painter then. . . .
>   (Pt. 1, *The Honest Whore*, 4. 1.)

Here may be seen how far Shakespeare could provide a model and copy-book for humbler writers. The value lies in its very stupidity, as presenting the lowest common denominator of the Revenge species.[19]

Minor species of Tragedy included the atrocity plays depicting the cruelty of Turks, Moors, Jews, Borgia Popes, Italians, Spaniards. Most of them were wretched stuff but they were very popular, and the recipe did not vary very greatly.[20] There were, on the other hand, plays of Stoic heroes: such invincible sufferers appeared largely in the drama of Chapman, Fletcher and Massinger, and by their fortitude and contempt for death were enabled to triumph over their Machiavellian opponents.

Domestic tragedy, based on some 'late horrible murder' was a fourth species with well-defined qualities. These plays depended on being lowly and unpoetic in their style, highly moral in their intention, familiar in their setting and usually based upon the eternal triangle in their plot. The title of one of them, *A Warning for Fair Women*, might equally serve for all.

Courtly comedy had sprung from the revels, as popular comedy from the interlude; and in some of Peele's and Lyly's plays the special link between life and art which distinguished courtly poetry still persisted. *The Arraignment of Paris* has something of the spirit of a charade.[21]

Lyly's plays, which are now too little read, were written by a court official for court performance and their artifice is obvious. But the decorative framework and the rhetorical pattern enclose a lively action; the words are good ripe colloquial English, and the prose has, at its lowest, the merits of *The Lady's not for Burning*.

> *Rixula:* Nay, if you set all on hazard, though I be a poore wench, I am as hardie as you both: I cannot speak Latine, but in plaine English, if things fall out cross, I'll run away.
> *Halfpenny:* He loves thee well that would run after!
> *Rixula:* Why, *Halfpennie*, there's no goose so grey in the lake, that cannot find a gander to her make.
> *Lucio:* I love a nut-brown maid, 'tis good to recreate.
> *Halfpenny:* Thou meanest, a brown nut is good to cracke.
> *Lucio:* Why, would it not do thee good to cracke such a nut?
> *Halfpenny:* I feare she is worm-eaten within, she is so moth-eaten without.
> *Rixula:* If you take your pleasure of me, I'll in and tell your practises against your masters.
> *Halfpenny:* In faith, sour heart, he that takes his pleasure on thee is very pleasurable.[22]

In this brisk exchange of catchphrases and proverbs, that 'diction of common life' which is Shakespeare's particular excellence makes its appearance; and the scene, it should be noted, is the Kentish landscape and the town of Rochester.

Lyly had a fine sense of rhythm and of idiom: his courtly prose has all the grace and control of Congreve. The pattern of the comedy depends on a symmetrical arrangement of characters: two pairs of serious lovers, one pair of comic lovers, a quartet of saucy pages, two or three fools and an aged parent or two make up the staple list. It might equally well provide the cast of *Love's Labour's Lost* or *As You Like It*. Lyly's characters interact, interlace, like singers in a madrigal, setting their voices against each other. The idiom of each group fixes its character: together they make up the consort of harmony. This is also Shakespeare's method: he 'nails' his characters through the individual accents of their speech.

It may well have been the existence of such an elegant and lively comedy as Lyly's that turned Shakespeare towards this species, although, starting from Lyly's mock simplicity, he achieved in the end that final air of spontaneity which is the reward of deeper and more complex resolutions of discord.

Other comic species were the revelling plays with a popular background, such as *The Shoemaker's Holiday*, to which species belongs *The Merry Wives of Windsor*. Fairy plays of magic and wonder were a popular form; on the other hand, the learned comedy of Chapman and Jonson is full of formal disguises, cross-purposes and farcical mistakes, of the kind Shakespeare employed in *The Comedy of Errors*. Comedy was as flexible and experimental as well could be imagined, but no less than tragedy each species was derived from a governing Idea, which gave it a peculiar decorum, of its own, an appropriate mode and vehicle.

In Shakespeare's embodiment of the governing Idea he begins with the particular and works up and outward to the general, at least in his more mature and characteristic works. Lyly on the other hand began with a theme which he proceeded to clothe in the characters of the stage. He, like Jonson and Chapman, used the players as the medium of an art which was above them; Shakespeare threw in his lot with the common stages, and was a working member of a team.[23] He began therefore with Bottom and the lovers and ended

with the theme of Enchantment instead of beginning with
Enchantment as Lyly did in *Love's Metamorphoses*. To start
from a principle or even a text, as Chapman sometimes did,
was never Shakespeare's way. He began with flesh and blood.
He looked at a young man and saw Youth, maybe:

He capers, he dances, he has eies of youth: he writes verses, he
speaks holliday, he smels April and May. . . .

but the young man was also one of his very good friends,
capering before him on the boards of the Globe. He could
not be, like Spenser's Calidore on Lyly's Endimion, Youth in
general with perhaps some 'shadowing' of a particular
Courtly patron.

v

Though in his earlier plays and in his lyric Shakespeare was
to some extent following Courtly models, anything which he
says on the nature of poetry appears to concur with Puttenham
and Daniel's view that poetry depicts Nature and does not
surpass her. In the seventeenth century he was known as a
poet of Nature, and he would have claimed no higher title.

Shakespeare's views on poetry as expressed in his plays[24]
cannot of course be taken as 'straight' pronouncements.
Even in the sonnets he is pleading against his learned rivals,
and it may be said:

How well he's read, to reason against reading.

Yet the plain unadorned truth-telling of some of the sonnets is
as remarkably unconventional as Shakespeare claims it to be.

Imagination as described by Duke Theseus is above all
comprehensive. The poet's eye gives to what it bodies forth,
a shape. *Shape* is the technical term for an actor's costume.
Writing assigns the bodies conceived by imagination to their
proper roles, and gives to airy nothing a local habitation,

something to *live* in. Hamlet declares that the end of playing is 'to hold, as 'twere, the Mirror up to Nature; to shew Vertue her own Feature, Scorne her owne Image, and the verie Age and Bodie of the Time his Forme and pressure'. The modesty of Nature here advocated is precisely what Shakespeare claims for himself in his sonnets. Yet, in this play, when Hamlet holds up to his mother a 'glass where you may see the inmost part of you', the picture of lust in action is as savage and violent as the play-scene itself. Hamlet does to Gertrude what the play did to Claudius: he embodies in words what she is. The modesty of nature can be a fierce modesty when occasion demands it.

The Induction to *Timon of Athens* contains a debate between Poet and Painter, which stresses the plasticity of the poet's medium and the spontaneous character of his art.

> Our Poesie is as a Gumme, which oozes
> From whence 'tis nourisht: the Fire i' the Flint
> Shews not, till it be strooke: our gentle flame
> Provokes itselfe, and like the current flyes
> Each bound it chafes. . . .
> My free drift
> Halts not particularly, but moues itself
> In a wide Sea of wax. . . .

on which the form and pressure (or impression) of the times is stamped and bodied.

In *The Rape of Lucrece*, Shakespeare had said 'men have marble, women waxen minds'—which was indeed a common-place—and in *Timon* he seems to give the poet a receptive, flexible, shaping spirit of imagination in contrast with the masculine vision of the Painter, who 'tutors nature' in the manner of the courtly ideal.[25] Shakespeare's Poet has only those merits of *easinesse* and *facility* which Heminge and Condell testified as his own most notable characteristic.

In the character of Berowne, Shakespeare sets out to attack the ideal of formal education. It is an adaptation of Sidney's plea for poetry as the most *effective* learning, powerful because indirect.

Studie is like the heaven's glorious Sunne,
That will not be deep searcht with Saucy looks

Navarre's court had been a very uncourtly place till the
arrival of the Princess and her ladies: it is they who teach
Berowne to shed his taffeta phrases, however. The older
style of sonnetting is as little in favour with them as 'painted
rhetoric'.

Yet in these early plays Shakespeare had clearly been taken
with the sweet flowers of fancy and the pretty conceits of
poet-apes. He models himself carefully, at times even laboriously, upon the correct line. His narrative poems belong
even more plainly to the courtly tradition: *The Rape of
Lucrece* has most of the features of courtly lamenting poems on
The Triumphs of Time or *The Tears of Peace*, and *Venus and
Adonis* belongs to the popular Ovidian species.

The debt is perhaps greatest where the younger poet seems
most in revolt. The generation of Nashe, Marlowe and
Shakespeare followed orthodox theory in employing the low
style for popular work: but they employed it more widely,
more wittily and for a greater variety of subjects than it had
been customary to do.[26] Parody was in the air. Some of it was
very crude. Nashe's bursten-belly-inkhorn orator in *The
Unfortunate Traveller* is a great deal more riotously done than
Holofernes of *Love's Labour's Lost*.

Yet unless the older tradition had still been powerful and
strong, the rebels would have had little pleasure in their revolt,
and the spirit of exuberance and defiance which is so brilliant
in Marlowe, Shakespeare, Nashe and Donne could not have
flamed so high. There is no fun in flogging a dead horse.
Wisdom and learning were not without their defenders;
Chapman, Drayton and the other Platonists were making
higher claims for their holy mystery than Sidney had ever
done.[27] Free mockery of the noble aspiring poet persisted
none the less. Pedants of language, of the duello and of the
proceedings leading up to it, peddlers of the orthodoxies of
consolation or good advice, lovers who spoke by the book are
glanced at not for their 'humours' but for their insufficiency.[28]

The wise man's folly is anatomiz'd
Even by the squandering glances of the fool

and in the humility of motley and the generosity of the comedian, Shakespeare dispenses with that shrewder and narrower anatomizing which his more learned friend Jonson was to practise later.

Moreover, his warmest defence of Nature was written in courtly style. *Venus and Adonis* established him as a poet in the eyes of his contemporaries; it was altogether in a different category from the work written for the common stages; a witty, gentlemanly poem, full of brave fancies and exactly to the taste of all youthful sprigs at Whitehall and the Inns of Court. It was novel, yet also traditional: for the tale from Ovid was the most popular 'species' of the nineties. The Elizabethan Shakespeare is most clearly discernible in *Venus and Adonis*.

CHAPTER IV

THE OVIDIAN ROMANCE

Lucretian Nature—II Lodge—III Marlowe—IV Shake-speare—V Chapman—VI Drayton and others

HERE and there among the ancients, there were heretical poets whom not even the ingenuity of the most accommodating gloss could bring within the bounds of propriety. Such a one was the atheist and Epicurean Lucretius. He was however known to the Florentine Platonists, in particular to Giordano Bruno.[1] That magnificent and spacious sense of the whole realm of Nature in growth and fecundity—Natura Naturans—which distinguishes Lucretius concurred precisely with the renewed delight in the physical world, in all its loveliness and all its transience, that characterized the early Elizabethan poets. Venus Genetrix was their goddess—that 'alma Venus' to whom Lucretius addressed his great invocation:

> Alma Venus, caeli subter labientia signa
> quae mare navigerum, quae terras frugiferentis
> concelebras, per te quoniam genus omne animantum
> concipitur visitque exortum lumina solis:
> te, dea, te fugiunt venti, te nubila caeli
> adventumque tuum, tibi suavis daedala tellus
> summittit flores, tibi rident aequora ponti
> placatumque nitet diffuso lumine caelum.
> nam simul ac species patefactast verna diei
> et reserata viget genitabilis aura favoni,
> aeriae primum volucres te, diva, tuumque
> significant initum perculsae corda tua vi.
> inde ferae pecudes persultant pabula laeta
> et rapidos tranent amnis: ita capta lepore
> te sequitur cupide quo quamque inducere pergis.
> *(De Rerum Natura, I, 2-16.)*

It was Lucretian Nature, not Lucretian metaphysics, that
Spenser adopted in the Garden of Adonis and in the Mutabilitie
Cantoes.[2] His translation of this particular passage might
indeed have found some support from the great proem to
Book III of Chaucer's *Troilus and Criseyde*, the Hymn to Venus
which precedes the consummation of Troilus' love:

> In heven and helle, in earthe and salte see
> Is felt thy mighte, if that I wel descerne;
> As man, brid, best, fish, herbe, and grene tree
> Thee fele in tymes with vapour eterne.
> God loveth and to love wol nought werne;
> And in this world no lives creature
> Withouten love, is worth, or may endure.
> (*Troilus and Criseyde*, III, ii.)[3]

> Then doth the daedal earth throw forth to thee
> Out of her fruitful lap abundant flowers,
> And then all living wights, soon as they see
> The spring break forth out of his lusty bowers,
> They all do learn to play the paramours. . . .
> Then do the savage beasts begin to play
> Their pleasant frisks and loath their wonted food.
> The lions roar, the tigers loudly bray,
> The raging bulls rebellow through the wood. . . .
> To come where thou dost draw them with desire.
> So all things else, that nourish vital blood,
> Soon as with fury thou dost them inspire,
> In generation seek to quench their inward fire.
> (*The Fairie Queene*, 4. 10. xlv–xlvi.)

This is Yeats's country of the young: it is the unregenerate
but lovely world of Comus's plea to the Lady, Nature's waste
fertility. Lucretian Nature, 'the too much loved earth' as
Sidney called it, had to be renounced by those who would
leave the love that reaches but to dust: nevertheless it was not
without its votaries. In the poetry of the nineties, Marlowe
and Shakespeare spoke up for the Flesh—and Marlowe, of
course, for the Devil as well. Spenser in his latest work seems
undecided: Mutability is 'put down and whist', as she ought

to be, but the final affirmation has all the suspicious marks of a death-bed repentance: and Spenser is honest enough to add the two stanzas of the VII Canto in which he admits that the conflict in his own mind is still unresolved. The natural flux and the constant merging and melting of shapes into each other, the cycle of birth and death, the seasons and generations had received embodiment in the work of a very different poet, and one who had been studied throughout the Middle Ages, whose works were among the most widely quoted and most frequently translated of all the ancients. Ovid's *Metamorphoses* depicted an anthropomorphic nature, where there was a story behind every flower, every tree, almost every stone and stream. The world was peopled with the transformed heroes and heroines of Ovidian story. Moreover in his *Heroides* Ovid had provided, in greater measure than any other poet of antiquity, studies of human passion. He was a psychologist with a strong sense of melodrama: he was the poet of Love, and of Nature seen as one gigantic love story. The *Heroic Epistles* were widely translated and imitated; and their influence combined with that of the *Metamorphoses* in the most popular literary 'species' of the nineties, the Ovidian Romance.

The answer to Mutability, to the transience of love and earthly happiness, to the death of the rose, was Metamorphosis. The Gods themselves are subject to change, as Spenser declared in the Mutability Cantoes: for the gods of the Pagan world became to the Elizabethans great natural forces—forces indeed greater than human—but yet within the jurisdiction and subject to the rule of the Goddess Nature.[4] In his subtle combination of the Ovidian theme of Protean change with the Lucretian theme of mortality and decay, Spenser drew on the Pythagorean part of the *Metamorphoses* and on the fifth book of *De Rerum Natura* to embody a vision which could belong only to his own age. The beautiful ripeness and strength with which the changing pageant of the Months is shown, the ironic contrast of the Titianesque warmth and solidity of each figure as it comes forward, and the gliding rhythm which bears it away on the final Alexandrine, has nothing to do with Lucretius or Ovid considered as doctrine. This is a poetic embodiment of a truth at once general and particular. In the tale by which Spenser introduces the great plea of Mutability to rule the whole world, adapted from Ovid's *Metamorphoses*,[5] the little stream which ran through his own countryside at Kilcolman was given its own story. The meaning should be plain. That most distressful country in which Spenser found himself set down, peopled with wolves and thieves, torn with violence, yet in itself so lovely, is the setting of this scene because it was the setting for Spenser's own experience. This is not Faeryland, it is the County Cork. Even the Faun is a particularly Irish faun, and the Molanna is certainly an Irish colleen: very charming and very feckless both of them are, but they contrive in the end, it will be noted, to outwit the incensed Diana. Spenser sets the most general statement of that melancholy which had haunted all his poetry—the melancholy which springs from the triumph of time and change—in a scene more precisely delineated than any other in all his poetry; he symbolized it, as he had so often done, in the transience and continuity of a stream.

This identification of a human story with a natural scene provided a focus; the situation was reduced to its basic terms. The instincts, passions and senses had play; but in the Ovidian Romance as such, as in pastoral, more exalted considerations were ruled out. Circumscribed in the world of Nature, the poem made its appeal largely by virtue of what was excluded. Spenser had a lofty aim and a high style. The followers of sweet witty Ovid had on the whole more humble ambitions.

The translations of Ovid in this period had a flavour of the Court or at least of the Inns of Court:[6] and the Ovidian poets of the nineties were clearly writing with a similar public in mind. They do not raise philosophical issues save by implications, but the personal reference of the love story was generally made clear. It was a mode of persuasion, and apparently, like pastoral, a customary first exercise for a budding poet. It offered a fixed tradition, the possibility of fairly literal translation if the author were so minded, together with a variety of overtones, satiric, Platonic, or merely complimentary. Narrative was on the whole a more interesting form for personal verse than the sonnet-sequence.

II

The first of such poems is Lodge's *Scilla's Metamorphosis* (1589). It is a courtly poem, adapted from the thirteenth and fourteenth books of *Metamorphoses*. The story tells how the sea-god Glaucus, in love with the disdainful Scilla, is cured by Cupid at the intercession of his mother Thetis and the sea-nymphs. Cupid also makes Scilla dote on Glaucus, and finally she is transformed into a monster by a troop of Furies—Rage, Despair, Woe and Wanhope—who are sent from hell.

The poem opens with the poet himself sitting on the banks of the Isis, thinking on the unkindness of his own lady, when Glaucus appears and comforts him by telling a similar story. The moral of the dejected god's story is the familiar one of mutability.

> Unto the world such is unconstancie
> As sapp to tree, as apple to the eye. . . .
> Take moist from sea, take colour from his kind,
> Before the world devoid of change thou find.

In the course of the narrative the position of the disdainful and the dejected lovers is exactly reversed; it might be called 'A symphony in dejection and disdain, set in the pastoral key', which in fact is not so different from the actual title 'Scilla's Metamorphosis, enterlaced with the unfortunate love of Glaucus . . . conteyning the detestable tyranny of Disdain, and the comical triumph of Constancie, very fit for young Courtiers to peruse and coy Dames to remember'.

The comical triumph is celebrated with a heartlessness on the part of the lover hardly to be justified by the fact that Cupid has cured him with a leaden arrow. Scilla becomes a monster and

Glaucus was glad, since Scilla was enthralled.

Its medieval Induction with the Form of the Poet and the
use of such key figures from the courtly code as Disdain and
Wanhope make it plain that the poem is a persuasion to love,
and that behind Glaucus and Scilla are the figures of the lover
and his lady. It is in the tradition of Chaucer's courtly love
poetry, and of the *Arcadia*. There is nothing individual about
the sentiments, but the study of the passion of love is not the
less delicate and precise for that.

> My Godhead's all in vain,
> For why, this breast includes immortal pain.
> Scilla hath eyes, but too sweet eyes hath Scilla,
> Scilla hath hands, fair hands, but coy in touching . . .

'The sense of musical delight', said Coleridge, 'is a gift of
the Imagination', and the turn of these lines controls the feeling no less surely than if the poet were here professedly
speaking in his own person. Instead, his feelings are embodied
in a beautiful world of appearance, which includes not only
the figures of the gods themselves but the landscape in which
they are set, the pastoral scene of meadow and shore. The
streams are sympathetically identified with the sea-god: they
withdraw their tides for grief at his complaints, they 'dance a
pleasant tide' when the sea-nymphs sing their invocation to
Venus—rhythmically the most beautiful thing in the poem.

> Born of the Sea, thou Paphian Queen of Love,
> Mistress of sweet conspiring harmonie,
> Lady of Cipris, for whose sweet behove
> The shephaerdes praise the youth of Thessalie,
> Daughter of Jove and Sister to the Sun,
> Assist poor Glaucus, late by love undone.

When Scilla swoons at her rejection, the grass curls round
her, trying to imitate both the sea where she lives and the
lover she desires:

> The soften'd grass like billows did arise
> To woo her breast and wed her limbs so dainty.

On the other hand, pain or sorrow are kept at bay by the
pastoral convention: the sufferings are not real at all:

> He that hath seen the sweet Arcadian boy
> Wiping the purple from his forced wound,
> His pretie teares betokening his annoy,
> His sighes, his cries, his falling on the ground,
> The Ecchoes ringing from the rocks his fall,
> The trees with tears reporting of his thrall.

Adonis is dying, yet his tears are only 'pretie'. This is not
callousness, it is a positive lack of interest in feelings inappropriate to the species.

The combination of natural beauty, symbolic and gorgeous
figures, and feelings conventional but not insincere had been
achieved by Sidney in his *Arcadia*, which Henry Reynolds
called a poem in spite of its form.[7] The splendid description
of the encounter of Phalantus and Amphialus—a mock-fight
conducted during a seige—embodies perhaps the memory of
some actual tourney in which Sidney appeared before Stella,[8]
thoughts of the early summer at Penshurst, with strawberries
and hare-hunting, and memories of May-games with a
contest of Hiems and Ver. Phalantus is armed and set

upon a horse milk-white, but that upon his shoulders and withers
he was freckled with red stain, as when a few strawberries are
scattered into a dish of cream. He had caused his mane and tail
to be dyed in carnation, his reins were vine branches, which en-
gendering the one with the other, at the end, when he came to the
bit, there, for the boss, brought forth a cluster of grapes by the
workman made so lively that it seemed, as the horse champed the
bit, he chopped for them and that it did make his mouth water to
see the grapes so near him. The furniture behind was of vines, so
artificially made that it seemed the horse stood in the shadow of the
vine, so prettily were the clusters of ruby grapes dispersed among
the trappings which embraced his sides. His armour was blue like
the heavens, which the sun did with his rays (proportionably
delivered) gild in most places. His shield was beautified with
this device: a greyhound which overrunning his fellow and taking
the hare, yet hurts it not when it takes it. The words were, *The
glory, not the prey.*

This is half-way towards a metamorphosis: yet it is not more extravagant than some of the actual tourney costumes recorded. Amphialus, crossed in love, melancholy and saturnine, with his black horse and trappings of autumn leaves, 'the straw-coloured livery of ruin', is not only the other half of the year, but also perhaps, the other half of Sidney: he is victorious, too, which would not be the case in a May-game. Their fight is conducted as rhythmically as a dance:

> Together they set spurs to their horses, together took their lances from their thighs, conveyed them up into the rest together, together let them sink downward . . . like music made of cunning discords.

III

Such magnificence and such symbolism contributed at all events to the most successful of all Ovidian poems, Marlowe's *Hero and Leander* (1593).[9] This 'amorous poem' was written by a professed mocker and scorner who was also a student of Ovid, a translator of the *Amores*, and a dramatist. Marlowe celebrates the triumph of Nature over Ceremony, erecting a Bower of Bliss upon a basis of truant learning. Mercury and Cupid are in league against the Destinies, and the familiar arguments used against Virginity by the 'sharp bold sophister', Leander, are amusing as parodies but quite unnecessary as weapons against the self-betrayed virgin, who, like all maids, 'says nay and takes it'. The exuberant joy with which Hero's victims are described in a state of unconditional surrender to her charms reappears when Hero herself is smote by Cupid. Pagan Nature rejoices in the conquest of chastity, mocks the defences which Hero erects while

> cunningly to yeeld her self she sought.

This again is the country of the young. The winds that caress Hero, the green waves that enfold Leander, the 'hot proud horse' to which he is compared,[10] are servants of the servants of love. The opulent pictures in the Temple are those of Spenser's House of Busyrane, but here there is no Britomart to rebuke the gods for their 'heady incests, riots, rapes': pleasure alone exists, and the beauties of Nature are adorned with the glories of Art. Hero's veil of *artificial* flowers and leaves, her singing buskins with the wanton sparrows carved in coral and gold, and the 'crowding images' which fill the poem are drawn 'from art and fancy rather than from Nature':[11] but only in the sense in which Sidney's horse is artificial: 'the art itself is nature'.

The two lovers are human in a way unknown to the earlier writers. Flesh and blood, not the Lover and the Rose, are before us. The lovely creatures are grouped with Botticellian grace but they have more than Botticellian relish of the flesh. The joyful and mocking comedy demands it. Hero is betrayed by her own body: in the betrayal is discovered the power which animates her whole world. The vivid touches in the dialogue, the realism of the final love-encounter are potent in a new way. The gods are subordinated to the mortals: Neptune's heavy amours, likes the loves of the Destinies, are ridiculous parodies of the 'breathing human passion'. This is an Epithalamion without benefit of clergy. At the centre of the world, as of the narrative, is no Platonic harmony, no changeless eternal calm, but Empedocles' warring of love and discord, the storm of atomic battle.

> She trembling strove, this strife of hers (like that
> Which made the world) another world begat
> Of unknown joy
>
> (ll. 291–292.)

As a Hymn to Earthly Love and Beauty, an anti-Spenserian manifesto, *Hero and Leander* is complete. There would be no way of ending this 'amorous poem' as a tragedy and preserving decorum. The celebration of the triumph of love rightly concludes it. There is no evidence whatever that Chapman's additions, or his divisions into Sestiads, had any justification in the state of the work as it was left by Marlowe, for of this nothing is known. It is conjectured that the poem was left unfinished at Marlowe's death but this again is pure hypo thesis.

It may be argued that to take a notorious tragedy as basis for a comedy is insolent, but such insolence is exactly what might be expected of Marlowe. As a matter of fact, in its most accessible form, the letters of Hero and Leander in Ovid's *Heroides*, the tragical conclusion is not given. It is from these letters that Marlowe probably took the hint for his picture of Hero 'like a planet, moving several ways', for Hero's letter is full of divided counsel, urging Leander to come and then not to come, shot with jealousy, and wholly inconsistent.

But of course there was never any need to take the whole of a classical story for literary purposes, but only so much as was relevant to the matter in hand and the literary species in question. In his edition of the *Works of Sir Thomas Malory*, Professor Vinaver has suggested that Malory deliberately left the story of Tristram incomplete, with the lovers enjoying happiness together at Joyous Garde, because his 'sen', his interpretation, did not require the tragic conclusion.[12] Similarly Chaucer hurried over the end of *Troilus and Criseyde*, and Shakespeare cut his version of that story short. The adaptation of a myth, like the conflation of a number of myths, was a perfectly legitimate practice. There are no loose ends in Marlowe's poem; the episodes of the Destinies and of Neptune are part of the mock-heroic design. They intensify the dramatic and complex human situation. Leander's sophistical speech against Virginity is an ancient tradition,[13] but Virginity is not allowed her usual crushing reply. His wit is by no means incompatible, it is ironically contrasted with his real ignorance of the 'amorous rites', a jest which Marlowe points by the absurd jingle and tumbling movement.

> . . . yet he suspected
> Some amorous rites or other were neglected.

The lovers are included in the circle of the comedy: they are both beautiful and absurd, sympathetic yet also ridiculous. In this, as in their battle of wits, they anticipate the lovers of Shakespeare's comedies.[14]

Chapman's continuation is related to Marlowe's poem exactly as Henryson's *Testament of Cresseid* is to Chaucer's great poem—to which in Elizabethan times it was appended— or as Ralegh's *Nymph's Reply* is related to *The Passionate Shepherd to his Love*. It is not a continuation but a 'correction', a tragic counterpart, moralized, full of emblems, and, in subject more 'grave and high' than Marlowe's. It is intended as a warning to lovers to 'shun loue's stolne sports by that these Louers proue'. Such a moral could not with any decorum be adduced from any tale written in the manner of Marlowe. The style is all wrong, and the matter is all wrong. Chapman's style—and therefore, in the real sense, his matter or 'cause'— are different.

Nor is Chapman's the only continuation: in 1598 Henry Petowe published *The Second Part of Hero and Leander*, in which after a happy life, the pair undergo metamorphosis. The extraordinary success of Marlowe's poem does not need to be stressed. Shakespeare quotes it more than once: in *Bartholomew Fair*, Ben Jonson puts garbled lines into the mouth of Lanthorne Leatherhead, the puppet master, who had evidently read the 'printed book' though he thought it too learned for his audience to understand: and Bartholomew Cokes, the gull of the play, admits that though he has also read it, he does not understand it either.

IV

In 1593, the same year in which Marlowe's poem was 'entered'—five years before it appeared in print—Shakespeare published *Venus and Adonis*. Like Lodge's poem, and perhaps like Marlowe's, this was evidently a 'persuasion' to love. The likeness of Adonis to the young man of the Sonnets and the close parallels between the poem and the sonnets in respect of imagery and theme, make it certain that the connexion exists.[15] From Lodge, Shakespeare adopted melodic variety, an interest in the pastoral setting; from Marlowe a more human treatment of the characters. The story is adapted from *Metamorphoses*, Book X: but Ovid's Adonis, unlike the young man of the sonnets, was not reluctant. The story is therefore conflated with that of Salmacis and Hermaphroditus, in the fourth book, to fit its special purpose.

The pace is slower than Marlowe's, for the stanza form is not so nimble as the couplet: the ornament is more elaborated, and the comedy not so sustained. There is indeed a lively enjoyment of the monstrosity of love; its power to breed self-deception and to cloud the judgment is treated as a jest.

> . . . lovers houres are long, though seeming short,
> If pleasd themselves, others they thinke delight,
> In such like circumstance, with such like sport:
> Their copious stories oftentimes begunne
> End without audience, and are never donne.   (842–6.)

So Venus checks the writhing Adonis, at the end of her very long speech:

> 'Lye quietly, and heare a litle more,
> Nay do not struggle, for thou shalt not rise . . .'   (709–10.)

The delightful *bravura* of Marlowe's mocking wit was all-pervasive: but Shakespeare still had some heavy provincial Warwickshire loam sticking to his boots. Indeed, the reminiscences of the countryside, especially the hunting of the hare, have often been praised as the most 'natural' parts of the poem, though in fact they are most carefully worked into the general symbolic design.

The poem is divided into two contrasted halves: the wooing and the hunt. Each has its characteristic images, and each is elaborately contrasted with the other. The commonest imagery is that of animals. The long accounts of the horse and the jennet, and of the hunted hare, repeat within the animal kingdom the themes of the wooing and the hunt. Adonis is compared with a snared bird, a dabchick, a deer and a hunted roe: Venus is an eagle, a vulture, a wild bird and a falcon. She is the beast of prey and Adonis the hunted quarry; this again links up the two halves of the poem. She had hunted Adonis, and to escape he hunts the boar. When the boar kills him, it seems only to be repeating Venus's insensate possessiveness:

> Had I bin tooth'd like him I must confesse,
> With kissing him I should have kild him first.   (1117–8.)

Freshly and naturally observed as it is, this pastoral background also gives humanity to the story. The detail—the small snail shrinking backwards in his shelly cave with pain, the trees and sprays of the wood which come to life and try to keep Venus from knowledge of Adonis's death are both decorative and closely observed.

> And as she runnes, the bushes in the way,
> Some catch her by the necke, some kisse her face,
> Some twin'd about her thigh to make her stay,
> She wildly breaketh from their strict imbrace.   (871–4.)

Venus and Adonis are both presented as lovely but purely instinctive creatures: their arguments are all conventional, and their life is given in terms of the senses. The early part of the poem is full of feeling presented in terms of flesh: its moistness, its texture, Adonis's sweating palm, his rose cheeks, his panting breath upon Venus's skin. The alteration of colour is particularly noticeable: it suggests the 'going hot and cold' of intense nervous excitement, and the coursing of blood beneath the skin. Venus will kiss Adonis until his lips are 'red, and pale, with fresh varietie'; but while she is 'red, and hot, as coles of glowing fire' he is 'red for shame, but frostie in desier'. Later he is

> Twixt crimson shame, and anger ashie pale,
> Being red she loves him best, and being white,
> His best is betterd with a more delight.
>   (76–78.)

Sometimes in violent contrast Shakespeare will adopt the heraldic manner for relief. An example is the much discussed stanza:

> Full gently now she takes him by the hand,
> A lillie prison'd in a gaile of snow,
> Or Ivorie in an allablaster band,
> So white a friend, ingirts so white a fo.[16]   (361-4.)

The lily, the snow, the ivory and the alabaster are all chosen for their chilly whiteness, which has nothing in common with that of flesh. They are all symbols of chastity: alabaster was used for the effigies on tombs and hence was opposed to blood, the symbol of life:

> Why should a man whose blood is warm
> Sit like his grandsire cut in allablaster?

asks Bassanio. Lilies were the emblem of virginity: snow was an ancient symbol of chastity and its coldness suggests death.

The ideas of death and chastity are precisely the opposite to those suggested in this passage. Again there is a direct contrast to the warm flexuous restraint of Venus's melting palm in the *hardness* of the ivory and alabaster which *binds* it, in the idea of *imprisonment* in a *gaol*, and the besieging force *engirting* the enemy. This passage is built on sensuous opposites: it is a definition by exclusion.

Often some cool generalization will interrupt the story at its most exciting point. Feelings which cannot be reduced to their sensuous embodiment are not given at all. Perhaps the most perfect example of implied emotion in the poem is the description of Venus hurrying to save Adonis, driven by purely animal instinct.

> Like a milch Doe, whose swelling dugs do ake,
> Hasting to feed her fawne, hid in some brake.   (875-6.)

Though a goddess, Venus has no supernatural powers: she is as helpless as any country lass to save Adonis or even to reach him quickly. She is not responsible for his metamorphosis into a hyacinth: it seems to be spontaneous. Shakespeare abandoned the supernatural: his gods are identified with Nature, physically one with it, enmeshed in its toils even more firmly than Marlowe's. Venus's cajolery of death, a pitiable echo of her cajolery of Adonis, is followed by a string of inappropriate conceits: her grief dazzles her eyes with tears till she sees double, and she tries to convey the grief by fantastic elaborations. Yet the horror of the blank glazed stare of the corpse is physically realized.

> She lookes upon his lips, and they are pale,
> She takes him by the hand, and that is cold,
> She whispers in his eares a heavie tale,
> As if they heard the wofull words she told:
> She lifts the coffer-lids that close his eyes,
> Where lo, two lamps burnt out in darknesse lies.
>
> (1123–1128.)

The sensuous beauty of Shakespeare's poem gave it a popularity equal to Marlowe's. It was frequently reprinted: the young gallants kept it under their pillows and used it as a model for their courtship. There are, I think, sufficient likenesses between the two to make it probable that Shakespeare knew Marlowe's poem before he composed his own. Similes which are perhaps commonplaces, like the terrified lover compared with a soldier awaiting capture (*Hero and Leander*, I. 121-122: *Venus and Adonis*, 893-894) can be found, but there is more in Marlowe's image of the 'hot proud steed', implying Leander's intractability:

> For as a hot proud horse highly disdains
> To have his head controlled, but breaks the reins
> Spits forth the ringed bit, and with his hooves
> Checks the submissive ground: so he that loves
> The more he is restrain'd, the worse he fares.

This is precisely the quality in Adonis's horse that is illustrated by his action, when he sees the jennet:

> The strong-neckt steed being tied unto a tree,
> Breaketh his raine, and to her straight goes hee ...

The yron bit he crushes tweene his teeth,
Controlling what he was controlled with.

(263–264, 269–270.)

Venus uses his behaviour to point the moral to Adonis, thus
making the relationship explicit:

How like a jade he stood tied to the tree,
Servilly massterd with a leatherne raine,
But when he saw his love, his youths faire fee,
He held such pettie bondage in disdaine:

(391–394.)

The unmanageable horse, symbol of the conquest of reason
by passion,[17] is the adopted 'impresa' of both poets.

v

Their great popularity led to a flood of Ovidian verse in the
second half of the fifteen-nineties. Drayton's *Endimion and
Phoebe;* Barnfield's *Cynthia;* two close plagiarisms of Shakespeare, T. H.'s *Oenone and Paris* and Henry Constable's or
Chettle's *Shepherd's Song of Venus and Adonis*, are only a few
of such imitations.

Other poems, such as the *Heroical Epistles* of Drayton, are
stuffed full of mythology and modelled on Ovid, though
their ostensible subject is English History. Chapman's
Ovid's Banquet of Sense and John Davies's *Orchestra* are philosophical poems which are tinged with the popular taste for
classical love stories. Marston's pornographic *Metamorphosis
of Pygmalions Image* is the low-water mark of the decade. It
appeared in 1598, and it was perhaps the appearance of such
poems which moved the Platonic poets, Drayton and Chapman,
to their heroic but unsuccessful attempt to reclaim the mytho-
logical romance for the service of virtue, and present once
more *Ovid Moralisé.*

Chapman's 'continuation' of *Hero and Leander* has an
emblematic and enamelled beauty of its own, if it is not

judged as an attempt to imitate Marlowe. In each of the four sestiads there is a long digression: the descent of the goddess Ceremony: the long description of Hero's scarf (a 'tapestry' interlude): the Tale of Teras: the final metamorphosis of the lovers into goldfinches. His moral is that without the endorsement of Ceremony, love is disastrous and therefore deadly. Hero is torn between her public role and her private feelings. This is symbolized by the descent of the Goddess Ceremony, and the angry Venus whose

> looks brought wrath, and urged fear:
> Her robe was skarlet: black her head's attire.
>
> (4. 27–29.)

It is symbolized more at length in the marriage which, as priestess of Venus, Hero attends, and in the 'ominous tale' which the nymph Teras tells there. The story of the marriage and deification of Hymen, Ceremonial Love, was borrowed from Attic legend.[18] The contrast between Hymen's torch and Hero's torch, as symbols of love and lust, reflects the elaborate use of light symbolism throughout the poem, which, of course, Chapman took from Musaeus. In his own translation of Musaeus, published in 1616, he begins:

> Goddess, relate the witness-bearing Light
> Of loves that could not bear a human sight . . .
> A light that was administress of sight
> To clowdy Venus . . .
> A light that took the very form of Love. . . .
> But Goddess, forth, and both one issue sing,
> The light extinct, Leander perishing. . . .

Symbolic colours and numbers are used throughout the poem: none of the sensuous detail is allowed to be merely sensuous, it has all to be given symbolical significance.[19] The use of mystical numbers and colours was of course part of the Hermetic philosophy, and it is to be found not only in Chapman, but also in Drayton and Henry Reynolds. This allows them to write decorative and extensive descriptive passages and at the same time to use these descriptions emblematically.

The tale of Hymen and Eucharis, the ceremonious and dutiful lovers, is deliberately contrasted with the loves of Hero and Leander. There is a lengthy account of their wedding rites which are a mixture of Roman and Elizabethan: the bride wears a red veil (for modesty) and the lovers are tied with white and blue ribbons (fidelity and chastity): the matron with her spindle, the exhibition of fire and water and the sacrifice of the jay are Roman. But the couple go 'to Church' and afterwards there are masks and shows, and the brideyouths scramble for comfits.

Then the mysterious nymph who had told this story vanished like an exhalation,

> O hapless Hero! that most hapless clowde
> Thy soon succeeding tragedy foreshewed.

The epithalamion is chanted 'while the torchie evening sprung'. In the sixth sestiad, Chapman moralizes at length on the torch. Light and harmony are associated with the rites of marriage whilst the Goddess tells Leander that because their union is unlawful:

> Fear fills the chamber, darkness decks the bride.
>
> (3. 154.)

Hero is described in this very darkness of fear after Leander had left her, as she sits wrapped in a black mourning veil.

> No form was seen, where form held all her sight,
> But like an embryon that ne'er saw light,
> Or like a scorched statue made a coal . . .
> Muffled with endless darkness she did sit.

Her plight makes her appearance indistinguishable from that of Shakespeare's ravished Lucrece. She is compared to a ransacked city: Lucrece to a 'late sact island'. Her Form is destroyed, and this is contrasted with the scene where in the Tale of Teras Love appears as Proteus, and in the form of a lily is given by Hymen to his bride:

> First, like the flower
> That Juno's milk did spring, the silver lillie,

He fell on Hyman's hand, who straight did spy
The bounteous godhead, and with wondrous joy
Offerd it Eucharis. She, wondrous coy,
Drew back her hand: the subtle flower did woo it,
And drawing near, mixed so you could not know it . . .
She viewed it and the view the form bestowd
Among her spirits: for as colour flows
From superficies of each thing we see
Even so with colours forms emitted be:
And where Love's form is, Love is: Love is form.

(5. 214-227.)

The symbol for Ceremony is that of Harmony; light or fire symbolizes love throughout the poem; and these two recur like *leit-motifs*.[20]

It must not be concluded that Chapman condemns Hero and Leander from a narrowly moralistic point of view. It is disastrous that their beauty and the beauty of their love must be destroyed because it will not fit into the scheme of things at large. Even physical beauty, however transient, should have some claims on Fate:

Ay me! hath heaven's straight fingers no more graces
For such as Hero than for homeliest faces?. . . .
Beauty in heaven and earth this grace doth win
It supples rigour and it lessens sin.

(3. 385-386, 395-396.)

The most direct piece of moralizing in the poem is the justification of Hero against her angry mistress Venus (4. 277-283). The beauty of the final metamorphosis of the lovers is coloured again by symbolic interpretation, yet it has a direct and natural appeal as well.

Two sweet birds surnam'd th' *Acanthides*
Which we call Thistle-warps, that neere no Seas
Dare euer come, but still in couples flie,
And feede on Thistle tops to testifie
The hardness of their first life in their last:
The first in thornes of loue and sorrows past.

And so most beautiful their colours show,
And none (so little) like them: her sad brow
A sable veluet feather couers quite,
Euen like the forehead cloths that in the night,
Or when they sorrow, Ladies use to weare:
Their wings blew, red and yellow mixt appeare,
Colours that, as we construe colours, paint
Their states to life: the yellow shows their saint,
The deuill *Venus*, left them; blew their truth,
The red and black, ensignes of death and ruth.

(6. 276–291.)

Chapman, throughout, complains against the hardness of the lovers' fate: he says at the end of the fifth sestiad that he uses digressions because he does not want to reach the point at which he must recount Hero's death. It is reminiscent of Chaucer's excusing of Criseyde and his shrinking from the end of the story. Yet, however sincere Chapman's feelings may have been, his poems remain a series of emblems, a gorgeous gallery of gallant inventions strung together by a very slender thread. The sudden appearance of such monsters as the figure of Dissimulation, created by Venus from the smoke of perjured Hero's sacrifice, the extended heroic similes, and the careful structure of the different sestiads, cannot compensate for the fact that as humanly convincing figures Hero and Leander have disappeared, overwhelmed beneath the tapestry of the symbols which profess to set them forth more illustriously. Perhaps his rival's *Rape of Lucrece* was his model.

VI

Drayton's *Endimion and Phoebe* is no less plainly written as a corrective to Shakespeare and Marlowe. Although deeply influenced by both, Drayton at the end makes pointed acknowledgment to Spenser, Daniel and Lodge (who was evidently a personal friend), but does not mention *Hero and Leander*, from which he borrowed the couplet form, and a good many devices that go with the couplet: or *Venus and Adonis*, whence the picture of a goddess wooing a mortal might have been derived.[21] Drayton's goddess however is as chaste as his shepherd: the whole poem is a celebration of Platonic love, as the subtitle, *Idea's Latmus*, would suggest. The poem is dedicated to Shakespeare's Phoenix, the Countess of Bedford, though inspired by Idea (Anne Goodiere), the goddess of Drayton's worship.

Like Lodge, Drayton writes in a pastoral strain: his Endimion is innocent, and there is a note of comedy reminiscent of Leander's wooing (the ultimate model is *Daphnis and Chloe*) in the scene where he rebukes the disguised goddess for offering love to him, as he is dedicated to Phoebe; he ends with a dash of Adonis's petulance.

> Then turns him from her in angry sort,
> And frownes and chafes that she had spoil'd his sport.
> And then he threatens her, if she did stay,
> And told her, great *Diana* came this way.

Phoebe's promises to her shepherd love have all the sensuous richness of *The Passionate Shepherd* and her person is presented, like Endimion's, in terms of a court masquer:

> An Azur'd Mantle purfled with a vaile,
> Which in the Ayre puft like swelling saile,
> Embosted Raynebowes did appeare in silk,
> With wavy streames white as mornings Milk,
> Which ever as the gentle Ayre did blow,
> Still with the motion seem'd to ebb and flow
> About her neck a chayne twise twenty fold,
> Of Rubyes, set in lozenges of gold,
> Trust up in trammels and in curious pleats,
> With sphery circles falling on her teats. . . .

Latmos itself is described with a rich artificial splendour that recalls on the one hand the April Eclogue and on the other Milton's Paradise.[22] The walks are full of symbolic trees which 'serve for hangings and rich Tapestry': the golden grapes and citrons are like 'gorgious Arras', the streams run in mazes over silver sand strewed with orient Pearl, and shadowed with Roses and sweet Eglantine. All the senses are feasted but none the less the outcome of the poem is the translation of Endimion to the heavens, Phoebe having appeared to him in all her splendour as a reward for his chaste love, and, even before that, having infused into him a celestial spirit which removes from him all the melancholy incidental to earthly passion:

> for why, the soule being divine alone,
> Exempt from vile and grosse corruption,
> Of heavenly secrets comprehensible,
> Of which the dull flesh is not sensible.

After this, it is not surprising that the splendid procession of the Graces and the Muses which accompany the chariot of Phoebe in Endimion's apotheosis should lead to a long philosophic discussion on the mystic significance of the numbers nine and three, involving the hierarchies of the angels, the nine worthies, the circles of the heavens, musical harmonies, the Trinity, musical modes, and the interior divisions of the senses.

The rich description of a golden world and the courtly splendours of the goddess and her attendants, set off by the full sensuous detail which pastoral authorized, might serve as a counterweight to the similar splendours of Marlowe and of Shakespeare. But all the nobility of Drayton cannot disguise the fact that once the characters of the Ovidian Romance had been given the humanity of Leander and Venus, it is impossible to put back the clock and return to the simplicities of an earlier way. Compared with Marlowe's and Shakespeare's dramatic characters, the figures of their Ovidian poems are developed only slightly: but still, it is enough to 'kill' Phoebe who is only interesting when she is disguised and 'merry', and to leave our impulse to mock Endimion insufficiently satisfied by Drayton's gentle banter.

Nevertheless Drayton's poem has such felicity of detail and such genuine simplicity of thought that on a total impression his integrity conquers, in spite of his naïvety. He is far less disjointed than Chapman: there is indeed a kind of rich and solid consistency in his style, which, like the very best plum cake, is so well compounded as to require a deliberate and not too unmeasured consumption.

Dramatic art had been injected into the Ovidian Romance with dangerous results: but the species itself remained one of the most popular forms throughout the seventeenth century. For the most part, the stories are decorative exercises, practised long after the particular conditions which made the courtly Platonism of Elizabeth's poets a living force had passed away. Fletcher's *Venus and Anchises*, Barksted's *Myrrha the mother of Adonis*, Reynolds's *Narcissus* are in varying degrees Spenserian, Hermetic and personal in their interpretations.

Beaumont alone, in his mocking, bawdy, aery *Salmacis and Hermaphroditus* has a touch of Marlowe's ironic wit. Of his poem he says:

> I use thee as a woman ought to be:
> I consecrate my idle hours to thee.

Giles Fletcher, on the other hand, could apply Ovidian myth in a most astonishing way to the consideration of religious themes:[23] and it was not till 1656 that Cowley—who himself in his youth wrote the Ovidian *Pyramus and Thisbe*—could dismiss as 'the *Cold-meat* of the *Antients*', these 'confused antiquated *Dreams* . . . of senseless *Fables* and *Metamorphoses*'.[24]

The significance of the Ovidian Romance is not to be measured altogether by the poet's achievements in that kind, magnificent as the best of them are. It was a liberating force whose combination of sensuous richness, with a certain classic simplicity and solidity, presented Shakespeare with his first great poetic opportunity. The impression remained with him, and as in *Henry VIII* he looked back to the poetry of Elizabeth's reign, so, in a speech which has often been read as a purely personal utterance, he turned back to Ovid.

> Ye Elves of hils, brooks, standing lakes and groves,
> And ye that on the sands with printless foot
> Do chase the ebbing Neptune, and doe flie him
> When he comes backe. . . .

Prospero's farewell to his art is not only Shakespeare's most important debt to Ovid, and one of the few direct and unmistakable quotations in all his work: it is also a measure of his debt to the whole Ovidian tradition of his youth, as the masque of Juno and Ceres which precedes it is the most perfect statement of what others had tried to put into the Ovidian Romance. Here, in these richly habited masquers and their pastoral attendants, the sunburnt sicklemen and the Nayades of windring brookes, transferred by a final metamorphosis to the celebration of chastity, the Gods and mortals of the antique world appear in all their purfled splendour, all their harvest ripeness, before their final dissolution into air.

CHAPTER V

THE FLOWING TIDE—SHAKESPEARE AND ELIZABETHAN ENGLISH

Medieval thought and Shakespeare's work—his innovations in language—his use of current literary theory

WITHIN the later Elizabethan period there may be seen in miniature something of the great shift from the medieval to the modern world; for this was in England a crucial point in the change. In my first three chapters, the early Elizabethan poetic style has been sketched, with its carefully distinguished species, its limited and strictly controlled decorum of style, its ordering of the natural world in reference to a governing Idea. In all these ways, as well as in the momentary integration of art and life in the figure of the Courtly poet, the Elizabethan world retained habits which were akin to those of the Middle Ages.

The poetry of Shakespeare's generation—which, in spite of Professors Baldwin and Hotson I take to be that of the nineties[1]—was in comparison fluid, experimental and multiform. In the field of language, Shakespeare was as bold an experimenter as Bacon in the field of science. Yet, as we have seen, he built on the work of his predecessors, and especially of his immediate predecessors, the poets of the eighties. He himself in some respects retained more of the medieval tradition, transmitted through the more popular forms of literature, than the courtly poets had done.

The hierarchical order of the world and society was still there, and still accepted: yet in Richard III, morally condemned as he is, there is a vitality which makes the morality of Richmond a little less convincing than it might have been. In Shylock appears a figure who, while in some respects clearly labelled for a certain circle of Dante's Hell, yet has

evoked an even wider sympathy. The mere existence of
Falstaff is a sign of the times: not that in himself he is un-
paralleled in medieval literature, for his descent from the
Lords of Misrule has been freely asserted, and he has a certain
likeness to the Wyf of Bath. But as he exists in relation to
other characters, he is as much of a novelty as Hamlet.

The medieval ascendancy of the law and the legal way of
thought can be found in the early plays, where debates and
disputations are frequent. Shakespeare's use of legal terms
has often been remarked. The famous speech on order and
degree in *Troilus and Cressida* has its parallel in Hooker's
encomium on law:

> Of law there can be no less acknowledged then that her seat is the
> bosom of God, her voice the harmony of the world: all things in
> heavne and earth do her homage, the very least as feeling her care,
> and the greatest not exempted from her power: both Angels and
> men and creatures of what condition soever though in different
> sort and manner yet all with one uniform consent admiring her as
> the mother of their peace and joy.[2]

(Yet Hooker was writing to justify a largely pragmatic settlement.)

Shakespeare's English histories, his most original contribution to the structure of the drama—for the history cycle was a
species of his own invention—depicts the evils of disorder
and divided rule. They look back upon the chaos of the
fifteenth century, to which Langland had apprehensively
looked forward, and as it were echo the lament of the older
poet. If we are to believe the evidence of the plays, Shakespeare detested violence, and in this he was neither of the old
age nor the new. He often adapts his stories to make them
less cruel than the original, so that he has been called an
Elizabethan Bowdler.[3] The blinding of Gloucester, the
murder of Lady Macduff, shock us because they are not what
we expect. They would shock much less in Marlowe or
Webster.

It has become fashionable to see in Shakespeare a representative of the older order of things—defending the traditional

view of society against Machiavellian 'politicians', natural *pietas* against modern individualism, Lear against Edmund. In *Timon of Athens* he has been said to defend the great households and their hospitality and good housekeeping against modern money-economy, the tightfisted and planned society of the tradesman and the capitalist. Professor Tawney's *Religion and the Rise of Capitalism*—a book so valuable and persuasive that its use should be very strictly controlled—has been invoked to defend Antonio and to blacken Shylock.[4]

But what we know of his own life does not suggest that Shakespeare lived in the past. Without making him out to be a villainous grinder of the faces of the poor, too close an adherence to older ideals can be postulated only by a sharp division between his life and his art.

II

However he may have looked backward in politics, Shakespeare certainly did not entertain old-fashioned ideas on poetry. He arrived in London during the great florescence which has been described in Chapter II and Chapter IV. The speed of development in the art of poetry at the time was greater than England has ever known before or since. Shakespeare was no theorist—indeed one of the least theoretic minds that could be imagined—but he could learn from such masters as Marlowe and Spenser by the direct method.

Naturally his learning took the form of revolt and remodelling—even if the revolt were only a subtle form of imitation, as it so often is. He broke away from theory but did not discard: nor indeed did he give up anything more than was absolutely necessary. When he abandoned the learned models, it was to go back to popular and unassuming traditions and transform them. His humility may not have been without some modest self-assurance behind it, like the humility of the 'lewd' and unlearned Chaucer.

The learned and rhetorical poets of the eighties had concentrated upon figures, schemes, conceits and the 'argument' of the new Ramist logic to loosen and free the language from the stiffness and awkwardness of the early Tudor style. The language was young, capable of rapid expansion, yet also of the clarity and pathos that are possible only in a comparatively unworked tongue. Much heavy lumbering verse, such as that of *Albion's England* and other verse chronicles, represented a manful drudgery which was absolutely necessary to gain flexibility and ease. In Spenser, it is the pattern of his stanza, the flow and ease of his movement that is his great contribution to English poetry. His vocabulary often sounds like that of a man trying to talk with his mouth full of toffee, and some of his stanzas are mere exercises in the muscular flexion of the sentence.[5]

The stiff pattern of sonnet and couplet, the careful doublings of the Euphuistic style, were a help to these early writers, and Shakespeare himself in his first plays uses rhetorical schemes of alliteration, repetition and climax. They are for example the staple of his style in *Richard III*, which depends upon the pattern of its arrangement[6] rather than upon imagery or depth of associative power in the words themselves.

Where Shakespeare was to break away from his predecessors was precisely in this matter of vocabulary. Of course there had been experiments before. The inkhorne terms of the mid-century reformers had called out a reaction, and the archaic Saxon terms of *The Shepherds Calendar* and of Peele were the result. It was in an attempt to *improve* the language that Peele put into the mouth of a classical goddess such lines as:

Yea, Vulcan, will ye so indeed? Nay, turn and tell him, trull,
He hath a mistress of his own to take his bellyful.
(*Arraignement of Paris*, 4. 1. 5–6.)

Our knowledge and sympathy for Elizabethan rhetoric has been much increased recently by the work of scholars, mostly American.[7] But when all is said, the theoretic attempts to improve the language were more well-meaning than effectual.

Sidney with his own good sense and good taste, Shakespeare
with his extraordinary power over words, achieved more
than all the theorists.

Shakespeare's achievement depends before all else on the
power, range and strength of his use of words. It is well
known that his vocabulary was about ten times that of the
average man of to-day. One of the difficulties of reading
him with an eye to what the immediate effect must have been
is that many words which to us are quite familiar would have
jumped out at an Elizabethan as new and startling. The whole
language was expanding at a prodigious rate and Shakespeare
not only coined, but borrowed, adapted and wrested words
to suit his own masterful will. The only writer comparable
to him in this respect is his contemporary Nashe. His linguistic
experiments and observations were suited to all classes. On
the one hand he would use a pun depending on a knowledge
of Latin: 'I am here among thy goats as the most *capricious* Poet
Ovid among the Goths' says Touchstone to Audrey. On the
other, the illiterate workman who had to learn new words by
ear is depicted in Costard: 'Remuneration! O, that's the Latin
for three farthings' or Mrs. Quickly: 'O thou Hony-suckle
villaine . . . O thou hony seed rogue, thou art a hony seed, a
man queller and a woman queller'.[8]

Shakespeare's English was not ours: almost every word
has suffered some change of meaning, and as Professor F. P.
Wilson points out,[9] the danger does not lie in those words
which are clearly obsolete, but those where their delicate
flavouring has changed and the reader is not put on his guard.
The language was in general rougher, more troubled, with
more body and more live metaphors. Dialects were stronger
and richer than they are now. Travellers brought back foreign
words as eagerly as new fashions and theatre-goers loved to
hear scraps of strange speech. Shakespeare uses French and
Welsh at some length in his English histories. The simple
soul who picked up any fine words he heard, like Sir Andrew
Aguecheek and Osric ('The concernancy, sir? why do we
wrap the gentleman in our more rawer breath?') are figures

of fun to Shakespeare; but twenty years earlier Osric and perhaps even Sir Andrew would have been commendable persons, attempting to beautify (vile word) their native tongue.

Shakespeare lived at a moment in the tide of time when the current of speech flowed strongly, and like a strong swimmer rejoicing in his art, he swam with the stream of common speech. Here he rejected the doctrine of decorum, which restricted the vocabulary to fitting terms. He used low words in tragedy and high astounding terms in comedy; and the complexity, power and range of his speech shows the same happy valiancy of style as his balance of plot and sub-plot, his reconciliation of tragic and comic.

III

Shakespeare had in fact always found difficulty in saying only one thing at a time. Such portmanteau phrases as 'inexecrable dog' and 'this knot intrinsicate', and his use of puns are symptoms of that power to see two objects or ideas related or superimposed which, on the larger scale, produced the contrasts between the different parts of *The Merchant of Venice* and *Much Ado About Nothing*.

The shift from the older patterns of rhetoric, where the vocabulary is fixed and simple, to the newer style, where the words themselves play into each other, where imagery and subsidiary meanings, echoes and puns play across from word to word, can be seen, as has been said, by contrasting the style of *Richard III* with that of *Richard II*. The style of the first is good early Elizabethan; that of the second is pure Shakespeare. Eventually he attained such a degree of control and freedom that in each play he presented a new and self-contained world. The doctrine of the species or different kinds had provided earlier writers with useful limitation of their intention. Shakespeare found these limitations of some use, not as conventions within which he worked but as a kind of climate to which he could conform. Yet each of his plays constitutes an individual species of its own. The recipe is not repeatable. The delicate blend of satire, pastoral, and romantic love in *As You Like It*, the subtle contrast of distinguished and divided groups in *Henry IV*, are each peculiar to that one play. They are its Stile in Puttenham's sense—*mentis character*.

In modern literature such limitations as the species provided are found only at the literary extremes of farce, grand opera, detective story or fairy tale. Shakespeare could on occasion make use of a learned species, such as the classical comedy which lies behind *The Comedy of Errors*. More frequently, he adapts and modifies a popular tradition. *Measure for Measure* is like a morality play, but it is not a morality play, and the differences are as significant as the likenesses. *Macbeth* may be based on religious conceptions of salvation or damnation, but it is not a religious drama, even to the same extent as Marlowe's *Faustus*. The species of the latest plays is that of 'tales, tempests and such drolleries' as Jonson scornfully observed— forms whose simplicity is such that they recall the unpretentious fables of the Bible: 'There was a certain man who had two sons. . . .'

When Berowne turned from learning to jest in a hospital, or Prince Hal learned to govern by putting himself into the shoes of an Eastcheap barman, they were practising the only creed which Shakespeare consistently preached by example. He submitted to learn of experience. The central core of each of his plays—its governing Idea, or germ—is an informing power radiating and glowing through every tissue and fibre of the whole, down to the single word. It is, as the Elizabethans would say, the 'soul' of the play, which is 'diffused quite through' to 'make it of a piece'. It is this central Idea or germ which determines the quality of the play, controlling and shaping the language and structure, the use of common material and the use of experiment.

Dryden's definition of the moral in dramatic poetry is the parody, the dead corpse of Shakespeare's central Idea.

The first rule which Bossu prescribes to the writer of an Heroic Poem, and which holds too by the same reason in all dramatic poetry is to make the moral of the work; that is, to lay down to yourself what that precept of morality shall be which you would insinuate into the people; as namely Homer's (which I have copied in my *Conquest of Granada*) was that union preserves a commonwealth and discord destroys it.[10]

This is not unlike the way in which Chapman wrote *Caesar and Pompey* upon the precept *Only a just man is a free man*, or Ben Jonson composed his comedies upon general principles; but Shakespeare, who began with holding the mirror up to Nature, produced work which cannot be resolved into a proposition or summed up in a maxim, because it has the organic unity of that Nature upon which it is based. No account of the speech on degree in *Troilus and Cressida*, taken from its context and paraphrased in terms of contemporary thought, will pluck out the heart of its mystery. The governing Idea of his most highly integrated work, *Twelfth Night*, could not be extracted without appearing absurd.

Working in restricted conditions and with many things laid down for him by the circumstances of his company and the state of public taste, Shakespeare triumphantly surmounted these disabilities and turned them to positive advantages. The story is one of a gradual emancipation and enlargement of literary boundaries. It was Shakespeare's generation who first made a profession of letters by trusting themselves to the favour of the public rather than to a patron. Nashe the journalist and pamphleteer, Greene, though less successfully, and Shakespeare himself, began in the late eighties and early nineties to write getpenny work. It was still ungentlemanly to publish, and more ungentlemanly to write for the common stages. The world of the theatre was the most mixed, the most lacking in decorum of all the fields of letters. To be popular and successful, yet not to be at the mercy of the lowest part of the audience, was a task which none but Shakespeare accomplished. Had he started as anything but an absolute Johannes Factotum, his full stature could hardly have been disclosed. He may perhaps have preferred the writing of courtly poetry such as *Venus and Adonis*; but the theatre won him and eventually kept him. In the theatre he had access to a world more varied, more violent and altogether more provocative than the world of the court. It was a mixed world; for the Elizabethan audience, unlike the Jacobean audience, contained a complete cross-section of society from the nobleman to the prentice.

In the years between the death of Marlowe and Greene, and the arrival of Jonson and Chapman, the critical years between 1594 and 1598, Shakespeare had the stage virtually to himself. This was the period of his most rapid development. He grew from the experimenter of *Love's Labour's Lost* and *Richard III* to the author of *Much Ado About Nothing*. It is an unequalled achievement. He was not only the greatest of the Elizabethan dramatists, but he did far more than any other man to create the drama and establish it. This was possible because he had the most complete facility for assimilation and rejection. He learnt and built on the work of his predecessors, yet the influence is generally so indirectly perceptible that we cannot often say with confidence 'Here is a trace of Marlowe: here of Spenser: here of Kyd'. Just as it is very difficult to pin down any passage in Shakespeare to a particular source (apart from the obvious ones like Holinshed and North), so there is nothing of the notebook method in his attitude to other poets. We do not know if he kept a commonplace book like Jonson and Webster, but if so he did not appear to consult it for his playwriting. He absorbed ideas from books, but still more perhaps from talk in taverns, chance encounters and the daily intercourse of the theatre. In this flexibility, this lack of one settled code, one clear line of study, one version of a story or even one characteristic style, Shakespeare is typical of his age, of its momentary but glorious embodiment of the old and the new worlds both together.

CHAPTER VI

THE MIRROR OF NATURE: CHARACTER IN SHAKESPEARE'S PLAYS

Character as relationship—II Life and Art as shown in Relation of Audience to Dramatic Characters—III Shakespeare's Characters—IV Nature of Relationship between Characters in the Drama

> Shakespearean fish swam the sea, far away from land;
> Romantic fish swam in nets, coming to the hand;
> What are all those fish that lie gasping on the strand?

IN Yeats's lines[1] the difference between the Elizabethan and the modern view of character is epitomized. The professional psychology of the Elizabethans—though *psychology* itself was of course a word they did not know and might not have approved of—has often been taken as a guide to the dramatic characters of Shakespeare, who are explained as studies in melancholy, anger or fear.[2] This summary proceeding is not without its uses; nor without its dangers. In the first place, as a number of critics have recently pointed out,[3] the Elizabethan 'psychologists' such as Bright, La Primaudaye and Coeffeteau were not concerned to erect a body of consistent, articulated science, for science in the modern sense had not yet been born. It was the creation of the seventeenth century. Therefore in deducing some theory of what the Elizabethans agreed upon, and what Shakespeare might accordingly take for granted, a false perspective of order is imposed upon the diversified material.

In the second place, Shakespeare, like other artists of his age, was capable of presenting as art something infinitely more complex than his age could know in any other terms. It is said that Leonardo da Vinci's sketches show a knowledge of human anatomy which did not receive scientific expression till the nineteenth century. In the same way, the drawings of Dürer and some of the illustrators of early herbals show a botanical knowledge far in advance of the scientific botanists of their time.

Shakespeare was not given to theory. He was not happy when he tried to theorize—as sometimes, in his early days, he did. But he had an unique power to use traditional beliefs as the basis of his plays, without allowing the belief to become 'fixed'—as the photographers say—or hardened into a theory. His learned contemporaries, Chapman and Jonson, were great theorizers. But Shakespeare preserved a negative capability, without any irritable reaching after fact and reason,[4] which keeps the heart of his mystery still a secret. We do not know his beliefs, though we know what he valued and what he condemned. Dover Wilson pointed out that in a play like *Hamlet*, which relies to some extent on contemporary views about ghosts, the Catholic, the Puritan and the rationalist might all find ground to believe that the ghost of King Hamlet was presented according to their own views.[5] The witches in *Macbeth* are sometimes seen as the sort of wretched old women who were arraigned at the Sessions for acts of petty revenge, sometimes as having the power of the great North Berwick coven which tried to bewitch King James, sometimes as having the powers of magicians or necromancers to command the devil with authority, foretell the future and prophesy, sometimes as superhuman emissaries of the Prince of Darkness, demons disguised as women, as one authority declared them to have been.[6] Yet they are the more convincing and horrifying because we do not know exactly what they are. It would have been perfectly in keeping with the story for Shakespeare to give Macbeth a regular compact with the devil; but it would have destroyed the power of the play to do so. The fog and filthy air which clouds the supernatural implications is more terrifying than hell-fire. This hell is murky, and depends upon a carefully controlled imprecision.

The surest evidence that a belief has been lived with is that it is no longer readily to be formulated as a belief. To take a modern example, the doctrinal and ritual character of Mr. Eliot's *Ash Wednesday* is far stronger than that of *The Four Quartets* or *The Family Reunion*, Creeds have their significance as shorthand, or as an Official Secrets Act. They are not meant to explain what they affirm.

When these considerations are applied to Shakespeare's character-drawing, it becomes impossible to treat single characters in isolation. Hardin Craig has compared the art of Shakespeare with the art of tapestry or Chinese painting. 'The prevailing type of unity in medieval art was unity and variety' and this multiple art lived on through the Renaissance'.

Can it be that Shakespeare had no one clearly definable thing to say about humanity when he put Hamlet on the stage, that he did not mean some one thing by Coriolanus? Did he mean to say "A representative human being once did, when so confronted and so situated, act and speak in such and such a way"? If so, that is a very different thing from saying "Human beings, if greatly perplexed, or if beset by inordinate pride, will in the presence of such issues always behave in these ways". There is more here than a mere matter of emphasis. . . . It puts the Renaissance conception of character in a new light, since it uses a pattern of life, rather than of art, enmeshes character in environment, and distributes dramatic interest over groups of characters.[7]

Hamlet, the greatest of Shakespeare's characters, is not susceptible of explanation, and innumerable explanations, many plausible, most of them mutually irreconcilable, do not exhaust him. For here is a character the core of whose being is a mystery, which remains no less a mystery to himself than to others. Aristotle might have said that Hamlet is consistently inconsistent.[8] In his isolation and self-consciousness he is the prototype of modern man. But nevertheless he remains a character in a play: he is defined in terms of his relations with his father, his mother, his uncle, Ophelia, Horatio and the rest. At every turn he is contrasted with the world he inhabits, so that he is not conceivable apart from that world. The tragic hero is the nearest the Elizabethans ever came to the portrayal of individuality in the modern sense. In their comedy, the sense of relationship is far stronger. The characters here are conceived of as existing in terms of mutual relationship throughout. For it is only in terms of relationship that the action of comedy can be sustained. The simplest clown must have another clown to fight with.

The favourite Elizabethan image of lovers seeing each other reflected in the pupil of the eye is a symbol of character defined in terms of relationship.

> In her eie I find
> A wonder, or a wond'rous miracle,
> The shadow of myself form'd in her eye;
> Which being but the shadow of your sonne,
> Becomes a sonne, and makes your sonne a shadow.
> (*King John*, 2. 1. 496–500.)

This is the doctrine of courtly love, whereby the universe becomes interpreted to the lover in terms of his relationship to his lady, focused through that relationship, so that in the end she becomes the mediator both of knowledge and of grace.[9] Shakespeare's version in full is to be found in Berowne's great speech in defence of love, 'Have at you then, affection's men at arms!' (*Love's Labour's Lost*, 4. 3. 290–365), where seekers after knowledge are told to find it in a lady's eyes.

Yet in Shakespeare's simplest play, the relationships are more complex than this would suggest. Romeo and Juliet without the Nurse and Mercutio, Navarre and his lords without Armado, Costard, Moth and the worthies, Richard without Bolingbroke, York, Gaunt and the Queen, would in effect cease to exist with the dramatic depth and significance which makes them what they are. The consort or harmony of characters may require a momentary brilliance to be cast on one of them, such as illuminates the Fool in Acts II and III of *King Lear*, or the playing down of a character such as Cymbeline: one central character may focus all the others in relation to itself, as Hamlet does; or the vast sweep of the plot may reduce all to a level as in *Troilus and Cressida*. In each play the interaction of the parts and the whole, which is a basic necessity of the actor's art, is also a consequence of the seamless continuity of the poetry. The images which Lady Macbeth uses, and the images which Macbeth uses, emanate from a single mind writing in a single mood. The storm scenes of *King Lear* present a single experience mediated through a group of characters, and the pattern of their speech is as strict, though of a different kind, as that of the Lovers' Madrigal in *As You Like It*. Nevertheless each part is distinct, though not divided—

Two distincts, division none—

and Pope said truly that the words of any character could be assigned to him by their individual accent and tone.

Compared with any other form of Elizabethan literature, the drama developed character both in distinctness and in power of growth. Spenser's characters are embodiments of states of mind. The exact quality of grief, despair, pride, can be most delicately rendered, but the particular embodiment of it is not 'enmeshed in environment', and need not sustain that particular role for long. It has been said that Spenser's characters have a tendency to fade like the wireless: and the characters of, for example, Daniel's or Drayton's historic poems have an even more limited function. Had the drama remained a closet drama of the Senecan type, it might not have been very different, but Shakespeare was himself a man of the theatre: he experienced the playing of parts in a repertory company, and knew that the successful performance depends upon harmony and co-operation between the performers, that is, upon mutual and manifold relations within a group of actors, and on the relation of the group to their auditory. Members of an orchestra, a games team or a small ship's company have analagous experience to that of the actor, who must be simultaneously aware of all his companions, quick to cover up a slip or repair a lapse on the part of the others; but in the actor the maximum degree of individuality is combined with this interdependence of the group. Each has his own part, his own moment of taking the limelight, his own strong lines or dramatic entry. All the parts are potentially of equal value, as in polyphonic music.

This was Shakespeare's school of practical psychology. What he learnt from the stage was the sympathetic ability to conceive the character from within—and this may suddenly happen with any character, large or small—together with the sense of that character's always forming part of a meshed continuity of action, in which other characters are involved.

II

The relations of an Elizabethan company with its audience were more intimate and complex than those which obtain between actors and audience to-day. Physically they were much closer, with part of the audience sitting on the stage: they were also more familiar with one another. At one extreme the clown might hold dialogue with a member of the audience or compose rhymes extempore on topics which they suggested: the tragic hero might point his moral directly at the audience, as Tourneur's Vindice does:[10] the Prologue and the Epilogue, in which the audience were openly addressed, might merge into the play proper. Owing to their belief in the direct moral power of literature, the presence of the audience, ready to be convinced, exhorted or edified, was considered necessary to the full life of the drama.

The characters were thus closely related to the audience as 'exempla', 'mirrors', or 'shadows'. In plays written for an especial audience, such as a wedding masque, they might reflect the principal spectators. When *The Arraignement of Paris* or *Endimion* were played before the Queen, the mirror was held up to Nature in a very special sense. As the golden apple was delivered into 'the nymph Zabeta's own hands' by Diana, the play dissolved into compliment. When Endimion's love was played before the Queen, the Prologue might well say:

> We present neither comedy nor tragedy nor story nor any-thing,

for Cynthia on the stage was but a pale reflection of Cynthia on the dais, and the whole point of the play was to allow Leicester to conduct his wooing by proxy.

> *End.* The time was Madam, and is, and ever shall be, that I honoured your highness aboue all the world; but to stretch it so far as to call it loue, I neuer durst. There hath none pleased my eye but *Cynthia*, none delighted mine eares but *Cynthia*, none possessed my hart but *Cynthia*. I haue forsaken all other fortunes to followe *Cynthia*, and here I stande ready to die if it please *Cynthia*. Such a difference hath the gods sette between our states, that all must be dutie, loyaltie and reuerence: nothing (without it please your highnesse) be tearmed loue. My unspotted thoughts, my languishing bodie, my discontented life, let them obtaine by princelie fauour that which to challenge, they must not presume, onelie wishing of impossibilities: with imagination of which, I will spend my spirits, and to myselfe that no creature may heare, softlie call it loue. And if any vrge to utter what I whisper, then will I name it honor'.
>
> (*Endimion*, 5. 3. 162–175.)

Such impudent ventriloquism was not often practised, but dramatic compliment of the kind which Shakespeare paid in *A Midsummer Night's Dream* to the 'Fair vestal throned by the West' derives from it. Plays which depicted the court—such as *Love's Labour's Lost*—must have had something of this mirror function; and as we learn from the play within the play, a courtly audience was quite as likely to intervene as a popular one. Later Dekker and Heywood dramatized the lives of tradesmen in similar fashion. With the possibility of a sudden incursion from the audience, whether banter from young gentlemen or intervention of the kind which occurs in *The Knight of the Burning Pestle*, the threefold relation of play-actors-spectators must have been constantly present to all.[11]

There is a curious parallel to this reflected inclusion of spectators within the play in some of the great paintings of the Renaissance, where the figure of a spectator is necessary to complete the composition. The well-known portrait of the Arnolfini by Van Eyck has in the background a mirror in which the artist's reflection can be seen. Velasquez' *Meninas*, a group of Spanish royal children painted for their parents, are standing in a semicircle, bowing and curtseying: the group was completed only when the king and queen stood in front of it in person and saw their reflections in a mirror hanging behind the children.[12] But if the picture required spectators to complete it, the composition in turn transmitted life to them. As the image of a Christ-child might bless the worshipper kneeling before it, so a Vice might warn the audience of its sins.[13] The 'lively image' depicted joy, grief, dissimulation and this 'life' moved the spectator by its excellence so that guilty creatures sitting at a play were brought to confession. Because life and art were so directly related, they could not be confused, except by clowns. Bottom expects the ladies to be afraid of the stage lion, but Hamlet is surprised that the First Player should work himself up to shedding real tears in the scene of Priam's death. The common experience for Shakespeare's audience probably lay somewhere between the two. In this mirror-quality of stage life the dramatist had an advantage over the earlier poets of the Court, who in the eighteen-eighties had centred their poetry upon the dramatic spectacle and the dramatic intrigues of the Queen, her adorers, and the lords and ladies of their train. I have suggested that the peculiar relation of the earlier poetry to the actual life of the characters who figured in it meant that there was originally a kind of air to which these words formed the song, a play of which they were no more than the scenario. This element of the art was transient, and died with the society from which it sprang.

When, however, Shakespeare turned from the courtly world

of the Sonnets (and also of his Ovidian poems) and subdued himself to what he worked in, the common theatres, the gain was almost incalculable. The life of a Court may be genuine enough, as the life of a mess, a convent or a ship may be genuine enough: but it is not *tidal* life. The poetry of the court was dominated by the rules of the different 'species' and their various 'decorums', which corresponded to the various roles which might be played upon the courtly stage by the noble actors. But on the public stages, whilst there were certain pragmatic 'species' and conventions, there was on the whole no organized Rule, as described in Chapter III.

So the basic sympathies of the plays lie not in this or that code, either moral or literary—if the two may be distinguished, as perhaps for the Elizabethan they could not—but in common humanity. Orlando appeals to the Duke for help in terms of daily experience which as Dr. Johnson said 'finds an echo in every breast'.

> If ever you have look'd on better days,
> If ever been where bels have knoll'd to Church;
> If ever sat at any good man's feast,
> If ever from your eyelids wip'd a tear,
> And knew what 'tis to pitty and be pittied,
> Let gentleness my strong enforcement be. . . .
>
> (2. 7. 113–8.)

King Lear kneels to pray for the 'poor naked wretches' who are out in the storm. Costard appeals for Sir Nathaniel as 'a marvellous good neighbour i' faith, and a very good bowler'. The fellowship which we have good testimony of in Shakespeare's life is embodied in his plays. Not that he is without moral sympathies and revulsions. In an excellent survey of Shakespeare's ethic, *As They Liked It*, Professor Alfred Harbage has pointed out that the interest which every age has taken in Shakespeare's characters and their problems has been a *moral* interest, although there has been but slight agreement about the moral standing of the characters or even about the nature of the problems. In other words, Shakespeare

avoided both judgments and dogmas, and kept to the
'high road of life' because the life that was mirrored in his
plays was so varied that a less inclusive attitude would not
serve. His instinctive judgment—all that distinguishes him
from the amiably complacent Dekker and Heywood—would
not prevent the whole concourse of gentlemen, and citizens
at the Globe from feeling at home in his world of common
humanity and seeing it as the reflection of their own.

No doubt there were both variation and development in the
relations of players and audience. The original function of
drama as religious ceremony made the spectator integral to it.
When the comic torturers scourged Christ in the miracle
plays, the audience would recognize themselve in these macabre
figures, since their guilt and sins were responsible for the eternal
act of crucifixion. In secular drama such complete identification is not possible. The open appeals to the spectators, which
are common enough in the interludes, become less common in
later Tudor drama: Robert Greene seems to have tried, in
ways that now appear confused and naïve, to work out the
relation between audience and actors.[14] Ben Jonson's Inductions,
the choruses to *Henry V* and the prologues and epilogues of
the Jacobean stage, are much more sophisticated. The masque,
pageant, or 'triumph' retained a closer connexion between
spectators and actors: in court masques, the players might
finally take out the audience to dance, and in triumphs the
leading figure might simply be dramatizing himself as Fortune,
Faithful Love, or Valour Triumphant.

As the nature of dramatic consciousness varied, so might
the nature of the characters in the play. Shakespeare has
characters of all degrees of naturalism and symbolism, and
even one or two allegorical characters, such as Revenge,
Rumour, Time, who appear in prologues or interludes.
Pagan gods and goddesses appear in *As You Like It*, *Pericles*,
Cymbeline and *The Tempest*. But far more frequently he will
use a representative figure like the Father and Son of *3 Henry
VI*,[15] the Old Man of *Macbeth*, Gower in *Pericles*, the French
Lords in *All's Well*. Other characters may approximate to

the generic, as Adam does in *As You Like It*: Orlando expressly says:

> O good old man, how well in thee appears
> The constant service of the antique world,
> When service sweat for duty, not for meed!
>
> (2. 3. 56–58.)

Adam is at least given a name (though a symbolic one perhaps): Bates, Williams, and Court in *Henry V* are likewise characterized to some degree; but in all such cases, the role is purely functional; to turn them into individual characters is not in accord with the parts as provided by Shakespeare.

III

The conventional stage types provided models of which Shakespeare sometimes availed himself, but attempts such as those of Professor Stoll to determine the nature of Shakespeare's characters by their theatrical pedigree were natural reactions from nineteenth-century criticism of the characters, and have by now almost run their course. It is nearly forty years since this type of criticism was first introduced by Schucking and Stoll, and the severe treatment bestowed upon it recently by Mr. J. I. M. Stewart seems rather like flogging a dead horse.[16] Mr. Stewart trounces Stoll for turning Falstaff into a morality Vice, only to reintroduce him translated into a Dying God, a dethroned and sacrificed king, a scapegoat. But here, as elsewhere in Shakespeare, it is necessary to remember his unique power of transmuting old conventions by new life. To ignore Falstaff's connexion with the Vice is perhaps as bad as to confuse him with 'the tradition', explain him in terms of the mid-Tudor interlude, and reject all that is most characteristically Shakespearean as 'modern misreading'.

Shakespearean characters have every gradation of being, from generic to specific: except that he seems to disclaim, in the person of the poet in *Timon*, the placing of real people on the stage.

> No levelled malice
> Infects one comma in the course I hold,
> But flies an eagle flight, bold and forth on,
> Leaving no tract behind.
>
> (I. I. 48–51.)

In this, modern criticism marches with him so far, that the contemporary reaction against 'character criticism' is liable to carry Shakespeareans into the opposite extreme. The vogue for symbolic interpretation presents us with Cordelia standing for Redeemed Nature, the Resurrection of Hermione as a Rebirth Symbol, and the murder of little Macduff as an image of the Atonement.[17] Such extravagances will always be counterbalanced by those who discover Leicester, Essex or Mary, Queen of Scots, behind various *dramatis personae*.[18]

Not only may characters range from the generic to the specific, their relations with one another may range through a wide variety of the direct and indirect, the implicit and the explicit, the contrasted and the superimposed. Sometimes there will be a complete and simple opposition, as between Cordelia and her two sisters: on the other hand, the opposition between Othello and Iago is of a subtler kind. In the brothel scene Othello speaks with the voice of Iago. Like Coleridge's *Christabel*, whose features imitate those of Geraldine, Othello reflects the image of his tormentor. In the first temptation scene it is almost possible to see the poison injected. In this scene a new relation is established between Othello and Iago. They grow closer and closer. 'I am your own for ever' Iago says: the demi-devil claims his victim, they grow horribly united. Othello blows his fond love to heaven and summons vengeance from the hollow hell. The cynicism of Iago issues through Othello's lips. His asides during the dialogue between Cassio and Bianca are like Iago's asides in the earlier scene between Cassio and Desdemona.

At the end Othello comes to himself, to find that in his madness he had butchered all he loved. Shakespeare is not using the doctrine of madness or possession in this play, but the relations of Iago and Othello are so interlocked that Mr. Stewart can declare that:

at certain cardinal moments in the play when poetically received, Othello and Iago are felt less as individuals each with his own psychological integrity than as abstractions from a single and, as it were, invisible protagonist. . . . It is less a matter of Othello's projecting concealed facets of himself upon an apt Iago . . . than of the dramatist's abstracting these facets and embodying them in a figure substantially symbolic.[19]

What this would mean in terms of Elizabethan thought I am not quite clear. But they would certainly have expected Othello as a negro to have all the characteristics which are given to Iago. All black men were cruel to an Elizabethan, classed with Turks and Jews in atrocity plays. Aaron, Eleazar, Muly Mohamet and the rest are perfidious Machiavels. The average audience would see Othello as untraditional and his expected character transferred to Iago.

Elizabethan psychology had an ethical aim, and attempted to expound to the reader the primary moral problem of human life and provide him with the requisite means to meet it.[20] Literature also had an ethical aim: it held the mirror up to Nature, and thereby enabled the children of Nature to correct their natural imperfections. Nature was plastic and could be moulded. Art was even more plastic than nature.

However much the physiological aspect of his character might predispose a man to act, the ultimate remedy for his disorders was ethical: the use of reason, prayer, and the exercise of the will in self-control. All theorists are at least agreed upon this. There was little sympathy even for the hereditary criminal, for the hunchback like Richard, or the bastard like John of Messina who was warped by the circumstances of his birth. The purpose of the classification of human beings according to types was often an ethical or political rather than a medical one: for instance a ruler who had studied the outward signs of various humours was enabled to detect traitors, distinguish the rash from the cautious by their appearance, and choose his counsellors accordingly. The immensely popular medieval *Secreta Secretorum* contains a long list of such characteristics for the use of the prince: Caesar is following this line of study when he wishes to have men about him that are fat.

Because reason was the supreme and governing faculty, dramatic characters may occasionally show themselves open to persuasion in a way that appears highly artificial. Truth *must* prevail: and if the mind is convinced, then the will and action will follow the lead of reason. In *The Honest Whore*, Part I, Hippolito undertakes to convert the courtesan Bellafront by force of reason and does so. In the second part, having lapsed into a sinful desire to possess her, he prepares to argue her out of her virtue again, and Bellafront agrees that *if* he can produce convincing reasons, she will yield.[21] In *The Revenger's Tragedy* Vindice's attempt to seduce his sister for the duke is repulsed, to his great joy: but he finds to his horror that his fallacious arguments have succeeded with his mother. Hence such scenes as the trial scene in *The Merchant of Venice*, Isabel's debate with Angelo, the King's attempt to show that Hellen is as noble as Bertram would have more than a rhetorical interest: for all these characters speak with the voice of reason, and if their opponents were not blinded or perverted, they would be irresistible. Brutus appeals to the reason of the Roman mob, Antony to its passions. Shakespeare was at this point in advance of his contemporaries, although his view derives from theirs.

A character might turn from a jealous man into Jealousy, as Malbecco does in *The Faerie Queene*. Leontes is like enough to Othello for everyone to feel the difference that makes him into a study of possession—the flooding of a character by the passion of Jealousy so that he ceases temporarily to *be* himself. This was readily acceptable to Elizabethans. John in a passion and Tom in a passion were more alike than John in a passion and John out of it.

But the representation of such passions belongs rather to the drama of Ben Jonson than of Shakespeare. Shakespeare could accept and transform the theory, but he did not use it undiluted. The relation of Othello and Iago remains therefore one which cannot be finally formulated but which can only be perceived. Nor can it be divided from the relations of Desdemona and Emilia. Desdemona transforms Emilia as Iago transforms Othello, so that at the end the coarse waiting woman puts on the image of fidelity and dies for her mistress. The two men who have murdered their wives face each other before the bed where Emilia lies 'by her mistress' side'. Yet the scene cannot be reduced to such a simple equation. Still less can the final plays, those exquisite embodiments of a vision in the form of the humblest and simplest tales, be reduced to a dance of symbols, variations upon a vegetation myth. Shakespeare always *embodies* his vision. To reformulate it in terms of character, ethics, or moral platitude is to leave the spectator with nothing but a ghost in a corpse—ideas dressed up in fine words.

In the realm of comedy, a different path led to the same conclusion. The characters of comedy were more fixed than those of tragedy—with the possible exception of characters in the revenge convention. The *commedia dell' arte*, the most highly developed professional comedy of Western Europe, depended on a group of stereotyped figures, the Harlequin, Pantaloon, Captain, Doctor and the rest, who had a stock of *lazzi* or farcical jests from which they might improvise the comic part of their play. In some of Shakespeare's plays there seem to be traces of these comic characters.[22] The old comedy of the English stage included various comic characters of tested popularity such as the 'frampole' woman, the witty page and the country bumpkin. There are for example a very fine pair of country bumpkins in *King Cambyses*, a play which Shakespeare certainly knew for he quotes bits of it in *Pyramus and Thisbe*.[23]

Whereas in tragedy Shakespeare had one or two stiff but heroical models, in comedy he had a miscellaneous collection of rather limited and outmoded types, together with the court comedy of Lyly. Shakespeare's earliest comedies depend on their models, whether Italian, as in *The Taming of the Shrew*, or classical, as in *The Comedy of Errors*; but they redouble the ingenuities, add further symmetry to the grouping of characters and further complexities to the intrigue. It was in the contrasting of groups of characters, such as the groups of *A Midsummer Night's Dream* and *The Merchant of Venice*, that Shakespeare developed his own technique. Variety strengthened his powers. The contrast of Portia and Shylock, or Theseus, the fairies and Bottom, gives a deeper life to each of these groups than is to be found in more homogeneous plays, such as *The Two Gentlemen of Verona*, built on the regular Italian pattern of serious lovers and comic clowns.

The variety of his character drawing is a measure of its complexity. In his mature work all might be subdued to a common atmosphere—the delicate mockery of *As You Like It*, the gracious and graceful absurdities of *Twelfth Night*. His characters live within a particular atmosphere, and move within the gravitational orbits of the other characters, each modifying all the others. Take away Sir Andrew Aguecheek, and not only is Sir Toby unprovided for, but the whole balance of the play is upset. These characters could not be summed up in the Theophrastian manner, as Ben Jonson sums up the characters of *Every Man Out of His Humour*. Such characters as his are variations upon a given theme; they are all gulls or knaves, sometimes, as in *Volpone*, variations upon one fundamental pattern of gull-and-knave. Yet Shakespeare's characters, like Ben Jonson's, exist, only in relation to each other, because they are all conceived as inhabiting a particular kind of world: they belong to a particular literary species and their speech, which in a sense *is* their character, is part of a single poem: they are

> matched in mouth like bells,
> Each under each.
>
> (*Midsummer Night's Dream*, 5. 1.)

IV

The governing Idea which produces multiplicity without division of parts is hardly to be found in modern literature. Personal relationships, 'the holiness of the heart's affections',[24] are not only the ground of modern fiction but the salt of modern existence. The great writers of the past fifty years have been concerned above all with exploring the relationships of highly individual characters. Proust reached the limits of individual sensitiveness, 'the small circle of pain within the skull' and the nightmares of a private world. His is a work designed for individual readers.[25] But the literature of Shakespeare's time was still largely communal. It was not perhaps altogether as communal as that of the fourteenth century, when many of the courtly class might be illiterate, and poetry was composed to be read aloud to a group—as was Chaucer's *Troilus and Criseyde*. Then all poetry was written for the general ear, love-poetry not least. The art of flirting had to be carried on in public. Although the notion of privacy had gained a little ground by Shakespeare's time, the upper classes of his day led nearly all their lives in public. Births and deaths in all classes of society were events which, far from being private, were occasions for some publicity, and even the bridal chamber was invaded in a way which would shock the most unembarrassed of our youth. Hamlet, the solitary muser, was an *innovation*; it is on the whole not till the seventeenth century that praise of solitude becomes a general thing.[26] Only villains, like Lorenzo and Richard III, will say, 'I'll trust myself: myself shall be my friend' 'I am myself alone' or 'Richard loves Richard: that is, I am I'.[27]

Such independence is diabolic. On the other hand, the relationship between different characters is often less than personal, and sometimes, perhaps, more than personal. Interpretation on a personal level yields the caddish Claudio and Bassanio, the proud and tactless Cordelia and 'that four-flusher Prospero'. Only cynicism could save the problem comedies or, for Lytton Strachey, the final romances, from incoherence. Personal relationship may at times be short-circuited, as that between Rosalind and her father. It is not needed in the body of the play, and so it is not developed. The useful convention of the twins enables Olivia in *Twelfth Night* to be made happy. A symmetrical grouping of lovers, such as those of *Love's Labour's Lost* or *A Midsummer Night's Dream*, allows the characters to be developed only in shallow relief—but here a certain shallowness in the characters is required for the effect Shakespeare is aiming at.

Disguise, conversion, or a magic potion will enable one of the *dramatis personae* to assume a completely different role, though usually one that is dramatically contrasted with that of his previous part. The most astonishing case in all Elizabethan drama occurs in William Heminge's *Fatal Contract* where the heroine disguises herself as a blackamoor. As all blackamoors are wicked, she commits the most appalling crimes in this disguise, which do not in any way pertain to her 'real' character.

Shakespeare uses disguise mainly for his heroines, where it has special charms, and special uses: and occasionally for his rulers, such as the Duke of Vienna and Henry V, where it stands in place of the power to walk invisible enjoyed by Prospero. Even a change of appearance may produce a transformation as when Henry V enters from his coronation, Prospero throws off his magician's robe, or Hamlet appears disguised as a common sailor. Edgar's disguise in *King Lear* is more like a change of role.

Shakespeare's use of such conventions, however, is far slighter than most of his contemporaries. It is not the popular playwrights alone who enjoy them but such learned writers as Chapman, who in one single drama (*May-Day*) provides a man disguised as a woman, a girl disguised as a page, and an old man disguised as a chimney-sweep. Shakespeare's comic plots are in general more leisurely, less crowded and more closely unified than those of other comic writers. In the tragi-comedy of *Cymbeline*, where he seems to be using means that are openly 'stagey', for a particular end, he is able to produce, in the final scene, twenty-four dénouements in the space of 455 lines. This is quite exceptional, whereas *May-Day* (which appeared a year after *Cymbeline*) is quite typical of Chapman, and depends throughout on 'catch-as-catch-can'. When Dr. Johnson observed that Shakespeare indulged his disposition and his disposition led him to comedy,[28] he was hardly doing justice to Shakespeare's tragic powers. But it remains true that in comedy no less than in tragedy, he profoundly modified what his age had to give, whilst availing himself of an unusually wide range of tradition.

There was also one other source which Shakespeare drew upon: his own compositions. He did not repeat himself, of course, yet the echoes and reformulations which can be traced between one play and another are surely significant. Antonio in *The Merchant of Venice* and Antonio in *Twelfth Night*, Hotspur and Coriolanus, the plots of *All's Well* and *Measure for Measure*, the themes of the final plays, Tarquin and Macbeth, Andronicus and Lear, Lear and Timon—these resemblances are more than accidental. There is a sense in which Shakespeare's work forms a single complicated whole—with a unity of the 'tapestry' kind discerned by Hardin Craig in the single plays. These successive attempts strive to formulate something of which perhaps they are each alternative embodiments, as Mr. Stewart has suggested:

. . . the subliminal falling now into one coherent pattern and then into another of the varied elements of his total man—elements many of which will never, except in his writing, find play in consciousness. It is this that gives the characters their independence as well as relation; their haunting suggestion of reality and of a larger, latent being unexhausted in the action immediately before us: their ability to beckon beyond the narrow limits of their hour.[29]

Or, put in its lowest terms, whilst the number of sources that Shakespeare is sometimes considered to have consulted may sound rather more in number than a busy professional man could find time to go round London borrowing, or more than would fit into his Bishopsgate lodging, there is one work with which we can be sure he was acquainted and which was at all times available to him: the poems and plays of Shakespeare.

To his contemporaries, and indeed to the greater part of the seventeenth century as well, Shakespeare's reputation did not stand as high as Ben Jonson's, who 'in every single decade of the century is praised more often than Shakespeare' and is mentioned three times to every single mention of Shakespeare.[30] Yet throughout the century Shakespeare's characters are better known. 'This particular aspect of Shakespeare's creative genius', according to Professor Bentley, 'triumphed over the critical standards which generally blinded the men of the time to his superiority'.

Falstaff, Othello, Desdemona, Brutus, Iago and Hamlet (in that order) were what Shakespeare's contemporaries and immediate successors thought of and spoke of whenever they thought of his art.

CHAPTER VII

MORAL HERALDRY

'Titus Andronicus'—II 'Rape of Lucrece'—III 'Romeo and Juliet'

TITUS ANDRONICUS and *The Rape of Lucrece*, Shakespeare's two 'tragical discourses' were in their time extremely well thought on. We have Ben Jonson's word that the public enjoyed *Titus*, and Gabriel Harvey's that the judicious read *Lucrece*.[1] They are now among the least studied of his work, and *Titus* has often been rejected from the canon, though its many echoes of *The Rape of Lucrece* should alone be enough to retain it.[2]

In these two works, where Shakespeare was trying his hand in the high style, he models from accepted designs. Early Elizabethan tragedy was closely connected with the nondramatic Complaint: *Lucrece* is comparable with Daniel's *Rosamund's Complaint*, and *Titus* is largely a dramatic lament. The Complaint was a late medieval form: in *The Mirror for Magistrates*, the medieval tradition was transmitted to the Elizabethans. The Vergilian journey to the underworld, the allegorical figures and wailing ghosts, the imagery of hell and judgment and the demonstration of the turn of Fortune's wheel as Chaucer described it:

> Tragedy is to seyn a certeyn storie . . .
> Of hym that stood in greet prosperitee
> And is yfallen out of high degree
> Into myserie and endeth wrecchedly—

are all transferred to the stage in the early revenge play, the other parent-stock from which *Titus Andronicus* derives. Kyd's *Spanish Tragedy* provided the dramatic model: Ovid's *Metamorphoses*, part of the story, which is based on the Rape of Philomel. Shakespeare was drawing on as many good authorities as he could: but the Senecan influence is now generally disallowed.[3]

There is an emblematic or heraldic quality about all the characters of *Titus Andronicus*. Formal grouping appears with the first great scene of lament where, after the procession of Titus's condemned sons, Lucius, his banished heir, stands with sword drawn, whilst Titus kneels and pleads with the stones under his feet.

> A stone is silent and offendeth not,
> And tribunes with their tongues doom men to death

he says, working out the emblematic contrast of the stony-hearted men at great length. Next, the ravished Lavinia is brought to her father; he invites the whole family to sit on the earth together and wipe one another's eyes in a kind of ballet of lamentation. Titus sees himself as a figure in a tapestry or a picture, something to move the sorrows of spectators.

> What foole hath added water to the sea,
> Or brought a faggot to bright burning Troy? . . .
> For now I stand as one upon a rocke
> Invirond with a wilderness of sea,
> Who marks the waxing tide grow wave by wave. . . .
>   (3. 1. 69–70, 94–96.)

His ravished daughter would be woeful enough if she were only a pictured figure, he says: but she is alive. Nevertheless the effect is that of a living picture rather than of life itself. Titus points out all his woeful family in turn and comments on them: when he has mutilated himself in a vain attempt to save his sons' lives, and receives as reward their two decapitated heads, his brother takes up the role of commentator, and points out the tragic spectacle, including himself

> Even like a stony image, cold and numme
>   (3. 1. 258.)

He invites Titus to rage and lament, instead of trying to restrain him. Instead, Titus bursts into a terrific laugh. It is the turning-point of the play: Titus has dropped the role of Lamenter to take up that of Revenger.

> Which way shall I find Revenges Cave?
>
> (3. 1. 270.)

he asks, as they go off in ghastly procession, bearing the severed heads and Titus's severed hand between them. The answering tableau is the grisly conclusion, with Titus, fantastically dressed as a cook, serving up his banquet of human flesh to Tamyra.

Moral heraldry is devised in the other scene of lament, the mourning feast at Titus's house, where he moralizes formally on his daughter—'this map of woe' he calls her. In this scene also he has a speech of madness in which he rebukes his brother for killing a fly, until told that it was a black fly, emblematic of the wicked Aaron. The comment is provided by a child:

> I have read that Hecuba of Troy
> Ran mad through sorrow
>
> (4. 1. 20–21.)

Such emblematic scenes, or mirror scenes as they have been called, occur in Kyd, Marlowe, and Shakespeare's tragic histories.[4]

The great precedents from the Trojan story are invoked again and again: in the final scene Marcus anticipates the ravished Lucrece when he speaks of 'the Sinon that bewitcht our eares' and brought Rome to her present ruin:

> The baleful burning night
> When subtile Greeks surpris'd King Priam's Troy.
>
> (5. 3. 83–84.)

It is Titus, Lucrece and their speeches of formal lament which are behind the First Player's speech in *Hamlet* upon the mobled queen. The play scene in *Hamlet* depends upon our taking this older species of tragedy seriously. Shakespeare was using it as he used ancient Gower in *Pericles*, to give remoteness and grandeur, not to parody or belittle an obsolete style.

The moral heraldry of *Titus Andronicus* is not confined to grouping and imagery. The figure of Aaron is the only one which beside Titus has any life in it. He is portentous and diabolic: his blackness an outward symbol of his diabolic nature, recognized by all. 'Aaron will have his soul black like his face', he says; and a similar character, Eleazer the Moor in *Lust's Dominion*,[5] is told

> Truth to tell,
> Seeing your face, we thought of hell,

and

> Here hell must be, where the devil governs you.

Aaron is clearly related to both Ithamore and Barabas of *The Jew of Malta*. In the long speech in which he confesses before his death, he echoes the Jew:

> Even now I curse the day and yet I thinke
> Few come within the compass of my curse,
> Wherein I did not some notorious ill. . . .

Murder, rape, perjury, the kind of crime against 'poor men's cattle' and their barns and haystacks which the common witch was accused of are all jumbled together, and neatly linked with Titus's lament by the final simile:

> Tut, I have done a thousand dreadfull things,
> As willingly as one would kill a flie. . . .
> (5. 1. 141–142.)

Aaron is half-symbol, half stage-formula. The medieval devil, witty and exuberant, has contributed to his character, and so has the conscienceless Machiavel, with his delight in plots, his manipulation of the poor victims to engineer their own undoing, and his rapid action by violence when 'policy' will not serve. He is an atheist of course, and regards an oath as 'popish' (5. 1. 76).[6]

His wit throws the laments of the tragic characters into high relief—whether he is crying 'weke, weke' as he stabs the nurse ('so cries a pigge prepared to the spit'), 'almost splitting his sides with extreme laughter' as Titus mutilates himself, or

dandling the coal-black baby which Tamora bears him, and
defying her sons:

> Yee white limde walles, yee alehouse painted signes. . . .
> (4. 2. 98–99.)

But when the Revenge action is on foot, Titus becomes
witty and ironic in turn, sends his ominous presents to the
young princes, shoots his arrows at the gods, and outplays
Aaron at his own game of countermining.

Murder and Rape are finally personified upon the stage and
the Empress Tamora herself appears as Revenge, the spirit
which had prompted her first acts, and which now prompts
Titus. Throughout the play the murders, rapes, mutilations
and other atrocities remain mere moral heraldry, with no
more sense of physical embodiment than if all the characters
had been given such names.

This is ensured by the formal quality of the writing, which
is learned, rhetorical, full of conceits. The imagery of 'black
night', 'hollow caves' and the gloomy journey to hell in
search of revenge belong to the tragic tradition of Kyd.[7] Yet
sometimes a decorous pastoral landscape appears, which jars
most violently against the subject with which it is related, as in
the description of the ravished Lavinia, when villains had

> lopt and hewde and made thy body bare,
> Of her two branches, those sweet Ornaments,
> Whose circling Shadowes, Kings have sought to sleepe in . . .
> Alas, a crimson River of warme blood,
> Like to a bubling Fountaine stirde with winde,
> Doth rise and fall between thy Rosed lips,
> Comming and going with thy honie breath . . .
> One houres storme will drowne the fragrant meades . . .
> (2. 4. 16ff.)

This imagery is meant to work by contrast, like some of the
imagery in the narrative poems.[8] The writer is saying by
means of the images, 'Look here upon this picture, and on
this'. The contrast of remembering happiness in misery is

the very material of the lament. Shakespeare's Queen Margaret and his Constance, when bereaved like Titus, were to do the same.[9] This remembrance is the cause of the madness of grief to which all three succumb. All personify Sorrow; all become larger than life, fixed in their statuesque pose.

> I will instruct my sorrows to be proud . . .
> To me and to the state of my great grief
> Let kings assemble: for my grief's so great
> That no supporter but the huge firm earth
> Can hold it up: here I and sorrows sit;
> Here is my Throne, bid kings come bow to it.
> (King John, 3. 1. 68ff.)

In King John, however, there is no decorum, no governing Idea. The laments of Constance, the personified figure of England that is called Falconbridge, and the moral theme, which is stated in the last lines, deriving perhaps from Andrew Borde's figure of an Englishman,[10] have no necessary connexions. Titus Andronicus, on the other hand, keeps decorum in its own species. It is a learned play, or at least it tries to be learned: it uses the grand rhetorical style, affixes scraps of Latin here and there, and the narrative has a fixed and stony quality which perhaps expresses the general idea of stern antique times. From Peacham's illustration it appears some attempt was made at historic costume. In all this it differs from a brawling headlong play like Lust's Dominion, and its manner, like its imagery, is nearer to the Ovidian Romance, such as Barksted's Myrrha, where the violent theme of incest between father and daughter is treated purely emblematically. Myrrha addresses her unborn child as brother and son at once with the kind of incongruous lyric metaphor that Shakespeare applied to Lavinia:

> Oft do two roses grow out of one stem,
> And one of them is blown before the other.

When she is turned into a tree and continues to weep,

> Two streams did run thorough each flower filld mead.

Myrrha is hardly a character; she is an embodiment of Natural Desire, and is constantly described under these images of Nature. The fact that Barksted was writing in professed imitation of Shakespeare's *Venus and Adonis* only emphasizes how greatly his work differs from that of his master; but it is in tune with *Titus*, where Tamora is a tiger and Aaron a devil, who like the negro bond-slave in the popular tale of Tom-a-Lincoln must be set in the earth and starved to death[11] to symbolize the end of Base Desire.

Titus Andronicus is then more like a pageant than a play. But unlike such pageants as those at the end of the third book of the *Faerie Queene*, it is not provided with an interpretation, and no doubt it was enjoyed by the groundlings as an atrocity play. They would take what it had in common with *Lust's Dominion* and ignore what was different. This learned and decorous work may have achieved popular success only through misunderstanding of the young author's intentions.

It is quite possible that Shakespeare himself did not know exactly what he meant by this play. But in the laments of Titus, which are the core of the piece, can be felt some faint foreshadowing of the pain and madness that were ultimately to issue in *King Lear*.[12] The play seems a first crude attempt to portray some experience that Shakespeare was only to recognize, understand and embody in a 'lively image' at a much later stage. Because that later image exists, we may guess at the unfulfilled intention of the earlier writing, where the meaning is given in terms of doctrine, not of experience: stated, not realized: shadowed, not portrayed.

II

The Rape of Lucrece is even more heraldic than *Titus Andronicus*. The combat between Lucrece and Tarquin, saint and devil (as they are called) is introduced by a passage in which the heraldry of Lucrece's face is set forth in a manner derived from the thirteenth sonnet of *Astrophel and Stella*, where Cupid wins the contest of arms from Jove and Mars:

> . . . on his crest there lies
> Stella's faire haire, her face he makes his shield,
> Where roses gules are borne in silver field.

In Lucrece's face there is a contest between the red and white of beauty and virtue:

> But Beautie in that white entituled,
> From Venus doves doth challenge that faire field,
> Then Vertue claimes from Beautie, Beauties red,
> Which Vertue gave the golden age, to guild
> Their silver cheekes, and calld it then their shield:
> Teaching them thus to use it in the fight,
> When shame assaild, the red should fence the white.
>
> (57–63.)

Tarquin, caught between these two armies, yields himself as many a Petrarchan lover had done. He sees clearly the result of his action: 'O shame to knighthood and to shining Armes'. The heralds will contrive some mark of abatement for his coat,[13] but

> Affection is my Captaine and he leadeth
> And when his gaudie banner is displaide,
> The coward fights, and will not be dismaide.
>
> (271–273.)

The long account of Tarquin's assault goes into minute detail of his 'drumming heart', his 'Burning eye', Lucrece's 'ranks of blew vains' which run pale when his hand like a 'Rude Ram' batters the 'Ivorie wall' of the 'sweet Citty'. Later his soul is compared with a 'sacked temple' and her body at the end to a 'late-sacked island'. Her shame is an abatement on Collatine's arms.

> O unfelt sore, crest-wounding, private scare!
> Reproch is stampt in Collatinus' face,
> And Tarquin's eye maie read the mot a farre.

All this imagery is centred in the great lament of Lucrece

before the tapestry depicting the Sack of Troy, in which she sees an emblem of her own state. In the figure of Hecuba she sees a mirror image of her grief and in the deceitful Sinon a mirror of Tarquin. The whole passage—it begins by describing the 'life' of the piece which seemed to 'scorn nature'—embodies the violence of war, and confirms the theme implicit in the metaphors describing Tarquin and Lucrece. The lament of the bereaved, the dignity of the commanders, the terror of cowards, are all depicted in little, and what is not depicted is implied by 'conceit deceitful, so compact, so kind' that a part was left to represent the whole which was 'left unseen, save to the eye of mind'. This insistence upon natural representation, within an artificial tapestry, set as an illustration to an artificially-devised poem has a strange recessional effect, comparable in some ways to the play-within-the-play.

The main body of the poem consists of the speeches of Tarquin and of Lucrece: his debate with himself, the debate between them both, the lament, testament and final speech of Lucrece. More than a third of the whole poem consists of her complaints, in which she 'rails' at Time, Night and Opportunity, the authors of her woe. Tarquin's debate with himself is more dramatic, since there is a conflict in his mind between conscience and will. As *Titus* in a simplified and distorted form presents some of the elements of *King Lear*, so the soliloquies of Tarquin are like a first cartoon for the study of *Macbeth*.[14] Here, too, there is an expense of spirit in a waste of shame, a figure of conscious guilt calling in night and the creatures of night for aid, an act of physical violence followed by as quick a repentance. Tarquin, like Macbeth, tries to pray in the very act of committing the act and is startled to find he cannot do it. The atmosphere of Rome is that of Inverness:

> Now stole uppon the time the dead of night,
> When heavie sleep had closd up mortall eyes,
> No comfortable starre did lend his light,
> No noise but Owles and wolves' death-boding cries
> Now serves the season that they may surprise

.The sillie Lambes, pure thoughts are dead and still,
While Lust and Murder wakes to staine and kill.

(162–168.)

Now o'er the one half world
Nature seems dead and wicked dreams abuse
The curtain'd sleep: Witchcraft celebrates
Pale Hecate's offerings; and withered Murther,
Alarum'd by his sentinel, the Wolf,
Whose howl's his watch thus with his stealthy pace,
With Tarquin's ravishing strides, towards his designs
Moves like a ghost.

(2. 1. 49–56.)

This figure of 'a creeping creature with a flaming light'
remained with Shakespeare as late as *Cymbeline* where Iachimo,
stealing towards the sleeping Imogen, says

Our Tarquin thus
Did softly press the rushes ere he wakened
The chastity he wounded.

(2. 1. 12–14.)

Imogen had been reading the tale of Tereus: Lucrece compares
herself, as Lavinia had so often done, to Philomel, and the
Ovidian story was evidently at the back of Shakespeare's
mind on all three occasions. It may indeed have inspired the
expository use of the tapestry of Troy.

Unlike Macbeth, however, Tarquin knows the emptiness
of his satisfaction before he ventures on his act of violence,
whereas Macbeth does not fully understand it till afterwards.
Tarquin's debate with himself is carried out with a clear sense
of the issues; too clear to be dramatically plausible. His
comments none the less would apply exactly to the later story.

Those that much covet are with gaine so fond,
That what they have not, that which they possesse
They scatter and unloose it from their bond,
And so by hoping more, they have but lesse. . . .
So that in ventring ill, we leave to be
The things we are, for that which we expect:
And this ambitious foule infirmitie,

> In having much torments us with defect
> Of that we have: so then we doe neglect
> The thing we have, and all for want of wit,
> Make something nothing, by augmenting it.
>
> (133–153.)

Sententious and explicit posing of the moral question is continued in the laments of Lucrece, in which she indicts the agents of her wrongs: first the allegorical 'Causes' and then the criminal person. Her formal and highly patterned apostrophes are the most artificial part of the poem. 'The well-tuned warble of her nightly sorrow' is copied in T.M.'s *Ghost of Lucrece*, a pure Complaint:

> O comfort-killing night, image of Hell,
> Dim register, and notarie of shame,
> Blacke stage for tragedies and murthers fell,
> Vast sin-concealing Chaos, nourse of blame,
> Blinde muffled bawd, dark harber for defame
> Grim cave of death, whispring conspirator,
> With close-tongd treason and the ravisher:
>
> (764–770.)

This recalls at once the laments over Juliet, and the absurd Pyramus:

> O grim-lookt night, O night with hue so blacke,
> O night, which ever art when day is not:
> O night, O night, alacke, alacke, alacke,
> I fear my Thisby's promise is forgot.
>
> (5. 1. 172–175.)

but even such parody cannot be taken as guarantee that by the time he wrote it, Shakespeare had rejected the style of *Lucrece*. Her long apostrophe to Time looks forward to the soliloquy of Richard II in his prison cell: the mental confusion and bewilderment which in the midst of all their speeches can strike the characters dumb prefigure those more dramatic moments when Romeo and Juliet see their hope destroyed.[15]

> Well, thou hast comforted me marvailous much.
> Is it even so? then I defie you, starres.

On the other hand *Romeo and Juliet* is not without those set
pictures or icons of the older fashion, such as the description
of Lucrece as she lies in her bed, or the description of how she
and her maid weep together:

> A prettie while these prettie creatures stand,
> Like Ivorie conduites corall cisterns filling
>
> (1233–1234.)

These deliberate similes help to give Lucrece her emblematic
character of Chastity personified. The Elizabethans saw her
as a kind of pagan saint: in *Bonduca* the Queen speaks scornfully to the Romans of 'your great saint Lucrece':

> Tarquin tupped her well,
> And mad she could not hold him, bled.

This blasphemy—for as such it is intended—is a measure of
Lucrece's significance. The particular crime was so shocking
that it allowed Shakespeare to leave a blank at the centre of
the picture. In this poem and *Titus Andronicus* he seems to be
trying to indicate the blind senseless horror of purely physical
outrage, which constituted for the moment his idea of tragedy.
Some atrocity that stuns its victim falls upon Lavinia, Titus,
Lucrece, and also on the victims of Richard III. They come
up against a stone. Titus kneels and pleads with the stones,
Lucrece pleads with the 'remorseless' Tarquin, in *Romeo and
Juliet* the lovers are literally brought up against a stone wall:
that of the orchard, and that of the grave. Tragedy is something that slaps you in the face: it is tragedy in the newspaper
sense. Lucrece

> the picture of pure pietie,
> Like a white Hinde under the grypes sharpe clawes,
> Pleades in a wildernesse where are no lawes.
>
> (542–544.)

Violence inexplicable and shattering overwhelms her.

The Rape of Lucrece is an ambitious poem. It is more than a
third as long again as *Venus and Adonis*, and while *Venus and
Adonis* was put out in an unimpressive little quarto, *The Rape*

of Lucrece is a handsome and much more costly piece of book-production. It has altogether the air of being more studied and deliberate: yet in the very centre of the poem there is a link with the most personal of the sonnets. The description of Tarquin's revulsion after his crime (693–714) is an expansion of Sonnet cxxix. The self-knowledge which Tarquin had is also present there:

> All this the world well knows: yet none knows well
> To shun the heaven that leads men to this hell.

III

While he painted the 'hell' of *Lucrece* more deliberately than dramatically, Shakespeare almost immediately achieved the Paradisal beauty of his first great poetic drama: *Romeo and Juliet*. Parts of the play are in a manner so rhetorical that they are emptied of all feeling. Romeo like Titus moralizes on a fly at the height of his laments. The modern actress can put across Juliet's reception of the news of Tybalt's murder only by treating it as an outburst of hysterics, which is certainly not how it would originally have been delivered.

> O serpent heart, hid with a flowring face,
> Did ever dragon keepe so faire a Cave? . . .
> Dove-feathr'd Raven, wolvish-ravening lambe,
> Despised substance of divinest show!
> Just opposite to what thou justly seemst,
> A damned saint, an honourable villaine.
>
> (3. 2. 73–79.)

Here is a dramatic presentation of that moment of confusion which in *The Rape of Lucrece* and other early work is merely elaborated. The fantastic play on 'I' and 'aye'

> I am not I if there be such an I,
> Or those eyes shot that makes thee answere I
>
> (3. 2. 48–49.)

reproduces the confusion that Venus feels when she looks at
the dead Adonis and sees double, or the confusion of Lucrece,
who dares not look at Tarquin but 'winking' sees ugly
'antics' dancing before her eyes.[16] Throughout *Romeo and
Juliet* there are plain traces of *Titus* and *Lucrece*—the sharp
contrast of brilliant light and deep darkness, the metaphor of
beauty as a triumphant conqueror, marvellously revived as
Romeo gazes upon the face he thinks is dead and ironically
recognizes life without knowing what he says:

> O my Love, my Wife,
> Death, that hath suckt the Honey of thy breath,
> Hath had no power yet upon thy beautie:
> Thou are not conquer'd: beauties ensign yet
> Is Crimson in thy lips and in thy cheekes,
> And Deaths pale flag is not advanced there
>   (5. 3. 91–96.)

The skeleton which Juliet sees as she drinks the potion is the
commonest of medieval symbols, but it is horribly envisaged
by Romeo as 'amorous'. The lights and feasting of the early
scenes, the processions, the sudden sharp bouts of fighting, are
on the other hand purely dramatic. This play as Granville
Barker noted calls for more sheer acting than any of the
previous plays had done. When Romeo hears of Juliet's death
he has only a few words. The rest is left to the actor. This
was an innovation and to an audience must have felt extremely
poignant. It was a new way of appealing to their sympathy.
What happened in *Romeo and Juliet* is that Shakespeare
became a dramatic poet. Mercutio and the Nurse are conceived from the inside: yet they are dramatic characters in
the full sense, placed and detached as the hero and heroine
are not. Both are comic: both have one scene that is deadly
serious. Angelica has the exuberance of the flesh, the natural
speech of Mrs. Quickly—Juliet's weaning is as good as Falstaff's proposal. She has the shameless amoral opportunism of
Sir John Falstaff himself—who was rejected by his nursling
for precisely the same *reason* though in a different manner
from the 'Ancient damnation!' which follows her sudden

unconscious betrayal of Juliet:

> Some comfort, *Nurse*,
> Faith here it is: *Romeo*
> Is banished . . .
> I think it best you married with the Countie
> (3. 5. 214–219.)

There is at once that element of surprise and of inevitability which marks character seen in the round. The shock is considerable: yet this is exactly what a woman like the nurse would say, even if it is what all nurses since Phaedra's have existed to say. Mercutio is a more subtle and more complex character, yet his 'cause' of being is to serve as foil to Romeo in a multiplicity of ways: his frank bawdry is a contrast, his quick wit a messmate, and his violent, pitiful, unnecessary death a foreshadowing of the hero's. The speed of the story, which all critics remark upon, and which is Shakespeare's own invention, is essential to the governing Idea. 'These violent delights have violent ends' says the Friar. The quenched torch, the meteor gliding through the night, the wedding cheer changed to a burial feast, all are embodiments of the same theme.

> Come what sorrow can.
> It cannot countervaile the exchange of joy
> That one short minute gives me in her sight:
> Doe thou but close our hands with holy words,
> Then love-devouring death doe what he dare,
> It is inough I may but call her mine.
> (2. 6. 3–8.)

These words of Romeo define the inward meaning of the tragedy. Fate and the feud may be the efficient causes which determine the cruel end of the star-crossed lovers; that which redeems it from mere cruelty is the sense that all

> quick bright things come to confusion—

that such intensity of living must be destructive. Put in terms of character, both Romeo and Juliet are too impulsive to live safely in the electric atmosphere that surrounds them; put in

terms of action, the speed of the plot carries everything along
at such a pace that we feel the momentum cannot be checked;
at this pace the smallest accident is fatal, the merest rub of
circumstance will throw a life away. All of which Shakespeare has built up from a lumbering and sentimental love-
poem. The invention in the Elizabethan sense, the discovery
of relations between different realms of imagination—which
put Queen Mab into the mouth of the blunt Mercutio, and
was soon to put her in the arms of Bottom—shows the kind of
daring that is possible only by a happy marriage of instinct
and skill. It is notable that in taking such a story as *Romeo and
Juliet* at all, Shakespeare was flouting convention. Tragedies
dealt with the falls of princes and the fate of kingdoms, they
were moreover bound to be true stories, and their theme should
be a high and lofty one. Shakespeare stooped to be popular.
He threw away the dignified apostrophes of Fate, Hell,
Vengeance, which he had used so profusely before. He threw
away the rule of kingdoms and took a simple love story.[17]
The contrast of the bridal bed and the grave is almost the
kind of thing that might have been found in a ballad. The
story is more like *Clerk Saunders* than any previous tragedy
of the English stage. It was overwhelmingly successful; but
quite as sharp a defiance to contemporary notions of decorum
as *Hero and Leander*.

The feud, the efficient cause of the lovers' deaths, is by no
means unimportant, and Shakespeare stressed it both at the
beginning and at the end. It makes all the violence natural.
In so far as this is a tragedy in the newspaper sense, the feud
provides all the motives. It is probably not more dangerous
than the feuds which broke out between the followers of
Ralegh and Essex at court. The Earl of Oxford's quarrel
with Sidney might very well have ended as Tybalt's quarrel
did. Life was cheap in Elizabethan London, though not
perhaps as cheap as in Italy; but the situation would be familiar
in kind if not in degree. It is worth noting how the code
works in detail. Old Capulet will not tolerate Tybalt's
attempt to start a quarrel at the feast. It is under his roof;

and he will not have his guests—even an uninvited Montagu —insulted, and his household disturbed in a merrymaking at which nobility are present. Yet he is quite ready to join in a street brawl himself if his wife did not mock him out of it.

In such matters a character may be realistically drawn, yet at another moment he may lapse into something near moral heraldry. All the fighting, the comedy, the stagecraft, are concentrated upon one end: throwing into sharper relief the love of Romeo and Juliet. It was the orchard scene which the young Inns of Court men learnt by heart, which is thumbed most heavily in the Bodleian First Folio. It is the final scene, in which Juliet's words

> My grave is like to be my bridal bed

are fulfilled before the spectator's eyes, that is dramatically the most subtle and poetically the most moving. The manipulation of suspense in this scene, the echoes of the first meeting in the 'feasting presence', the contrast between Romeo's *canzone* and Juliet's quick sharp action, are in keeping because Shakespeare has abandoned his models and taken simply and solely to writing like himself.

The theme in general was that of the age. There never was a period in which more love-poetry appeared. The sonnet sequences, many of them written earlier no doubt, were pouring from the press. Ovidian Romances, Heroical Epistles, lyrics of all kinds abounded. So far as the subject went, Shakespeare swam with the stream. He had almost certainly read *Hero and Leander*. In the year that Shakespeare wrote *Romeo and Juliet* Spenser wrote *Epithalamion*[18] in which something like Juliet's voice can be heard through the music of the bridal.

> Ah! when will this long weary day have end,
> And lend me leave to come unto my love? . . .
> Has thee O fairest Planet to thy home
> Within the Western foam:
> Thy tyred steeds long since have need of rest.
>
> (ll. 330–336.)

Gallop apace, you fiery-footed steeds
Towards Phoebus' lodging. . . .

(3. 2. 1–2.)

Both may be echoing Catullus, 'Vesper adest, iuvenes, con-surgite', or Ronsard: but whether the resemblance be acci-dental, or whether the debt be Shakespeare's, in this poem Spenser rises above all his customary limitations and comes nearer than anywhere else to the fullness of Shakespearean imagination. Yet there is the significant difference that his is a social poem. *Romeo and Juliet* exist only as lovers, only in the relation of love. Society is outside. 'Call me but Love and I'll be new-baptised' cries Romeo: he is Everyman in Love and though Verona and the feud, the Nurse and Mercutio exist as supporters to the star-crossed lovers, the play's core and heart is a love-duet. In courtly poetry there is always the chorus. The Elizabethans would, then, have seen *Romeo and Juliet* as 'an amorous tragi-comedy' if any Polonius had essayed its classification. They would have recognized—though for different reasons than the modern ones—that it was not a full tragedy. They might have been content to agree that *Measure for Measure*, when it appeared, was the more tragical of the two, dealing with the high and grave matter of Justice and Mercy, in terms more lofty. Claudio's vision of death and judgment is more serious than the skeleton who keeps his 'feasting presence' in a grave.

Above all, the theme of love was 'comical' for the Eliza-bethan. The course of true love never did run smooth; personal affection was bound to cut across social exigencies among great ones, except by some such lucky accident as married Hotspur to his Kate. They took it as unquestioned presupposition that the odds were heavy against Hero being anything but a nun, Criseyde being anything but a middle-class young woman and Troilus out of her sphere. In real life, Juliet was married to Paris. Nevertheless young love will not obey an old decree. In stealing a marriage, Romeo and Juliet, like Florizel and Perdita, justified the rebellious blood among the auditory; they would have this extra claim upon the sympathy of youth. Society is flouted and takes revenge; yet the lovers' deaths heal the feud which caused them.

Shakespeare was established as a love poet and a poet of the personal relation, in delicate interweaving with social custom and habit, but dominating custom and habit by a natural and spontaneous power. The inevitable field for him was comedy. His comedy now seems so normal that it is difficult to realize how novel it was to the audience of his day. To find the Elizabethan norm, the modern reader may imagine a slice of sociology and politics served up with a sauce of clowning. At its best, something like Itma: at its worst, something like the bright modern sermon of the new curate.

CHAPTER VIII

TRAGICAL-HISTORICAL

'Henry VI'—II 'Richard III'—III 'Richard II'

THE 'New Look' in the reading of Shakespeare's histories first appeared in the nineteen-thirties and became general in the nineteen-forties. The moral theme is stressed by Dover Wilson, Tillyard, Miss Lily Campbell, Theodore Spencer, Zeeveld and others.[1] According to this view Shakespeare's histories are designed as moral *exempla*, illustrating the evils springing from rebellion and disorder. The basic pattern is that set down in Hall's Chronicle with its moral interpretation of history—deriving of course from the medieval view: the ethics are those set forth in the Homilies on obedience[2]: the structure is that of the secular morality play, in which factions or troubles show 'a contention between order and chaos for the state of man'.[3] *Magnifycence*, *Gorbuduc* and *The Troublesome Reigne of King John* are instances of such plays. On this reading, history is seen always as a guide to the present; its lessons are always relevant, and perpetually applicable: Clio holds up to Nature a particularly truthful dial, looking-glass, or mirror, which enables the judicious to plot their future actions in confidence of the outcome.

> There is a historie in all mens lives,
> Figuring the nature of the times deceast;
> The which observd, a man may prophesie
> With a neere ayme of the maine chance of things
> As yet not come to life, which in their seedes
> And weake beginning lie intreasured.
>
> (2. *H. IV*. 3. 1. 80–85.)

A particular use of history as mirror is provided by the staging of *Richard II*, which the conspirators ordered before the

123

Essex rebellion. The arrest of Ben Jonson for writing sedition in *Sejanus* (presumably it was considered to reflect on the private pleasures of King James) is proof that the magistrate took these reflections seriously.

This 'tragical-historical' view of the plays has corrected the focus in which they are seen, and in some cases over-corrected it. Appreciation of homiletic satire and the tradition of the Morality play may lead to the temptation to organize Shakespeare as the middle term between *Gorboduc* and Ben Jonson, having all three as common theme ' The Wounds of Civil War'.[4] Viewed in this light, *Richard III* might eventually turn out to be Shakespeare's best history, the difference between *Henry VI* and *Henry IV* of less importance than the likenesses: all of Falstaff that could not be identified with Riot and the Vice would have to be popped behind the arras, and Hotspur drowned like a kitten or blind puppy-dog.

It is the garments of style, phrase and character which distinguish *Richard II* from *Richard III;* and these apparellings are preicsely what distinguish Shakespeare from other writers. The mid-Tudor period had been one of very slow growth, but the speed of development between say 1590 and 1598 was such that those medieval habits quite proper to the age of the University Wits had been very rapidly overlaid. The decade of the fifteen-eighties, which saw such an immense development in non-dramatic poetry, made its mark on the stage in these years. Cambridge and the Inns of Court were reading Machiavel: Hooker is not quite so medieval as it has been usual to suppose:[5] the mid-Tudor earnestness had given way to the generation of Nashe and Marlowe. The curve of development in these few years was so steep that it is risky to lay down moral tramlines; especially, where the development can be seen, in the work of Shakespeare himself. The pattern of 'moral history' can be discerned fitfully but not regularly in the trilogy of *Henry VI:* it is clearly present, mixed with the conventions of 'Senecan' tragedy in *Richard III.* The change of style between *Richard III* and *Richard II* is so

striking as to constitute one of the great moments in Shakespeare's development as an artist, but the moral theme, though
now handled in a very different way, is yet the core of the
play. In *Henry IV* and *Henry V* it is less prominent, and what
remains is largely an echo of what has gone before: but the
main interest of these plays is elsewhere, and they are too
complex to be reduced within the framework of any pattern
which would apply to the earlier work.

Hall's moral view of history sprang from More's *History of
Richard III*: both belong to the reign of Henry VIII when
the moral view of history was worked very hard in the
interests of the Tudor dynasty. Richard III, especially in
Tudor eyes, was a perfect example of God's judgment, and his
story was always popular with dramatists. Buckingham's
lament in *The Mirror for Magistrates* is largely a portrait of
Richard. Even his effigies were redesigned to give him a
suitably villainous appearance. Hall was writing to glorify
Henry VIII, and the lesson of his story may be equated with
that of the Homilies on obedience which, it is frequently
noted, provide the basis for Shakespeare's most impressive
speech on a well-ordered commonwealth.[6]

Henry VI has a great deal of drum and trumpet fighting.
Only with the great scenes at the end of the third part does
moral history clearly emerge from the hurly-burly; especially
in the killing of York, Henry's speech on the miseries of kingship, and the soliloquy of Gloucester.[7]

H. T. Price has given the name of 'Mirror Scenes'[8] to these
symbolic moments in which the theme of the play is directly
embodied and fully stated, by figures who are often grouped
in the statuesque manner which has been noted in *Titus
Andronicus* and *The Rape of Lucrece*. Such scenes have something of the quality of an Induction, or a play within the play,
and may be written in a heightened style to emphasize their
special function. Henry VI's speech on kingship, following
on the laments of the father who has killed his son and the
son who has killed his father in the recent battle, constitute
such a scene. At this stage of Shakespeare's development,

such a scene called out all his powers. Action is suspended, whilst the king and his subjects mourn alike the 'fatal colours of our striving houses', horridly depicted in the red blood and pale faces of the dead. The whole theme of contest, disorder, and unnatural division is stated. Henry's description of the chaos of battle in terms of the contests of dark and light at dawn, or of wind and sea in a storm, is the prelude to a full lament in which the natural images of the shepherd's life and the progress of the seasons are contrasted with the unnatural life of the king, surrounded by pomp and treachery. In its formal pattern, and in the beauty of its imagery, this speech stands out from the play, and the theme it sounds is of such permanent significance in Shakespeare's work that Richard II on time, Henry IV on sleeplessness and Henry V on ceremony, all seem to find their germ and origin here.

The lament of a great man was the medieval form of tragic statement, which Shakespeare knew through the *Mirror for Magistrates*. In the *Induction* to the *Complaints* which make up the body of that work, the atmosphere is set in terms of the scene, the desolate scene with which the poem begins. Nature is sympathetic to the griefs which ensue.

> The tapits torn, and every bloom down blown . . .

> And soote fresh flowers, wherewith the summer's green
> Had clad the earth, now Boreus' blast down blew.

> The sturdy trees so shattered with the showers,
> The fields so fade that flourished so beforn.

Between these flat lines came ones which Shakespeare was to remember:

> Hawthorn had lost his motley livery,
> The naked twigs were shivering all for cold,
> And dropping down the tears abundantly.

(Compare Sonnet lxxiii.) The landscape of tragedy is defined in these lines: it is that of the trampled garden of *Richard II*, and of the prologue to *Antonio's Revenge*.

The setting makes tragedy as inevitable as the seasons, so

that the allegorical figure of Sorrow which presently appears
seems a part of the scene:

> Her body small, forwithered and forspent
> As is the stalk that summer's drought oppressed,

while her tears drop down abundantly like rain.
Sorrow is a figure from a pageant or tapestry: she is fixed
in one attitude. She tells the poet that she will show him a
true image of his mood, and leads him to the Entrance to Hell,
which is filled with allegorical figures. Here appear the
Ghosts whose laments form the main body of the poem. The
great distance between Sackville and Shakespeare should not
obliterate the connexion. Shakespeare broke into history
from the tragic lament.

King Henry is fixed in a pose of Sorrow: the father and the
son are 'supporters' who uphold the heraldic device. Henry's
lament is marked off by the strictness of its rhetorical 'Schemes'
—the most elaborate in the trilogy—and by the sympathetic
beauty of the images or 'Tropes'. Both are interwoven to
form a pattern, the poetic equivalent of the pattern provided
by the action and the story.[9]

Henry begins by describing the uncertainty of the issue
in highly schematic terms, but suddenly two lines of pure
Shakespeare appear:

> What time the shepherd, blowing of his nails,
> Can neither call it perfect day nor night.

The shepherd reappears later as the king contrasts his own
hard life with that of a swain. The elaborate Scheme used here
looks forward to the verse of *Richard III* in style:

> So many hours must I tend my flock;
> So many hours must I take my rest;
> So many hours must I contemplate;
> So many hours must I sport myself;
> So many days my ewes have been with young;
> So many weeks ere the poor fools will ean;
> So many years ere I shall shear the fleece:
> So minutes, hours, days, months and years,

> Passed over to the end they were created,
> Would bring white hairs unto a quiet grave.
>
> (2. 5. 31–40.)

Such flat use of 'figures of speech', i.e. verbal pattern or Schemes is suddenly modulated into a deeper style evoked by 'figures of thought', i.e. images or Tropes where the depth, associative power and sensuous qualities of the language are called out.

> The shepherds homely curds,
> His cold thin drink out of his leather bottle,
> His wonted sleep under a fresh trees shade,
> All which secure and sweetly he enjoys,
> Is far beyond a princes delicates,
> His viands sparkling in a golden cup,
> His body couched in a curious bed,
> Where care, mistrust and treason waits on him
>
> (2. 5. 47–54.)

The variety of sensuous imagery (*cold thin drink*) and of rhythm (*a prince's delicates*) are hardly to be found again in Shakespeare's dramatic poetry for some years. The father and the son are poetically very indifferent, but the visual pattern is highly dramatic and is recalled at the end of *Richard III* in the speech of the triumphant Richmond:

> England hath long been madde and scard herselfe,
> The brother blindlie shed the brother's bloud,
> The father rashlie slaughterd his own sonne,
> The sonne compeld been butcher to the sire
>
> (5. 4. 36–39.)

The son had in fact been pressed by the Lancastrians, whereas the father was apparently blind with battle-fury and hope of loot. (The source is *Gorboduc*, 5. 2. 374–6.)

The internecine strife of Edward III's descendants has infected the whole land. It is from the dissensions of 'the seven branches growing from one root' that all the evil springs. In his work *The Tree of Commonwealth* (1549) Edmund Dudley saw the whole realm as a great tree, whose fruits and roots he allegorically expounded; and in Shakespeare the genealogical tree of the Plantagenets—which might be depicted as a real tree, as the Jesse Tree depicted in so many church windows—was identified with the Tree of Commonwealth. Hence the imagery of England as a garden, which is found in *Richard II*. The two common soldiers of *Henry VI*, like the gardeners of the later play, are representative of the humbler undergrowth, the life of the soil. They are the Peasants, who in the medieval symbol of 'The Five Alls', should Work for All,[10] and their presence is an ironic reflection upon Henry's praise of the shepherd's life, which is no less disorganized by war than his own. The poor men who lament with him might well be shepherds; they belong to the humble people and represent their plight symbolically. They are no allegorical figures of Wrath or Contention, but as solid as Piers the Plowman.

II

In Hall's phrase, 'the troublous season of Henry VI' was succeeded by 'The tragical doings of Richard III'.[11] The fear of civil war and a disputed succession did not need a mirror for most Elizabethans; but this play records the climax of a hundred years' disorder. Shakespeare, like Wagner, began his cycle at the end of the story. Yet the disorder is 'mirrored' in a play whose symmetry and balance are its most notable characteristics. *Richard III* is Shakespeare's most patterned play. There is the rhetorical pattern of the Schemes: the alliteration, antithesis, rhetorical symmetry of all kinds. There is the pattern of the characters, who are set in opposing groups. There is the pattern of the theme, which is Nemesis. This is the final phase of a long story; vengeance for all the crimes past is exacted, and in Richard the hundred years of wrong becomes embodied: he is a 'scourge of God' and with him the evil is finally separated and cast out. The ghosts, who appear between the tents in the Mirror Scene of this play, bidding Richard 'despair and die' and Richmond 'live and flourish', represent the whole train of victims stretching back to Richard II at Pomfret.[12]

The two branches of the Plantagenet tree are symmetrically equal in woe. Queen Margaret prophesies at the beginning of the play:

> Edward thy sonne which now is Prince of Wales,
> For Edward my sonne which was Prince of Wales
> Die in his youth by like untimely violence,
> Thyself a Queene, for me that was a Queene,
> Outlive thy glory . . .
> (I. 3. 199–203.)

and the fulfilment of her prophecy is recalled in the great scene where York and Lancaster unite to curse Richard:

> I had an Edward till a Richard kild him;
> I had a Harry, till a Richard kild him;
> Thou hadst an Edward, till a Richard kild him;
> Thou hadst a Richard, till a Richard kild him.
> (4. 4. 40–43.)

This symmetry is of the same nature as Hall's antithetic pattern of the kings' reign. In various forms it runs throughout the play. There are dozens of omens, curses and prophecies whose fulfilment is recorded in words which echo the original passages.

Anne, Buckingham, Stanley's curse, that which Margaret utters and the curses laid on her are all recalled. His own mother solemnly curses Richard, which is but the climax of many curses laid on him throughout the play: they are all summed up in the imprecations of the Ghosts[13] on the eve of the final battle. His crooked back, the signs and portents attending his birth, and even his own words mark him out as completely diabolic: he is himself the greatest of the many portents which point the signs of the evil times.[14]

Prophecies are scattered throughout the play,[15] and those of the earlier plays recalled: in the four great scenes of lament which form the pivotal points of the play, the three widows, the orphans of Clarence and Richard's own wife appear to bewail, denounce and record the fulfilment of ancient curses.[16]

The rhetoric of this play recalls Kyd: there is of course plenty of evidence that Shakespeare knew *The Spanish Tragedy* well.[17] In both plays the basis of action is ironic: the pleasure of a fitting revenge is to see the engineer hoist with his own petard. 'The Pedringano trick' by which a murderer is made to bring about his own death is echoed in Richard's treatment of Hastings and Buckingham, his accomplices. Ironic echoes in the dialogue, caused by the intrusion of some sinister eavesdropper, repeat the ominous symmetry:

Belimperia.	But whereon dost thou chiefly meditate?
Horatio.	On dangers past and pleasures to ensue.
Balthazar.	[aside] On pleasures past and dangers to ensue.

(Spanish Tragedy, 2. 3. 26–28.)

Gloucester.	Farre be it from my heart the thought of it!
Queen Eliz.	As little joy my Lord as you suppose
	You should enjoy, were you this countries King,
	As little joy you may suppose in me,
	That I enjoy, being the Queene thereof.
Queen Marg.	[aside] As little joy enjoys the Queene thereof;
	For I am she and altogether joylesse.

(Richard III, 1. 3. 150–156.)

In the cut-and-thrust debate of Richard and Lady Anne which opens the play Shakespeare used figures from the cut-and-thrust between Belimperia and her suitor Balthazar. In his last soliloquy Richard uses the figure called by the Elizabethans 'a tracer' to build up a feeling of inevitability: Balthazar had used it for the same purpose.[18]

The treacherous violence of the villains is introduced by the same type of phrase: the laments in duets and trios, the final judgment delivered by the ghosts are similar in both plays. The terrifying figure of Queen Margaret, who dominates the great laments, recalling all the earlier plays in which she had appeared, owes something to old Hieronimo[19] and something also to the triumphant Revenging ghost Andrea.

Shakespeare is of course far more skilful than Kyd: his writing is tighter and more elaborated, his dramatic climaxes more powerful, and the integration of speech and action is beyond the earlier writer.

The descriptive and atmospheric colouring for the play comes, through Kyd, from the medieval Complaints and from the *Mirror for Magistrates*. Night, darkness, a murky vast and echoing gloom may give way to images of eternal torment. A brooding sense of the 'four last things' hangs over the play.

The Vergilian Underworld is the ultimate source of this imagery, which Sackville uses to describe the journey of Sorrow and the Poet down to Hell.

> Then came we to the horrors and the hell,
> The large great kingdoms and the dreadful reign
> Of Pluto in his throne where he did dwell,
> The wild waste places and the hugy plain,
> The wailing, shrieks and sundrey sorts of pain,
> The sighs, the sobs, the deep and deadly groan,
> Earth air and all resounding plain and moan.

In the tragedy of *Gorboduc* which, like *Richard III*, is a study of crime and punishment, the same atmosphere obtrudes. *The Spanish Tragedy*, more than a quarter of a century later, reproduces it in Hieronimo's meditations on death and judgment. They have the same ring: the same gloomy underworld colours the play, the same tormented figures appear; visions of a hard brilliant splendour abound, and give a peculiar tang, a 'taste of brass and metal sick':

> There is a path upon your left hand side,
> That leadeth from a guilty conscience
> Unto a forest of distrust and fear,
> A darksome place and dangerous to pass. . . .
> *(Spanish Tragedy*, 3. 12. 15ff.)

In Clarence's dream, Shakespeare evoked the same imagery, and implied the same conception of tragedy, as Sackville and Kyd.

> I passed, methought, that melancholy flood
> With that grim ferryman the poets write of
> Unto the Kingdom of perpetual night . . .
> . . . What scourge for perjury
> Can this dark monarchy afford false Clarence?
>
> (1. 4. 45-51.)

In these lines, Kyd's influence is far clearer than Marlowe's; he makes little use of patterned speech[20] and little of this particular imagery of Night and Hell.

Machiavellian Richard has been introduced at the end of 3 *Henry VI:* his soliloquy there (5. 6) together with York's great tirade against the 'she-wolf of France' and King Henry's lament form the three mirror scenes of that play. York's curse upon Margaret establishes the form of the curse which she herself, reduced to the misery which she had inflicted, was to utter in the subsequent play. Richard's soliloquy establishes his character, which is inherent in the quality of the verse he speaks. Richard is a dramatic character; although he talks so much about himself, it is his idiom, his accent of wit and scorn, which individualize him. His language, like his person, is diametrically opposed to the main pattern of the play. It is proverbial, full of old saws, the 'diction of common life' used as disguise. He cuts short Henry's prophecy on his future crimes with a word and a blow:

> Die, prophet, in thy speech:
> For *this,* among the rest, was I ordained.
>
> (3. H.VI., 5. 6. 57-58.)

There is something approaching his wit in earlier villains, and in Shakespeare's own Aaron, but none of them have Richard's virtuosity. He enjoys playing a part, whether that of the plain blunt soldier or that of the pious recluse.[21] His two wooing scenes, and his dissembling with Clarence and Hastings, his dupes, are entertained with such zest that in spite of morality the spectators find themselves engaged on his side. He scoffs irreverently at blessing and cursing alike[22] and though no doubt this is diabolic, it sounds sometimes very good sense. He defies the power of Nemesis, which all the other characters acknowledge: his scepticism cuts across the fatalistic gloom, as his brisk wit slashes the heavy brocade of the rhetoric. He has a touch of Antony's oratory as 'the plain blunt man', a touch of Edmund's wit in his unfilial jests, and at the base of his character is a touch of Iago's envy: but gradually the witty comedian sinks in the tyrant, and so he is one of the earliest examples of Shakespeare's particular skill in portraying the *development* of a character, a skill which indeed no other writer except Marlowe possessed. In the character of Richard, the new drama is seen bursting the husk of the old.

The four groups of murders for which he is responsible record a descending scale of vice. Clarence, though treacherously killed, is left to conduct his own plea with the murderers, whilst Richard plays his diabolic but witty role of Prisoner's Friend at Court. The murder of Hastings and the Queen's relatives is a sudden violent act of treachery, openly conducted by Richard himself: the murder of the little princes is an atrocity whose very nature stamps the perpetrator, and which has been stigmatized by Buckingham in advance, although Buckingham has hitherto been Richard's most hardened accomplice. The final execution, that of Buckingham himself, occurs when the counter-movement is already begun. With the achievement of his ambition, Richard has no further need to play a role, and his witty dissimulation gives way to hectoring. The wooing of Elizabeth has not the brilliance of the wooing of Anne, with which it stands in ironic contrast. To introduce the name of Elizabeth of York was in effect, for an Elizabethan audience, to sound the theme of the Union of the Roses.

In his final soliloquy, Richard's irony is turned inward upon himself:

> I am a villain, yet I lie, I am not,
> Foole of thyself speak well, Foole do not flatter.
> (5. 3. 192–193.)

The nervous, broken rhythm has a new power: the inward mind of Richard achieves self-recognition. 'I am determined to prove a villain': 'I am a villain, yet I lie, I am not'. In these two speeches lies all the difference between the presentation of a character in action and the embodiment of a character in words as a suffering and sensible being. The consciousness of his own nature, which comes to Richard III at the end, links him with Richard II, who has it from the beginning. In this achievement Shakespeare reached the 'dramatist's mood, his characteristic differentiation, which we may think of as sympathy. He enters into the minds of his characters . . . and speaks as it were from within them, giving thus a kind of impartiality to his picture of life, sorrowing with him that sorrows, rejoicing with him that rejoices'.[23] Whilst the whole theme and structure of the play is bent to show Richard as a devilish monster, Shakespeare's power of sympathy gives him the accents of an individual being, so that we pity him as being, at his lowest, a man.

III

In *Richard III* very little is said of England or the troubles of the realm: the citizens' scene (2. 3) is feeble, and there are no representatives of the common people. In *Richard II* the background is not heaven and hell, but the sceptred isle, and instead of Senecan imagery of night and death, the dominant image is that of England, 'the garden of the world'[24] laid waste, her fields manured with blood and her 'fair rose', Richard, withered. The image of the trampled garden runs through the play and it is embodied in the Mirror Scene of the gardeners, when the first news of Richard's capture reaches his foreboding queen. This scene, the stumbling-block to all naturalist readers, sets out the main theme of the play. The gardeners who expound the art of government in terms of their own labours are none the less something of an archaism in this play. For the device of the mirror scene which enabled Shakespeare to focus his poetry in *Henry VI* is now outgrown, so rapid was his development at this time. The groom who appears in the final scene is a fully dramatized character who 'quarrels' with these choric gardeners: yet in spite of such minor inconsistencies, *Richard II* presents a wonderful balance between the theme and the character, between the image which is poetically embodied and the image which is dramatically embodied. The prophecy of the Bishop of Carlisle (which Shakespeare did not find in his sources, and which appeared only in the later editions of the play) constitutes the fullest statement of the moral history, the destruction of order and degree by the usurpation of Bolingbroke.

> The bloud of English shall manure the ground,
> And future ages groane for his foul act.
> Peace shall go sleepe with turks and Infidels,
> And in this seat of peace, tumultuous warres
> Shall kin with kin, and kinde with kind confound:
> Disorder, horror, feare, and mutiny
> Shall heere inhabit, and the land be calld
> The field of Golgotha and dead mens skuls.
>
> (4. 1. 137–144.)

In place of flat verbal patterns Shakespeare develops in this play recurrent or, as it has been called, 'symphonic' imagery[25]: and this change of style is the outward and visible sign of a changed conception of structure. The tableaux, set debates, laments in chorus, give way to more complex groupings of characters, each character contrasted not only in function but in temper and idiom; each character a sympathetically conceived being, not conceived indeed in isolation from the others or from the general theme, but still conceived from within. It is the multiplicity of points of view which gives its tragic character to this play: even as on the early stage a multiple setting allowed the dramatist to set several scenes on the stage side by side, so this multiple characterization allows the dramatist several centres of sympathy. Richard, Gaunt, York, Bolingbroke are all animated in this way. To a modern reader this may not sound a very remarkable achievement: yet it was something none of Shakespeare's predecessors had

done since Chaucer wrote *Troilus* and *The Canterbury Tales*.
In *Richard III* he presented one man contending against 'the
main sway of things': here he presents a whole world.

Richard himself, defined both through speech and action,
has something in common with Henry VI, the weak king
crushed by his violent subjects, as far as his history goes; but
there is little in common between their persons. The dicho-
tomy between Man and Office 'the deputy anointed by the
Lord' and the man who

> lives with bread like you, feels want,
> Tastes grief, needs friends. . . .
>
> (3. 2. 175–176.)

is one which Shakespeare was to treat again and again under
many aspects: in Bolingbroke's uneasy nightwatching, and
his son's meditation on Ceremony: in Hamlet, King Lear,
the Duke of Vienna and the Duke of Milan. Here it serves as
basis for the reconciliation of opposites within a single role:
Richard loves his land, with an almost passionate devotion
to its very soil, but hopelessly misuses his office; he is sensitive
and brutal, variable and obstinate, witty but not wise. The
variety of his speech reflects the variety of his moods—his
fanciful poetry to Aumerle or the Queen, his nervous irony to
Bolingbroke and Northumberland, his cruel petulance to
old Gaunt and his pitiable family likeness to old York make him
consistently inconsistent, as Aristotle would say: give that
peculiar depth and many-sidedness to his character which is
the mark of Shakespeare's dramatic and poetic power, and
by which he creates the illusion of life itself, multiform yet
one.

The trampled garden of King Richard's land, in which he is
the withering rose or the setting sun, is an image peculiarly
fitted to govern the play of which such a man is hero. Here
Shakespeare first evolved that method of embodying the
main theme in a dominant image which he was to use in the
greater tragedies, particularly *Hamlet* and *Macbeth* with their
darkness, disease and blood. There is a fine balance between

the natural and sensuous evocation of this image, as in the scene of farewell between Richard and his Queen, and the more emblematic or heraldic use of it.

Heraldry is behind the lines,

> Downe, downe I come, like glistring Phaethon;
> Wanting the manage of unrulie Iades
>
> (3. 3. 178-179.)

which derive from Richard's personal badge of the sun in glory. The image is used in this sense elsewhere (3. 3. 62-67: 4. 1. 221, 260-262), and it is as fully heraldic as Richard III's badge of the boar.[26]

Here it is blended with a notion also of the turning wheel of Fortune, on which Richard is now descending, and with the image of the horse, which had been since Plato the symbol of instincts managed—or not managed—by reason the charioteer. The prominence of horsemanship in courtly education gave it particular power at this time and it is no dead simile for Richard. The account of his ride into London and the final scene in which the groom tells Richard of his ungrateful 'roan Barbary' develop the image as symbol of harmonious relations between king and subject, body and soul.[27]

This wealth and fecundity of meaning within a single image is matched by the wealth of significance in the great dramatic tableaux. Richard's incompetence in the lists at Coventry, where all the pomp and order of the fight is broken up by his gesture, reflects directly upon his government: the confusion symbolizes the greater confusion to come. In the deposition scene, the old formal properties—the stage crown and the Mirror itself—are used in a symbolic manner warranted by tradition,[28] yet the formality of the scene is a completely adequate presentation of the personal conflict between the despairing Richard and the 'silent king' who confronts him. Bolingbroke's character, indeed, as has been noted often enough, is largely built up from what he does *not* say, and this dramatic use of a silent figure implies a grasp of full theatrical perspective. His early rejection of the conventional

consolations offered for his banishment by Gaunt marks Bolingbroke as one who despises mere words: his silence in the
abdication scene is as bitter a reflection upon Richard's weakness as Northumberland's taunts: and in the scene where
York and his Duchess plead before the King, after Aumerle's
conspiracy has come to light—a scene where Bolingbroke's
mastery of the situation contrasts sharply with Richard's
behaviour at Coventry—a single word suffices to give his
judgment on the whole affair. It puts all his clamorous
relatives in their place, and, with the neat clinching of a rhyme,
adds the spice of wit to his irony. York and his son have been
high in speech, the Duchess is crying without the door, when
Bolingbroke turns to the culprit with:

> My *dangerous* cousin, let your mother in:
> I know she is come to pray for your foule sinne.

The scene then changes to something pretty near farce.

The use of contrasting groups in this play is dependent on
the complex family likenesses and differences between Richard,
Aumerle, Bolingbroke, Gaunt and York: at Coventry, Gaunt
and Bolingbroke are grouped in opposition to Richard:
later Gaunt and Richard, age and youth, confront each other.
The variations of interplay are far more subtle than those of
Richard III, and recall rather the plays immediately preceding or following—*Romeo and Juliet* and *A Midsummer
Night's Dream*—where Shakespeare is clearly experimenting
in contrasted groups or contrasted figures.

A further measure of the complexity of conception which
distinguishes *Richard II* is found in the complexity of the
source material upon which it is based.[29] Hall, Froissart,
two French pamphlets and Daniel's *Civil Wars* seem to imply
such unusually academic interests that Dover Wilson attributed
all the spade-work to the unknown author of a hypothetical
source-play. It might be hazarded that Shakespeare wrote
this play at a moment when he had attracted the notice and
perhaps the friendship of a noble patron, and that therefore he
composed for the judicious and learned part of his audience
and that it is the historical partner of *Love's Labour's Lost*.

The first recorded reference to *Richard II* is a letter dated 7 December 1595, written by Sir Edward Hoby, the son of Sir Thomas Hoby, translator of *Il Cortegiano*, to invite Sir Robert Cecil to a private performance of the play at his house in Cannon Row, after supper (E. K. Chambers, *William Shakespeare*, ii. p. 320–321). Though it is not absolutely certain that this is Shakespeare's play, both Chambers and Dover Wilson regard it as highly probable.

It is known that this play was later of particular interest to Essex's friends, who included Southampton and Sir Charles Percy: and it is not impossible that it might have been composed with an intention specially directed towards them. Its sense of the beauty of courtesy and the graces of life might arise from Shakespeare's first encounter with the life lived according to Castiglione.

Certainly the meaning of history had changed for Shakespeare: perhaps the poetry of Daniel and of Drayton, which softened these harsh stories into decorative lyrics of love,[30] had something to do with the change. But like a later poet he had

> learnt to get the better of words
> For the thing he no longer had to say or the way in which
> He no longer had to say it.
> *(East Coker, V.)*

For the subsequent history plays differed as widely from *Richard II*, as *Richard II* had done from its predecessors. England is no longer embodied in tragic images but in comic characters.

CHAPTER IX

THE FASHIONING OF A COURTIER

Sonnets—II 'Two Gentlemen of Verona'—III 'Midsummer Night's Dream'

SHAKESPEARE'S 'sugred sonets' were as popular as *Romeo and Juliet* in the mouths of young gallants. Though unpublished till 1609, without clue to the order of their disposition or their relation to Shakespeare's personal life, the relation to his other work would seem to place them in the early and middle nineties. This is also where they would naturally belong in the history of sonnet-writing as a whole, and where, in spite of Dr. Hotson, I would place them. They tell a story too obscure, too odd and too closely linked with recurrent themes in the plays to make it likely that they were either a coronet for his Mistress Philosophy or a bait for some other man to fish with. Such theories belong to an age which could not accept Dante's Beatrice as a real woman, and which saw everything which was not spontaneous as impersonal.

The range of the sonnets is startling. Petrarchists and anti-Petrarchists who wove their flowery sequences through the eighties were generally consistent in their tone, imagery and style. On the whole the sonneteers were more gentlemanly than fiery:[1] the conventions were well established, and translation was allowed a broad interpretation. The character and exploits of Cupid, the warfare in which the lady ambushed, attacked, slaughtered or enslaved her unresisting victim: his own melancholy, wasting, sleeplessness and pangs of absence are the regular themes. The praise of the lady is no less conventional. Demetrius at the first sight of Helena after he has been anointed with the love philtre, runs through his stock in trade of compliment:

> O Helen, goddesse, nymph, perfect divine,
> To what, my love, shall I compare thine eyne?
> Cristall is muddy. O how ripe, in showe,
> Thy lippes, those kissing cherries, tempting growe
> That pure coniealed white, high *Taurus'* snow
> Fand with the Easterne winde, turns to a crowe
> When thou holdst up thy hand. O let me kisse
> This Princesse of pure white, this seale of blisse.
>
> (3. 2. 137–144.)

Florizel, some fifteen years later, is still talking of the fann'd snow, though he allows Perdita's hand only to equal and not to surpass its whiteness (*Winter's Tale*, 4. 3. 374–377).

The Petrarchan lover was a despairing lover: perhaps when the lady was won, sonnets became unnecessary. Yet Spenser's charming banter

> See how the Tyrannesse doth joy to see
> The huge massacres that her eyes do make
>
> (*Amoretti*, x.)

or

> Sweet Warrior! when shall I have peace with you?
>
> (*Amoretti*, lvii.)

has more weight when seen as the product of one of the English Garrison, living in what had been a stronghold of the dispossessed Fitzgeralds, and consequently liable to reprisals of the kind that eventually cost him his all. Sidney too, in his military metaphors writes as a professional soldier,[2] and often with an ironic twist.

Nor were Elizabethan ideas of decorum always equivalent to what the word might now imply. Spenser's *Amoretti* xlvi is in a good medieval tradition;[3] it is as broad as the most notorious of Shakespeare's sonnets, or the broadest of Mercutio's jests, and like Mercutio, witty enough to justify its impropriety.

Sidney approaches nearest to Shakespeare in the range of his mood, in his logical and closely articulated form, in the

AN UNKNOWN MAN
AGAINST A BACKGROUND
OF FLAMES

HENRY WRIOTHESLEY
3RD EARL OF SOUTHAMPTON
AGED 20 IN 1594

natural tenderness and humour which plays over the surface of his conventional despair, and in his easy blend of the conventional and the personal, the formal simile and the colloquial phrase, giving an impression both of sincerity and control. Stella has at last been undeniably identified with Penelope Devereux,[4] a woman of whose charm and beauty there are other testimonies than Sidney's. Yet a series of laments for Sidney under his name of Astrophel could be dedicated to his widow, Frances Walsingham—though not indeed before she had become the wife of Stella's brother, the Earl of Essex. The tangled relationships of Elizabeth's court circle could to-day be equalled only in some small remote country village. How much of the love-making was genuine and how much was fashion will never be known, for the whole object of the system was to conceal that very fact; and even the ladies of *Love's Labour's Lost* miscalculated completely In addressing a friend and not a mistress Shakespeare deprived himself at once of a good deal of the sonneteer's stock-in-trade; the promise that he will 'eternize' the virtues which he celebrates is of course a commonplace,[5] and some of the conceits, particularly in the first eighteen sonnets, the most formal and distant of the group, are of the traditional kind.[6]

The one convention which provided Shakespeare with the means of making something new, something that went beyond the convention itself, was that in which the lover described the exchange of hearts between his lady and himself. Sidney had used this conceit in the song from *Arcadia*:

My true love hath my heart and I have his.

The eye and the heart were both invoked in songs of this kind ('Send back my long strayed eyes to me'), and debates between the eye and the heart on their mutual responsibility for the singer's plight went back to medieval poems of the Courts of Love.[7] But the interchange of hearts is used as symbol for that 'marriage of true minds' which makes the natural self-centred life of any individual reverse itself, establishing the centre of all hopes, needs, desires, plans, pleasures and pain in the beloved. Throughout the Sonnets this theme appears, playfully, painfully, triumphantly and bitterly.

> In our two loves there is but one respect,
> Though in our lives a separable spight
>
> (xxxvi.)
>
> Oh how thy worth with manners may I singe,
> When thou art all the better part of me?
>
> (xxxix.)
>
> All mine was thine, before thou hadst this more
>
> (xl.)
>
>   my friend and I are one,
> Sweete flattery, then she loves but me alone.
>
> (xlii.)
>
> I in thy abundance am suffic'd,
> And by a part of all thy glory live.
>
> (xxxvii.)
>
> Bring your slave what should I doe but tend,
> Upon the houres, and times of your desire?
>
> (lvii.)
>
> Oh let me suffer (being at your beck)
> Th' imprison'd absence of your libertie
>
> (lviii.)
>
> Sinne of selfe-love possesseth al mine eie . . .
> Tis thee (my selfe) that for my selfe I praise,
>
> (lxii.)
>
>   I love you so
> That I in you sweet thoughts would be forgot
> If thinking on me then should make you woe.
>
> (lxxi.)
>
> When thou shalt be disposde to set me light,
> And place my merrit in the eie of skorne,
> Upon thy side, against my selfe Ile fight
>
> (lxxxviii.)
>
> For thee, against my selfe Ile vow debate,
> For I must nere love him whom thou dost hate
>
> (lxxxix.)

But doe thy worst to steale thyself away,
For tearme of life thou art assured mine . . .
Thou canst not vex me with inconstant minde,
Since that my life on thy revolt doth lie

(xcii.)

yet like prayers divine,
I must each day say ore the very same,
Counting no old thing old, thou mine, I thine,
Even when as first I hallowed thy faire name.

(cviii.)

In the Dark Lady's sonnets, the friend is called 'my next selfe'
(cxxxiii) and 'that other mine' (cxxxiv). Such complete
devotion can almost invite the charge of 'idolatry' which
Shakespeare rebuts in Sonnet cv; yet it also justifies the un-
commonly plain speaking which is so unusual a feature of his
sonnets:

You to your beautious blessings adde a curse,
Being fond on praise, which makes your praises worse

(lxxxiv.)

the reproaches of Sonnets xciii–xcvi—matched by the self-
reproaches of cxvii–cxx—and the agonized defiance of:

Then hate when thou wilt, if ever, now,
Now while the world is bent my deeds to crosse

(xc.)

Instead of the comparatively simple relationship of other
sonneteers—where all subtlety dwells in the art of the chase,
the lady's powers of coquetry and the balance between pose
and feelings, courtship and passion—Shakespeare presents a
dramatic and flexible situation. It has neither the distance of
Spenser's respectful worship of his 'Angel', or the Platonic
calm of the Phoenix and the Turtle, 'two distincts, division
none', of Sidney's *Eighth Song* or Lord Herbert of Cherbury's
Ecstacie. But it springs from the convention of the exchange
of hearts, set out in an early Sonnet:

all that beauty that doth cover thee,
Is but the seemely rayment of my heart,
Which in thy brest doth live, as thine in me,
How can I then be elder then thou art?

L

> O therefore love, be of thy selfe so wary,
> As I not for my selfe, but for thee will,
> Bearing thy heart which I will keepe so chary
> As tender nurse her babe from faring ill,
>   Presume not on thy heart when mine is slaine,
>   Thou gav'st me thine not to give backe againe.
>
> (xxii.)

If this be compared with Sidney's song, it will be seen already how far personal feeling has informed the argument. Shakespeare developed his sensibility in the sonnets, far beyond anything which he achieved in the drama of the nineties; but the sonnets must have helped in the very rapid growth of the years 1594–1596, to which Chambers assigns *Two Gentlemen of Verona, Love's Labour's Lost, Romeo and Juliet, Richard II, Midsummer Night's Dream,* and *The Merchant of Venice.* 1594 saw also the publication of *The Rape of Lucrece,* and the foundation of the Lord Chamberlain's Company, the great and stable fellowship which replaced the shifting groups of earlier days, providing Shakespeare with his true dramatic environment. He now was thirty years of age, old enough to write about youth with an understanding mind. His subject in general was the world of the court, or as Spenser said, the fashioning of a gentleman. He had learnt enough of courtly manners to be able to laugh at them, and at the same time to admire. He could disclaim the conventional poetry of praise (Sonnet cxxx) and then write a sonnet to his mistress' eyes (never, it must be admitted, to her eyebrow) in a manner which borrows quite shamelessly from Sidney's praise of the black eyes of Stella (Sonnet cxxxii: compare *Astrophel and Stella,* vii). Both ladies' eyes are in mourning for the cruelties they have inflicted upon their lovers. Detached enough for mockery, sympathetic enough to absorb the manners to which he held up a mirror, Shakespeare achieved, through the depiction of a world, the eventual delineation of persons.

II

The earliest and most colourless of Shakespeare's romantic comedies, *The Two Gentlemen of Verona*, has been passed over by critics, except for its textual problems.[8] Yet behind the prefiguring of so many later characters and the first draft of so many lines there is a particular germ or 'cause'.[9]

The title indicates the subject, the friendship of two Italian courtiers. The virtues of a courtier, which were the four cardinal virtues, included first of all, as a part of Justice, Fidelity or Constancy.[10] Proteus' name marks him out as a sinner against this requirement, as Valentine's name marks him the true lover. But friendship remains here the personal relationship; love, the courtly one.

The courtier's occupation was largely discourse, at least according to Castiglione, who devotes the whole of his second book to this important subject; and Platonic love was his religion. *The Two Gentlemen* is a study of manners rather than of sentiments, of behaviour rather than emotion; there is little feeling anywhere. Proteus' wooing of Julia is purely Petrarchan: his phrases are all out of the sonnets— 'Love-wounded Proteus', 'poor forlorn Proteus'—and Julia's tearing up of his letter can be paralleled from Spenser's *Amoretti*:

> Innocent paper; whom too cruel hand
> Did make the matter to avenge her yre:
> And ere she could thy cause wel understand
> Did sacrifize unto the greedy fyre
>
> (xlviii.)

Silvia loves Valentine, Valentine Silvia; but they are never left alone together, and do not exchange one intimate word. It is Courtly love: Valentine has all the marks which Rosalind failed to find in Orlando—he cannot even put on his hose properly. His wit combats with Thurio, the rival, are 'a fine volley of words quickly shot off': he cherishes a glove and in all ways 'does penance for condemning love', though his earlier condemnation has been also spoken by the book. When he is accosted by the outlaws, he conceals his love according to the best courtly code[11] and pretends he is banished for manslaughter; while some of the outlaws, less nice, confess to 'stealing a wife'. At first Proteus is shown as a student, whereas Valentine is more active and looks forward to education at Court;

> to practice tilts and tournaments,
> Hear sweet discourse, converse with noblemen,
> And be in eye of every exercise
> Worthy his youth and nobleness of birth.
> (1. 3. 30-33.)

He finds however that his chief occupation is in the School of Love, where he proves an apt pupil. Although deep in the study of *Hero and Leander*—

> a deep story of a deeper love
> (1. 1. 23.)

with crossed arms and ungartered hose, Proteus is outdone by Valentine, whose new role of despairing lover is set forth and most robustly mocked at by his servant. When Proteus arrives at the court of Milan and is entertained by Silvia as one of her 'servants'—note that there is so little personal implication about this that Valentine entreats the honour for his friend—he receives so magnificent a panegyric on love from the converted Valentine that he is impelled to call it 'braggardism'. Valentine is himself aware of his own absurdity, and rejoices in it. He is completely identified with his idol.

'Call her divine' he says and when Proteus replies, 'I will not flatter her' his besotted friend retorts, 'O! flatter me, for love delights in praises'. Valentine knows he dotes, but his senses, pleased with madness, do give it welcome. In the midst of all this his true human relation to Proteus is not forgotten:

> Forgive me that I do not dream on thee
> Because thou see'st me dote upon my love.
> (2. 5. 174-175.)

His agreeable madness is unfortunately infectious; Proteus' fancy, bred in his eye, is altogether unstable, and Valentine's praise has been too rhetorically telling. He announces in soliloquy that he is now in love with Silvia. This may be unworthy of *homo rationale*, but we are not in the presence of *homo rationale*. Had Puck been at hand with his little western flower, Proteus would be justified. He does not give much thought to Julia: it is his discourtesy to his friend, his 'dissembling' which makes him culpable in his own eyes: he is most of all foresworn in wronging his friend (2. 6. 3.). Proteus' argument with himself is not so much a revelation of perplexity, as an exercise in self-excuse. It may be contrasted with Shakespeare's own 'salve for perjury' which in its ingenuity goes beyond anything Valentine could reach:

> But here's the joy, my friend and I are one,
> Sweete flattery, then she loves but me alone.
>
> (*Sonnet* xlii.)

The mind of a lover was by definition changeable, a 'very opal', and the fickleness of Proteus is a more dangerous symptom than the perversity of Julia or Valentine's rapid oscillation between rapture and despair, but not different in kind. Only the divine Silvia remains constant; and like Imogen importuned by fool and knave in turn, she can spare pity for the unknown Julia in the midst of her own distress. Valentine is made stupid by love, so that he cannot detect Silvia's courtly trick of making him write a letter to himself, and has to be enlightened by the clown. Proteus is made treacherous, like Helena of Athens, and Julia driven to reckless venturing, like Hellen of Narbonne.

The play is full of prefigurings, which throw the reader's mind forward to greater works. The Duke's impulsive rejection of his daughter

> Let her beauty be her wedding dower

anticipates Capulet: Julia's debate on her suitors, the debate of Portia and Nerissa: her embassage to Silvia, Viola's to Olivia; there are frequent echoes of Romeo in Valentine's part, of Moth in Speed's, and of Costard in Launce's. There is even a Friar who helps Silvia to escape. The play in its turn furnished hints to other dramatists. In Chapman's *Monsieur d'Olive* (1606) there is a direct recollection of that most abused and universally rejected scene in which Valentine releases his interest in Silvia to the repentent Proteus.

> And that my love may appear plain and free
> All that was mine in Silvia I give thee

he says, although not twenty lines before Proteus was attempting to ravish her.

The schoolboy cries of 'cad' and 'scoundrel' with which Valentine is pelted by critics, the epigrams of Q ('By now there are *no* gentlemen in Verona') would have struck Shakespeare's audience as simply a failure in understanding. If an interpolator thrust this bit of business into the scene it is very surprising that Chapman should recall it fourteen years later: for him it was evidently a genuine climax.

In his play, the widowed Earl of St. Anne is sent in trust a-wooing on behalf of his brother-in-law and falls in love with the lady. His justification is the same as Proteus'

> Yet in this case of love who is my brother?
> Who is my father? who is any kin?
> I care not, I am nearest to myself.
> I will pursue my passion, I will have her
> > (*M. D'Olive*, 4. 1.)

> I to myself am dearer than a friend,
> For love is still most precious in itself.
> > (*Two Gentlemen*, 2. 6. 23–24.)

He is overheard by his brother-in-law, who after upbraiding his treachery, relents almost in the words of Valentine

> Heaven bless both your loves as I release
> All my feigned love and interest to you.

though finally explaining that it was all a plot to make St. Anne happy in a second wife—but this St. Anne and the audience was hardly to know.

In releasing Silvia, Valentine was displaying in transcendent form the courtly virtue of Magnanimity, the first and greatest virtue of a gentleman. It was essentially competitive, the prize for the highest bidder and not to be won by qualifying merely. 'Magnanimity sent a man into high enterprises which taxed to the uttermost the power of mind and body and before which lesser men would quail';[12] in the definition of Herrault, it was 'a certain excellencie of courage, and different from valiantness or prowess, in that prowess respecteth chiefly the feats of warre and magnanimitie respecteth honour'.[13] The magnanimous man ignored wrongs done to him, so that the question of forgiveness did not even arise. He sought always to confer benefits rather than receive them, and any benefit which he received must at once be repaid with interest. This free spirit constrained Antonio to pledge his life for Bassanio, impelled Antony to forgive Cleopatra's treachery with a kiss—'even this repays me'—and to send treasure after the renegade Enobarbus, and did not distinguish between liberality and prodigality. It is his Magnanimity which is the justification of Timon. So when Proteus says simply

> Forgive me, Valentine,

Valentine responds equally simply

> Then I am paid
> (5. 4. 77.)

The brevity of their exchange—some twenty-four lines in all—should not prevent recognition that it is the germ or core of the play. When he is banished from Silvia, Valentine's despair is philosophical, full of nice respects. It is an exposition of Platonic doctrine in rhetorical terms:

> What light is light if Silvia be not seen?
> What joy is joy if Silvia be not by?
> Unless it be to think that she is by,
> And feed upon the shadow of perfection.
> Except I be by Silvia in the night
> There is no music in the nightingale;

> Unless I look on Silvia in the day,
> There is no day for me to look upon:
> She is my essence: and I leave to be
> If I be not by her fair influence
> Foster'd, illumin'd, cherish'd, kept alive.
>
> (3. 1. 174–184.)

This can be paralleled from the sonnets (cxiii is a variation on the same argument); but Valentine's reproach of Proteus has the accent of direct speech; it is deeply personal and strikes a note to be heard again—incongruously—in Henry V's reproach of the traitor Scroop, in Antonio's reproach of Sebastian in *Twelfth Night* and faintly echoing even in the speech of Prospero to his brother.

> Thou hast beguil'd my hopes: naught but mine eye
> Could have persuaded me: now I dare not say
> I have one friend alive: thou would'st disprove me.
> Who should be trusted, when one's right hand
> Is perjur'd to the bosom? Proteus,
> I am sorry I must never trust thee more,
> But count the world a stranger for thy sake.
>
> (5. 4. 64–70.)

Trust is more dangerous than love, for it commits to the keeping of another not only our happiness and affections, but our values and beliefs, of which they are taken as the embodiment.

At this point the two young men may be well down on the forestage, but with Valentine's forgiveness and proffer, Silvia and Julia are brought into the action again. It has been asked how Silvia should be expected to react to this summary disposal of her favour. Clearly she should not react at all. She is the prize, for the purpose of argument, and must not call attention to herself, but stand like the 'mistress' in *Cynthia's Revels* before whom the courtiers conduct their amorous verbal duels, a lay figure.[14] Leading ladies may not relish this, but leading boys would have been more tractable.

Julia swoons. She has been accused of calculation: a Julia who throws herself on the grass at what she adjudges the critical moment is absolutely unthinkable in Elizabethan terms. It is part of the modern vulgar search for 'personality' at all costs. Her action precipitates the dénouement. Julia contrasts herself quite formally with Proteus—he has changed his mind, she has changed her 'shape' or costume. Proteus matches her with a little panegyric of constancy. Valentine treats the reasonable Thurio with an unmeasured ferocity he had not shown the unreasonable Proteus, for this distinguishes the action proper to a lover where friendship is not involved. Everything ends happily:

> One feast, one house, one mutual happiness.

The mirror which is here held up to nature reflects your fine gallant. His world is an artificial one, except for the clowns, and they can sometimes make play on the dramatic convention by a direct appeal to the audience. 'I speak this speech in print, for in print I found it', says Speed after one of his gems of proverbial wisdom. Launce's 'parting' from his family completely kills Proteus' parting with Julia (which it immediately follows) using even the same puns. Julia's praise of love or Valentine's satiric character of women, given to the Duke, are set speeches; this last is in the quipping vein and aptly describes Julia's coquetry but has nothing in common with his own feelings or practice. It might be anyone's. As for the action, whenever Shakespeare can think of nothing else to do, he puts in a misdirected letter, of which there are a record number in this play. The parody of the clowning acts impartially against all—Launce's dialogue with his dog is in such a powerful contrast with the elegance of the courtier that a modern audience cannot do justice at once to Silvia's divinity and her befouled farthingale; but this indecorum was decorous in the literary if not the social sense, as long as the heroics and the clowning, the high style and the low were used in contrast, as black and white, and not allowed to blend. It is like the juxtapositions in Chaucer between the Knight and the Miller, or the story of patient Griselda and the prologue of the Wyf of Bath.

Courtly writers, Sidney and Lyly, have something of the same sort. The clowns of *Arcadia*, Mopsa and the rest, the fools of courtly comedy offered a simple burlesque, not unlike that which the antimasque of professional players might afford the courtly dancers of the masque proper.

On the popular stage there was no compelled decorum. The clowns who popped into tragedy, the fairies who darted into history, and the complete disregard of chronology which could put Ben Jonson into the court of William Rufus and a modern clown in *The Rape of Lucrece*[15] were the fruits of licence and not the consequences of emancipation. Shakespeare, who had practised a regular style in *The Comedy of Errors*, did not continue on those lines. His own recipe was the bold one of blending different species, or 'kinds', to form a balanced and harmonious pattern. In this he even did not scruple to mix figures of the tragic stage, such as Shylock, with those of romantic comedy.

III

In *A Midsummer Night's Dream*, Shakespeare did not rely either on old stories or old plays. There may be faint traces of Chaucer,[16] but the whole thing is virtually his own. Three contrasted worlds—the lovers', the rustics', and the fairies'—have each their own idiom and their own codes, but in the woods of Athens, as in the Forest of Arden, divided worlds meet and intermingle. This simple trick of contrasted plot and subplot has in it the germ of all Shakespeare's later construction —it shows the artist's eye that could pick out an old chronicle play, crude but serviceable, and a story from the most elegant fiction of the day, put them together and make *King Lear*. His mind full of images of the countryside, and *Ovid's Metamorphoses* (for he had not long since written *Venus and Adonis*, where the two combined) the distressed lovers who were parted by their family, and a picture of Queen Mab (for he had also not long since written *Romeo and Juliet*) Shakespeare combined them, perhaps for a wedding masque, and wrote *A Midsummer Night's Dream.*

The lovers of the Athenian Court are drawn in a spirit of parody perfectly in keeping with an occasion which would mark the triumphant end of a real courtship. They are moreover contrasted with the heroic loves of Theseus and Hippolita.

The opening scene, daylight and Athens, maintains a formal style which sets the death penalty hanging over Hermia and the treachery of Helena in their proper perspective. The bouts of wit between Hermia and Lysander or Hermia and Helena are on professedly serious subjects, but their manner is that of Valentine's exchanges with Thurio:

Hermia. I frowne upon him, yet he loues me still
Helena. O that your frownes would teach my smiles such skil . . .
Hermia. The more I hate, the more he followes mee
Helena. The more I loue, the more he hateth mee
Hermia. His folly, *Helena*, is no fault of mine.
Helena. None but your beauty; would that fault were mine.
(I. I. 194–201.)

Yet here and there, within the scene, there is heard an impersonal note of description, depicting love in terms of the natural world, which brings into the rhetorical stiffness of the dramatic exchanges such lively contrasts as that of the holy maids 'chanting faint hymnes to the cold fruitlesse Moone', and the sound of Hermia's voice:

> More tuneable then Larke, to shepherdes eare,
> When wheat is greene, when hauthorne buddes appeare.
> (I. I. 184–185.)

So after Egeus' speech—quite in the tone of Old Capulet—on Lysander's wicked use of love tokens, songs at the window by moonlight, and other means 'of strong prevailment in unhardened youth' there is a more powerful echo of the loves of *Romeo and Juliet.*

If there were a sympathy in choice,
Warre, death or sicknesse did lay siege to it,
Making it momentary, as a sound:
Swift as a shadow short as any dreame,
Briefe as the lightning in the collied night,
That (in a spleene) unfolds both heauen and earth,
And ere a man hath power to say, behold,
The iawes of darknesse do devour it up,
So quicke bright thinges come to confusion.

(I. I. 141-149.)

Yet, taken in a different key, this confusion of darkness, swift
brevity of love, and dangerous portents of the collied night
are to be the lot of the quartet of lovers in their woodland
wanderings. The enchantments of the night were a topic of
the hour: Nashe had recently written a not altogether serious
pamphlet on them, in a tone of rustic credulity.

The nocturnal was itself a recognized species at a later date,
with 'the mistakes of a night' providing the opportunity for
broad farce. The *Two Angry Women of Abingdon* is the best
known example[17] where the wrangling of the good wives
and the runaway antics of Moll and Frank weave a homespun
version of some of Shakespeare's scenes. Shakespeare's only
models were the fairy plays of Greene and Peele, *James IV*,
Friar Bacon and *The Old Wives' Tale*, all charming, innocent
and completely shapeless, depending upon the inconsequence
of the folk tale and the 'shows' with which the early stage
abounded. *A Midsummer Night's Dream* combines in the most
paradoxical way the natural and to Elizabethan eyes pastoral
and humble beauty of the woodland and its fairies with the
highly sophisticated pattern of the lovers' quarrel and the
straight burlesque provided by the loves of Pyramus and
Thisbe. Seen from the courtly point of view, the play has
many elements of the masque, as Miss Welsford pointed out:
'*A Midsummer Night's Dream* is a dance, a movement of bodies.
The plot is a pattern, a figure, rather than a series of events
occasioned by human characters and passions, and this pattern,
especially in the moonlight parts of the play, is the pattern of a

dance'.[18] The enchantments of Puck are a deft parody of the normal operation of fancy, which is

> engenderd in the eyes,
> With gazing fed,

and little more reasonable than his magic. Theseus describes the lover's power of metamorphosis:

> Louers and madmen haue such seething braines,
> Such shaping phantasies, that apprehend more
> Then coole reason euer comprehends . . .
> Sees *Helen's* beauty in a browe of *Egipt.*
>
> (5. 1. 4–11.)

This is a theme which was to be more subtly and fully explored in later plays, but the jests of Puck are not much beyond the ordinary scope of Cupid.

Bottom and his friends are drawn, as Mr. Sidgwick observed, 'from observation', but also from the stage clowns who have already been allowed to mock Valentine and Proteus. Their mimic play apes the flight from Athens, though of course the parallel is not visible either to them or to their highly condescending auditory: it is part of the 'mirror' technique of the play-within-the-play, where Bottom so laboriously makes everyone comfortable with explanations of the difference between life and art, and where the fun puts both players and audience together inside the jest of professional actors pretending to be mechanicals trying to be amateur actors before an unreal audience. There is a special pleasure in this play within the play from the actors' point of view, and the hilarious bit of business which is preserved by a contemporary reference, 'Like Thisbe in the play h'as almost killed himself with the scabbard',[19] shows that it was played with gusto.

The mechanicals are out of their element when they get into the wood but the heroical Bottom is ready to adapt himself to any situation. His transformation may recall the tricks of witches, who sometimes loved and were loved by transformed animals: it may recall the *Golden Asse:* it may be mockery of the legend of Circe which held a tragical implication for Elizabethans:[20] but it is primarily a comic Metamorphosis, a simple and splendid opportunity for the low comedian to bring off a telling stage hit. When Falstaff is transformed into a horned beast under the magic oak of Windsor Forest, the fairies might plead their most moral intentions, as they pinch him black and blue:

> Fie on sinneful Phantasie: Fie on Lust and Luxurie:
> Lust is but a bloody fire, kindled with unchaste desire. . . .

but the fairies of Athens have no such highmindedness.

Oberon, Titania and Puck, though they were figures of folklore, are completely transformed in Shakespeare's imagination. (Greene's Oberon is a wizard who acts as Presenter to *James IV*.) It was he who devised the tiny fairy of modern fantasy, and his charming inventions were seized upon by his contemporaries almost at once. Drayton's *Nimphidia*, Herrick's *Oberon's Palace*, *Oberon's Feast* and *Oberon's Chapel*, and the fairies of the Jacobean masques, derive from Shakespeare.[21] In all his supernatural creations, he seems to have created completely new species of creatures, and these of all his characters were most eagerly copied by his contemporaries and immediate successors. The Witches in *Macbeth* were not the first attempt to present a serious treatment of the evil supernatural on the Elizabethan stage, but they set a fashion for witch plays; the spirits of *The Tempest* again set a fashion: Caliban is the prototype of the Witch's Son, a popular stage figure in Caroline drama, and Ariel made a deep impression on the Restoration stage. Throughout the seventeenth century Shakespeare's spirits and fairies served and inspired other playwrights and poets of all kinds.

The fairies are spirits of the woods and the flowers—their names betray them. The description of their life is a description of the woodland itself, its freckled cowslips, its wild thyme, oxlips and nodding violets, its luscious woodbine. Titania woos Bottom in the accents of Drayton's Phoebe wooing his Endimion, even promising to transform him to a spirit, 'purged from earthly grossness'.

Her little fairies who attend on him and offer him their courtesies are exquisitely set off by his earthly if laboured politeness. The contrast is even bolder than that which put the description of Queen Mab into the mouth of the gracelessly broadspoken Mercutio:[22] and perhaps in this clumsy response to the queenly proffer of love, the author of *Venus and Adonis* is providing a 'squandering glance' at his own earlier and somewhat fleshly idyll. Some light parody of *Romeo and Juliet* is also discernible. The fairies are born of that same minute observation which depicted the hunting of poor Wat, dew-bedabbled and scratched with briars, the snail:

> whose tender hornes being hit,
> Shrinks backward in his shellie cave with paine,

and from the chidden hounds of Adonis's hunt come the hounds of Theseus.[23]

The whole anthropomorphic world of the Ovidian romance, the world of Lodge's *Scilla* and of Drayton's *Endimion and Phoebe*, is embodied in the magnificent speech of Titania which places the fairies in control of the whole natural scene, and evokes so richly and powerfully Nature's waste fertility, all to disorder wandering. This speech may be reminiscent of Vergil in his pastoral poetry;[24] Titania's later appeal to Bottom recalls the Eclogues quite directly.

> tibi lilia plenis
> ecce ferunt Nymphae calathis, tibi candida Nais,
> pallentis violas et summa papavera carpens,
> narcissum et florem iungit bene olentis anethi;
> tum casia atque aliis intexens suavibus herbis
> mollia luteola pingit vaccinia calta.
> ipse ego cana legam tenera lanugine mala
> castaneasque nuces, mea quas Amaryllis amabat
> (*Eclogue* II. 45.)

In their recriminations over Theseus and Hippolita, Titania and her Oberon seem to be deputizing for the ancient gods, for Juno and Jove himself, so that their final appearance to bless and hallow the marriage bed is not unfitting for a king's bridal. They are masquers like the Masquers of Prospero's Vision, but the Masque is that of the whole flowery natural world—Natura Naturans—blossoming, ripening, decaying and renewing. In spite of the fact that the picture in Titania's first speech is one of disorder, the effect is not destructive, or horrifying, or at all akin to the tragic speeches of *Richard II*, for example, which is of the same date as the *Dream*. If Titania's speech be compared with the gardeners' scene, it becomes clear that the natural beauties of the Queen's territory are not being used as symbols, or reflections in another mode, of the fairy quarrel, as she asserts they are; but rather that in the fairies themselves, as in those later 'elues of hils, brooks, standing lakes and groves' which Prospero invokes,[25] the very quality of the too-much-loved earth has been given a local habitation and a name. Here if anywhere is the 'cause' and germ of the play:

> Neuer since the middle Summers spring
> Met we on hil, in dale, forest, or mead,
> By paved fountain or by rushie brooke
> Or in the beached margent of the sea,
> To dance our ringlets to the whistling winde. . . .
> The Spring, the Sommer
> The childing Autumn, angry Winter change
> Their wonted Liueries, and the mazed worlde
> By their increase, now knowes not which is which. . . .
> (2. 1. 52ff.)

The voice of Venus Genetrix is the same in Vergil's Sicily, or Shakespeare's England; the particular countryside, heavily wooded, with rushy streams, broad water meadows and rich undulating pasture, is that of Warwick. As a faint light beside the full splendour of Shakespeare's play may be set Nashe's *Summers Last Will and Testament*,[26] with its figures of Winter and Back-Winter, its song of

> Spring the sweet spring is the years pleasant king

alternating with the grim picture of the plague-stricken city from which the entertainers have fled to the safety of Croydon. But compared with Shakespeare, this is an artless piece of revelry. His first completely individual comedy was to remain, *sui generis*, a 'species' of which only one specimen was found in nature.

M

CHAPTER X

POLYPHONIC MUSIC

'All's Well that Ends Well'—II 'Merchant of Venice'— III 'Much Ado About Nothing'

HOVERING uncertainly in date between early and late nineties, *All's Well that Ends Well* is a play which is of its age rather than for all time.[1] It might have as sub-title 'Two plays in one', for the reason of its neglect—and the reason why in spite of the title, all did not end well, and it is not a successful play—is that a personal and an impersonal theme are here in conflict. It began by being a 'moral play', a grave discussion of the question of what constituted true nobility, and the relation of birth to merit. This was *the* great topic of the courtesy books, and in a court that included such a high proportion of self-made men as Elizabeth's did, the question was not without practical consequences. Such questions were the equivalent of a political discussion to-day. But in *All's Well* the 'social problem'—to give it the modern term—of high birth, exemplified in Bertram, and native merit, exemplified in Hellen,[2] is bisected by a human problem of unrequited love. The structural centre of the play is the King's speech on nobility, by which he justifies Hellen's marriage: the poetic centre is Hellen's confession of her love to the Countess. Few readers would deny that this speech is different in kind from anything else in the play:

> I know I love in vain; strive against hope;
> Yet in this captious and intemable sieve
> I still pour in the waters of my love,
> And lack not to lose still. Thus Indian-like,
> Religious in mine error, I adore
> The sun that looks upon his worshipper
> But knows of him no more.
>
> (I. 3. 209-215.)

This is the voice of Juliet.

> My bounty is as boundless as the sea,
> My love as deep; the more I give to thee
> The more I have, for both are infinite.
>
> (2. 2. 133–135.)

Seen through Hellen's eyes, Bertram is handsome, brave, the glass of fashion and the mould of form: seen through older and wiser eyes, he is a degenerate son, an undutiful subject, a dishonourable seducer. The two images blend in the action as he sinks from irresponsibility to deceit, but makes a name for himself in the wars. He ends in an abject position: no other hero receives the open condemnation that Bertram does. Modern taste may disrelish Claudio, Bassanio or Orsino; but Shakespeare does not ratify it.

Here all the harsh words are spoken upon the stage: all but Hellen condemn Bertram. After suffering rebukes from his elders, his contemporaries, and even his inferiors, he ends unable to plead any excuses[3], in danger of the law. The characters of the Countess and Lafeu were invented by Shakespeare, and the King's role much expanded, in order that judgment might be passed on Bertram. By these three, who have an equal share of blood and merit and are therefore impartial judges, he is compared with Hellen throughout the play, to his increasing disadvantage.[4] In the end she alone can restore the honours he has lost.

Bertram is very young, perhaps seventeen or eighteen at most, left without a father's direction and highly conscious of his position. He is handsome, courageous, winning in manners; but also an inveterate liar. Yet the Elizabethan code of honour supposed a gentleman to be absolutely incapable of a lie. To give the lie was the deadliest of insults, not to be wiped out but in blood. Honour was irretrievably lost only by lies or cowardice; a gentleman, as Touchstone remembered, swore by his troth, as a knight by his honour. Crimes of violence were less dishonourable: the convicted liar was finished socially. Bassanio, though he thinks of a lie at the end, to get himself out of an awkward situation, does not utter it.

Bertram's fall is due to ill company: Parolles, or Words, another character of Shakespeare's own invention, is perceived in the end by Bertram himself to be the Lie incarnate, a fact which everyone else has known from the beginning.[5] He is that principal danger of noble youth, the flatterer and misleader, the base companion against whom all books of behaviour issued lengthy warning. The relation of Bertram and Parolles resembles that which every one except Prince Hal takes to exist between himself and Falstaff. Parolles claims to be both courtier and soldier but his courtship is entirely speech, as his soldiership is entirely dress. Even the clown calls him knave and fool to his face; he is ready to play the pander, and at the end he crawls to the protection of old Lafeu, the first to detect and, with provocative insults, to 'uncase' him.

The model of a perfect courtier is set before the young man by the King, in a 'mirror' or portrait of his father.

His father's 'morall parts' are what the king wishes for Bertram: their physical likeness has already been commented on. The elder Rousillon was a soldier first of all, but also a courtier.

> . . . in his youth
> He had the wit, which I can well observe
> To day in our yong Lords, but they may iest
> Till their owne scorne returne to them unnoted
> Ere they can hide their levitie in honour:
> So like a Courtier, contempt nor bitternesse
> Were in his pride, or sharpnesse: if they were
> His equall had awakd them, and his honour
> Clocke to it selfe, knew the true minute when
> Exception bid him speake: and at this time
> His tongue obeyd his hand. Who were below him
> He us'd as creatures of another place,
> And bow'd his eminent top to their low ranks. . . .
>
> (1. 2. 30 ff.)

Such is Bertram's inheritance of conduct, and he had a duty to live up to it. Hellen's miraculous cure of the king, which is proffered by her and accepted by him and the court as an act of Heaven,[6] makes her a candidate for nobility, though she is only the daughter of a poor gentleman belonging to the least dignified of the professions.[7] The recognized causes for ennobling the simple were headed by 'virtue public' that is, some great public service. Sir Thomas Elyot had declared that nobility is 'only the prayse and surname of virtue' and set forth the eleven moral virtues as the model for his Governor. Desert for virtue is Hellen's claim, and this, all but Bertram allow her.

By making his social climber a woman Shakespeare took a good deal of the sting out of the situation. The question of blood and descent versus native worth was an ancient subject of debate on the stage: indeed the first secular play to survive, *Fulgens and Lucres*, deals with precisely this matter. Here the lady's verdict was given for the worthy commoner against the degenerate nobleman. Though noble descent was prized as giving a disposition to virtue, and the opportunity of good education and good examples, yet 'one standard commonplace on nobility took shape; that lineage was not enough, but that the son of a noble house should increase and not degrade the glory of his ancestors'.[8]

Hellen has been conscious throughout of her humble station, and has urged the Countess that though she loves Bertram she would not have him till she should deserve him (1. 3. 199). Before and after marriage she thinks of Bertram as her 'master' as well as her lord, a title Parolles will not give him. It was within the power of the King to confer honour where he chose; and Hellen had already been ennobled in a superior way by being marked out as the instrument of Heaven towards the King's recovery.

When therefore she is offered her choice of a husband, none save Bertram think of refusing her. The 'lottery' is like a reversal of Portia's caskets, for here the lady makes her choice, sure to win. In bestowing a wife upon his ward, the King was certainly doing no more than Elizabeth or any other monarch might do. Yet Bertram's cry, 'A poor physician's

daughter my wife!', would not sound so outrageous to an
Elizabethan ear as it does to-day, for marriage out of one's
degree was a debasing of the blood which blemished successive
generations. The King, in his great central speech, whose
formality is marked by the couplet form, replies and sets out
to Bertram the causes why he should not disdain merit. This
speech contains the germ of the play—or one of the two plays
which together make up this story.

> Tis only title thou disdainst in her, which
> I can build up: strange is it that our bloods
> Of colour, weight and heat, pour'd all together
> Would quite confound distinction: yet stands off
> In differences so mighty. If she bee
> All that is vertuous (saue what thou dislik'st,
> A poor Phisitians daughter), thou dislikst
> Of vertue for the name: but do not soe:
> From lowest place, whence vertuous things proceed,
> The place is dignified by th' doers' deede.
> Whence great additions, swells, and vertue none,
> It is a dropsied honour. Good alone
> Is good without a name: Vileness is so:
> The propertie, by what it is, should goe,
> Not by the title. She is young, wise, faire,
> In these to Nature shee's immediate heire:
> And these breed honour: that is honour's scorne,
> Which challenges it selfe as honour's borne,
> And is not like the sire: Honours thrive
> When rather from our acts we them derive
> Then our forgoers: the meere words, a slave
> Deboshed on every tombe, on every grave:
> A lying Trophee, and as oft is dumbe
> Where dust, and damn'd oblivion is the Tombe
> Of honour'd bones indeed . . .
>
> (2. 3. 129 ff.)

This is doctrine of a kind which ought to convince Bertram.
It is only after he has objected, 'I cannot love her, nor will strive
to do it', that the King exercises his power to compel submission.

The customary formula when presenting young people to each other in such circumstances was, 'Can you like of this man?', 'Can you like of this maid?', in other words, can you make a harmonious marriage? Love was not expected. If Bertram is thought to show peculiar delicacy in demanding passion as the basis of marriage, he removes all such notions at the end of the play by his alacrity in accepting Lafeu's daughter, a match which the King had planned since their childhood. In the original story, Beltramo protests his unwillingness but he does not defy the King, nor does he recant as Bertram so abjectly does under the King's threats, protesting that he now sees Hellen to be ennobled by the royal choice. The King's fury, far more reasonable than old Capulet's when Juliet exercises a right of rejection, depends on his, and everyone else's conviction that Hellen is 'vertuous' and the special favourite of heaven. Not only his king but his mother accepts it. That Bertram should misprize her is not in keeping with the decorum of the play. This is not *Romeo and Juliet*; it is written upon quite different premises, the social premises which that play so pointedly omits. And Bertram has no precontract; for his vamped-up excuse in the fifth act that he was really in love with Mademoiselle Lafeu is patently one of his fibs. He dislikes Hellen on social, not personal grounds. He is being wilful; and in running away after the marriage ceremony, he is evading obligations which are imposed by the Church as well as the State, as Diana does not fail to recall to him (4. 2. 12–13).

His rejection of Hellen must be seen then not in isolation but as linked with his choice of Parolles. The first dialogue of Hellen and Parolles, the Liar and Vertue as she herself designates them, must be seen as the encounter of Bertram's good and evil angels, who, if this were a morality play, would contend for his soul in open debate.[9]

The exposure of Parolles' cowardice and lies precedes but foreshadows the exposure of Bertram. The last scene, which is Shakespeare's improvement of his source, is a 'judgment', like those which conclude so many of Chapman's comedies.

The most extraordinary stratagems are practised by Diana and Hellen to extract Truth from the Accused. The jewels which are bandied about have symbolic significance; they stand for a contract and an estate of life. The King's gem derived from him to Hellen, and Bertram neither knows nor cares what it is. His own monumental ring symbolizes all he has thrown away.

> an honour longing to our house
> Bequeathed down from manie Ancestors,
> Which were the greatest obloquie i' th' world
> In me to lose
>
> (4. 2. 42–45.)

This jewel, with which he had taunted Hellen, is found at the end to be in her keeping. Hellen too is a 'Jewell' (5. 3. 1) which Bertram has thrown away. In this scene the King appears as the fount of justice, as earlier he had been the fount of honour: he deprives Bertram of all honour (5. 3. 183–185) and the rapidity with which he jumps to thoughts of murder is prompted as much by his affection for Hellen as his well-merited distrust of her lord. Lafeu and the Countess also recall Hellen's memory with sorrow. The likeness with the later play of *Measure for Measure*,[10] which was evidently modelled in part on *All's Well*, is particularly strong in this judgment scene, with charge and countercharge piled up in bewildering succession till they are resolved as if by magic in the appearance of the central figure. The ingenuities of Hellen, like those of the Duke, are not to modern taste but their purpose is conversion.

Bertram's conversion must be reckoned among Hellen's miracles. It is notable that on the fulfilment of the bargain she turns to seek, not her husband, but the King. What is achieved is public recognition of her right, which he concedes her. She has been acknowledged by her lord; that her personal happiness is simply irrelevant, and the ending neither hypocritical nor cynical, can be granted only if the play is seen as a moral debate on the subject: Wherein consists true honour and nobility?

This is a grave subject: more lofty than that of *Romeo and Juliet*, for example. But such a subject needed to remain upon the level of debate. An Elizabethan audience might have been quite willing to see it worked out as a species of morality play, without taking the personal aspect into account. What is now called 'the love interest' is generally overweighted in the modern view of Shakespearean comedy. His audience would be well accustomed to see a love-intrigue provide the spring of the action without providing any of the interest or body of the play, as it does in the comedies of Jonson or Chapman, where it is like the love interest in a detective story, strictly subordinate to the disguisings. But here the nature of the story makes it extremely difficult to insulate the marriage as a social and religious contract.

Two incompatible 'species' are mingled because the personal aspect awakened to life. The play is a genuine hybrid, one of the few examples of Shakespeare's failure to master and control his form. Bertram is magnificently drawn: his petulance, his weakness, his cub-like sulkiness, his crude and youthful pride of rank. His charm has to be accepted because Hellen loves him, but there is little other evidence for it. Hellen's love, as expressed in her three great speeches, is a devotion so absolute that all thought of self is obliterated; yet her action cannot but make her appear, however much more modestly to an Elizabethan than to us, a claimant, and a stickler for her bond.[11] The parallels between her love speeches and the sonnets (expecially xxxv, lxvii, lxxxii, lxxxiv, xcv, xcvi), something in common between the lineaments of Bertram and those of Adonis, Bassanio, and Proteus, suggest that the theme of high birth versus native merit, first approached impersonally, had touched off reactions which could not properly be related to the story as it originally stood. The figure of Bertram, so radically changed from that of Boccaccio's Beltramo, is drawn with a fullness, a kind of uncynical disillusion which makes Hellen as a person still more unsatisfactory. She is a voice of despair breaking into the play; at other times a pliant lay-figure on which the characters drape their admiration. No crude and direct personal equation can be thought of; Shakespeare would certainly not wish to unlock his heart on the public stage. But here for once the poet and the dramatist are pulling different ways. He set out to start a discussion on the fashioning of a gentleman, and found himself impelled to draw the likeness of one whom Lafeu called an 'asse' and Hellen the god of her 'idolatrous fancie', but whose portrait stands out clearly as something more complex than either.

II

The interweaving of a moral theme and a romantic story was successfully accomplished in *The Merchant of Venice*. Here too there is a 'marriage by lottery', the achieving of an almost impossible success in love, and the rescue of man by the wit of woman. Hellen confronting Parolles is matched by Portia confronting Shylock, and more than matched, for in this play the contrasts are deeper, the issues more fully realized, more truly embodied in lively images. It is among the most vivid of Shakespeare's works in tone and colour. The golden world of Belmont and the heavier splendours of Venice are yoked together by something that, if it were not mastery, would approach violence. Shakespeare has carried his new method of contrasting different species within a single play to the very limits of its capacity. In Shylock he has imported the stage villain of Marlowe—upon whom his own Aaron had been modelled—and set him down within the limits of a love story. True, he found the Jew in his source, but had he not chosen to make a play of such boldness he might easily have looked elsewhere.

Modern humanitarianism has run riot on Shylock; like Falstaff, with whom he has little else in common, he is held to be wronged in the end. Though the abuse of Bassanio's fortune-hunting, Antonio's manners and the Duke's notion of

mercy has abated a little of recent years, there is still a tendency
to overwork that phrase:

> Out upon her, thou torturest me *Tuball*, It was my Turkies, I
> had it of *Leah* when I was a Batchelor: I would not haue giuen it
> for a wildernesse of Monkies.

Such an admission of conjugal fidelity is almost held to out-
weigh a taste for judicial murder.

But Shylock is in search of Revenge.   So indeed was
Barabas, and they have the same excuse:

> I learn'd in *Florence* how to kisse my hand,
> Heave up my shoulders when they call me dogge,
> And ducke as low as any bare-foot Fryar,
> Hoping to see them starue upon a stall,
> Or else be gather'd for in our Synagogue;
> That when the offring-Bason comes to me,
> Euen for charity I may spit intoo't.
>
> (Jew of Malta, II. 784–890.)

> Shall I bend low and in a bond-mans key
> With bated breath and whispring humblenesse,
> Say this: Faire, sir, you spet on me on Wednesday last;
> You spurn'd me such a day: another time
> You cald me dog: and for these curtesies
> Ile lend you thus much moneys.
>
> (I. 3. 124–130.)

Revenge, even in the most extenuating circumstances, was
for the Elizabethan a crime; Shylock's injuries were not
per se any further justification than Edmund's grievance of
illegitimacy, or the predisposition to vice which his crooked
birth gave Richard III.   Nothing less monstrous than the
theatre's prize bogyman, linked in the popular mind with
Machiavelli and the Devil in an infernal triumvirate, would
serve for the villain of a romantic comedy.   Were he less
diabolic, Shylock would not be tolerable.   It might be said of
Shylock, as Swinburne said of Mary of Scots:

> Surely you were something better
> Than innocent!

A human Shylock, devoted to Jessica, smarting under what Antonio can do in the way of spitting on his gabardine, is something less than Shakespeare's. Still less can he be looked on as an embodiment of the Rise of Capitalism, Shakespeare's protest against the new money economy.[12] Naturally Shakespeare used his feeling about 'the breed of barren metal'— later to be used to more potent effect in *Timon*—but only as a similitude, shadowing in a baser manner the theme of his play; which is very plainly set forth as Justice and Mercy,[13] the law and love that is the fulfilling of the law, the gold of Venice and the gold of Belmont.

Shylock, in so far as he stands for anything, stands for the Law: for the legal system which, to be just to all in general, must only approximate to justice in particular cases. Shylock's creed is an eye for an eye, and in a later play Shakespeare set out the measure to be meted in the name of strict justice. The Bible would be sufficient lead to the identification of a Jew with legal concepts of justice, and for the opposition of the Old Law to the New. Portia's famous speech is the most purely religious utterance in the canon—the most directly based upon Christian teaching, with its echoes of the Lord's Prayer, the Christian doctrine of salvation, and the words of *Ecclesiasticus*, 35.20:

> Mercy is seasonable in time of affliction, as clouds of rain in the time of drouth.

As addressed to a Jew, the argument loses its cogency, but it is intended rather as contrast to Shylock's

> What iudgement shall I dread doing no wrong? . . .
> I stand for iudgement, answer, Shall I haue it? (4. 1. 89ff)

As in so many trial scenes of the Elizabethan drama, the pleading is addressed directly to the audience; it is exposition. In Shylock's and Portia's case it is also self-revelation; but it is the peculiar virtue of this play, and of the later *Measure for Measure*, that the characters are at the same time fully human, and symbolic or larger than human. Shakespeare has achieved here what he failed to do in *All's Well that Ends Well* and written a 'moral play'—that is a play in which the lively image of a general truth is embodied with such decorum and in so fitting a form that it has all the immediacy, the 'persuasion' as the Elizabethans would say, of a particular instance.

Hath not a *Jew* eyes? hath not a Jew hands, organs, dementions, senses, affections, passions, fed with the same foode, hurt with the same weapons, subiect to the same diseases, healed by the same meanes, warmed and cooled by the same Winter and Summer as a Christian is? . . .

(3. 1. 63ff)

This is so powerful a plea, ending as it does with an echo of Barabas,

The villanie you have taught me I will execute, and it shall goe hard but I will better the instruction

that it produces a natural rush of sympathy, and Salarino is given no answer. But of course the answer is provided later:

My deedes upon my head.

(4. 1. 206)

It is the sentence which drew down the Curse upon his race:

Then answered all the people and said, His blood be on us and on our children.

(*Gospel of St. Matthew*, 27. 25.)

So when Portia asks him to have a surgeon ready lest Antonio bleed to death, Shylock says:

It is not nominated in the bond?
Portia.   It is not so exprest: but what of that?
           Twere good you do so much for charitie.
Shylock.   I cannot finde it, tis not in the bond.

(4. 1. 260)

There is a sense in which Shylock has not the eyes that a Christian has—the sense which Gloucester implies when he says:

I stumbled when I saw.

The doctrine of grace and the second birth of baptism, the new man and regeneration were such commonplaces that

Portia's allusion to the 'sceptred sway' which is 'enthroned in
the hearts of Kings' would suffice as reminder of the inward
and outward kingdom, and the inward and outward senses.
Gratiano has already made a cruder statement of Shylock's
privation, but Gratiano here plays much the part that Emilia
does at the end of *Othello*: by his vehement and violent
assertion of the truth he relieves the tension, while in a kind of
exasperated crescendo continuing to work up the excitement.

> O be thou damn'd inexecrable dogge,
> And for thy life let iustice be accus'd:
> Thou almost mak'st me waver in my faith;
> To hold opinion with *Pythagoras*,
> That soules of Animals infuse themselves
> Into the trunkes of men. Thy currish spirit
> Gouern'd a wolfe, who hang'd for humane slaughter,
> Euen from the gallowes did his fell soule fleet;
> And whilst thou layest in thy unhallowed dam,
> Infus'd itself in thee: For thy desires
> Are woluish, bloody, steru'd and rauenous.
>
> (4. 1. 128–138.)

This is Metamorphosis in its tragic vein: 'O tyger's hart
wrapt in a woman's hide'. Humanity lapsing back into the
beast was to become one of the central themes of *King Lear*.[14]

> If that the heauens doe not their visible spirits
> Send quickly downe to tame these vild offences,
> It will come
> Humanity must perforce pray on it self
> Like monsters of the deepe.
>
> (4. 2. 46–50.)

It is no belittlement of Shakespeare's achievement to say
that in Shylock he has drawn a man lapsing into beast. The
personal responsibility of Shylock for his horrible state is
very small; it is the result of his wrongs, his birth and his
creed. But to remove all guilt from him on this account, and
to treat him as a sympathetic criminal would not have occurred

to any Elizabethan. Few would have had Shakespeare's insight and awareness of the natural case to be made out for Shylock's revenge; but that case, and the figure of Shylock himself, is very much weakened if his crime is seen as anything less than damnable. The present generation has been taught by bitter examples that persecution breeds criminals, and sometimes criminals of so violent and perverted a nature that their only end, in a world that does not believe in the efficacy of forcible baptism, would seem to be despair. The concentration camps of Nazi Germany bred many heroes and martyrs but also a few Shylocks.

The legal quibble by which Portia saves Antonio is triumphantly and appropriately a quibble. Any sounder argument would be giving Shylock less than his deserts. The bare letter of the law nooses him; and mercy takes the form of another legal instrument. The deed of gift balances the 'merry bond'.

The whole play is built upon contrasts of this sort. The original story and Marlowe's stage Jew require stronger counterweights than the heroine of *Il Pecarone* provided. Portia and Belmont are Shakespeare's creation; the casket story, which he added to his original, stands in precise and symbolic contrast to the story of the bond. In this play Shakespeare makes more direct use than anywhere else of dramatic *impresa*: the bold physical contrasts of the Jew with his curving knife and the boy-Portia in doctor's gown. The splendours of the Doge's court and the moonlight of Belmont would probably be outdone as sheer pageantry on the Elizabethan stage by the highly symbolic casket scenes.

The Prince of Morocco who comes first wearing 'the shadowed liuerie of the burnished sun' is described as 'Morochus a tawnie Moore all in white'. He has the accents of Tamburlaine:

By this Symitare
That slew the Sophie and a Persian Prince
That won three fields of Sultan Solyman . . . (2. 1. 2–46)

and ruled by his planet Sol, he chooses the Golden Casket with its motto, 'Who choses me shall gaine what men desire', in a

speech that deliberately recalls Tamburlaine's praise of Zeno-
crate:

> The Hircanion deserts, and the vaste wildes
> Of wide Arabia are as throughfares now
> For princes come to view fair *Portia*.
>
> (2. 7. 41–3

The answer is a death's head. Mortality conquers those who
like Tamburlaine are more 'bold' than 'wise' (2. 7. 71).
The Prince of Arragon is a Spaniard, incarnation of Pride.
He chooses silver which promises 'as much as he deserves'.
The answer is a fool's head; and unlike Morocco, he is not
only dismissed but rebuked by Portia; his wisdom only
makes him a 'deliberate fool' (2. 9. 80).

Bassanio chooses the lead casket: 'Who chooseth me must
giue and hazard all he hath'. The hazards of love in this
venture are Antonio's; Bassanio invited him to hazard
(chance) a second arrow after the first, and the hazards (dangers)
of the venture are no less than his life. The scene of Bassanio's
choosing is made into a tapestry picture by Portia's magnificent 'augmentation':

> Now he goes,
> With no lesse presence but with much more loue
> Than yong *Alcides* when he did redeeme
> The virgine tribute paid by howling Troy
> To the Sea-monster: I stand for sacrifice,
> The rest aloof are the Dardanian wiues
> With bleared visages come forth to view
> The issue of th' exploit.
>
> (3. 2. 53–60)

The heightened language (almost with a touch of Hamlet's
First Player), the tableau, the soft music whose significance
Portia has explained so fully, are all designed to isolate this
moment, the turning point of the story—the song, warning
Bassanio against the fancy (or love) that is 'engendered in the
eyes'. His dangerous hazard brings him to a moment of
blind and naked choice: and his choice is based on negatives.
He will not take the *seeming* beauty. The speech of his choice
echoes a theme which was to recur in the tragedies, and even

before the tragedies, was to appear with almost tragic significance.

To work so much morality out of a pretty fairy tale may appear too much like breaking a butterfly upon a wheel; but the fairy-tale quality of the story serves to keep these significances unemphatic, not to obliterate them. Some such technique, but far subtler, was to be used in the final plays. To ignore the moral significance of the casket story—familiar commonplace morality, but the Elizabethans enjoyed the familiar and doted on the commonplace—is to ignore the main counterbalance to Shylock. He is symbolic in an all but tragic manner: these scenes are symbolic in an all but fairy-tale manner. The thrust of the opposing stresses maintains the arch of the narrative.

Portia, whose sunny locks hang on her temples like a golden fleece, whose suitors come from all corners of the earth to woo her, is set against the wealth of Venice, the mart where all the trade of east and west flows in. Antonio's argosies sail to Mexico, England, Tripoli, Lisbon, Barbary and India. The pledge and bond of matrimony—which is both a sacrament and a legal contract—is set against the bond of the Jew and Antonio's pledge of his flesh. Bassanio has won all, for with the ring Portia gives power as

> her Lord, her Governour, her King.
> Myself and what is mine, to you and yours
> Is now conuerted.
> (3 . 2166–8)

The exchange of property is an exchange of the very self, which leaves Bassanio confused, as his powers recognize the voice of their sovereign[16] in Portia's voice.

The rings which are exchanged reappear in the final scene as the pledge of this bond. It is as parody of the trial scene that the final episode becomes something more than a jest out of the Hundred Merry Tales. The gold of the rings is not the gold which Shylock deals in, and to which Portia and Antonio are both so superbly indifferent, which Bassanio has rejected in the casket scene, and which the unthrift Lorenzo acquires in so light-fingered a fashion. It is the gold of Belmont, and in parting from the ring, for Antonio's sake, Bassanio has supplied some backing for his second choice, made in the trial scene:

> Antonio, I am married to a wife,
> Which is as deare to me as life it selfe,
> But life it selfe, my wife, and all the world,
> Are not with me esteem'd aboue thy life.
> I would loose all, I sacrifice them all
> Heere to this deuill, to deliuer you. (4. 1. 283ff)

So that in the dispute between husband and wife, Antonio reasonably intervenes, with the offer of a new and even more reckless bond, though of the kind that may not be registered in law.

> I once did lend my bodie for thy wealth,
> Which but for him that had your husbands ring
> Had quite miscarried. I dare be bound againe,
> My soule upon the forfeit, that your Lord
> Will neuer more break faithe aduisedly. (5. 1. 249–253)

The pretty jests about cuckoldry are far from modern taste (like the jests which Diana makes with Lafeu and the King at the end of *All's Well* over Hellen's ring). Yet it is as hopelessly anachronistic to boggle at them as to treat Bassanio as a fortune-hunter. He is luck and young love personified, given as much character as the object of Portia's and Antonio's devotion requires; but, like Bertram though without any of the condemnation that Bertram receives, he is there to be the *object* of devotion, and he must look and move his part. I have seen it suggested that if his feelings for Antonio are all that he proclaims, he has only to run Shylock through with his rapier in the open court and stand to the consequences. Let anyone try to write a play on these lines. *The Merchant of Venice* is in the best sense artificial; Portia's successful disguise, the nature of the bond itself, the set pleas of Justice and Mercy are all artifice, designed not to make the story slighter but to control, direct and focus the emphasis upon the theme or 'cause' of the play. Every piece of artifice is

there for a purpose, and a purpose which an imaginative
reading discloses readily enough. For *The Merchant of Venice*
is not a subtle play; it is a recklessly bold and obvious sort of
play. The symbolism is almost blatant, the violence of the
contrasts almost glaring. It can be turned about and viewed
from many aspects; the personal relationship between
Antonio and Bassanio—which is mostly Antonio's—is so
familiar from elsewhere in the Works that the only danger is
lest the connexion with the sonnets should be pressed too
far.[17] The reproachful sonnets should not be invoked. Nor
must the economics of the situation be taken on economic
lines. In an age when economic treatises could be written by
city merchants in the form of allegory and called *St. George
for England*,[18] there would have been little danger of misunderstanding, even from those members of Shakespeare's
audience who smelt most strongly of ink and counters. For
the groundlings he had provided a magnificent villain, some
exciting scenes of pageantry and a tale which might have been
authorized by their grandam. For the young gentlemen of
the Inns of Court, he had provided some lovely speeches of
wooing and some of morality and good life; for everyone
the contrast between Justice and Mercy, gold and love,
embodied in figures of so winning a grace that the critics
talk of them as if they lived. It is the first of Shakespeare's
plays which invites the moral judgments of real life in this
way.

III

If *Romeo and Juliet* was a tragedy with its full complement
of comedy, and *The Merchant of Venice* a comedy with an
infusion of tragic pity and fear, *Much Ado About Nothing* is a
comedy of Masks where the deeper issues are overlaid with
mirth, and appear only at the climax of the play, the church
scene. It is for this reason that so very mechanical a villain

as Don John becomes a necessity of the plot. A true villain, like Shylock or Edmund or Richard III, would destroy the comedy: those who protest at the insufficiency of Don John should consider what would happen to the total composition if he were other than he is.[19] The old worn device of a maid dressing up in her mistress's clothes—one of the commonplaces of European fiction for centuries—is also used for a special purpose. It is not perhaps so incredible as modern readers tend to think it: the story of Gratiano and Nerissa should have served as reminder that gentlewomen really might ape their mistresses,[20] and talking with a man out at a window had happened in Shakespeare before without incurring moral disapprobation, even of the strictest; it was only as it happened on her wedding eve to the betrothed Hero that it took on the colouring of perfidy as well as lightness. Nevertheless the convention is used in a frankly conventional way; Margaret does not intervene when Claudio lodges his accusation, and Claudio does not fall upon the interloper and run him through like the hero of *A Blot in the Scutcheon*, both of which are obvious, natural, and probable, but inappropriate things for them to do.

In *Much Ado*, as Masefield pointed out,[21] the two plots are linked by the common theme of credulity and self-deception. Claudio believes first that Don Pedro, then that Hero plays him false: Benedick and Beatrice believe the stories of their friends, thereby building a truth upon a fabulous basis. Dogberry and Verges need no one to lay them a trap; they are perpetually deceiving themselves, and invent a wonderful fabrication from the conversation of Borachio and Conrad. Yet it is they who unmask the villainy, thus robbing it of a good deal of its sinister value.

Credulity and foolish mistakings are the natural effects of love: we have already seen Valentine unable to fathom Silvia's meaning in asking him to write a love-letter, and the courtly ladies of *Love's Labour's Lost* are unable to distinguish between jest and earnest—though here perhaps the fault lies rather with their lovers, who are so unpractised at expressing their feelings. Love's power to trip the heels, baffle the wits, and transform the person is a staple of Shakespearean comedy. Within the frame of a formal narrative, with its set situations—their staginess underlined rather than disguised—Shakespeare develops the personal and natural feelings of his lovers, working by implication and by strong use of contrast.

It does not need a critic to observe that Benedick and Beatrice are flirting from the beginning. The technique of a 'merry war' is not unknown to clowns, and if Shakespeare had not happened to have met it in real life, he could have found it plentifully enough in literature.[22]

Nevertheless discussions as to whether Benedick and Beatrice are 'really' in love will lead precisely nowhere. That in a sense is the point of their wit-combat; what they think they are, what their friends think they are, what they really might be, are left as a series of alluring possibilities. 'I confesse nothing nor I deny nothing' says Beatrice at the climax of the church scene; it was a situation to which the practice of courtship must have given precedents enough. The dancing spray of the dialogue could not, at all events, rise from mutual boredom.

As in *Love's Labour's Lost*, but not in *Two Gentlemen of Verona* and *Twelfth Night*, the jesting is extremely broad. If Beatrice is translated into modern English some of her language would not be heard far west of Leicester Square. Yet she is hit, as Phoebe and Olivia were to be hit, by a good scolding from another woman. It seems to have been Shakespeare's grand strategy for subduing the female sex. Benedick on the other hand is caught with an appeal to his pity. The means are nicely varied; so are the responses. His long, natural and entertaining soliloquy, 'Love me? why it must be requited', is based on the soliloquies of Berowne (*Love's Labour's Lost*, 3. 1. 184-215: 4. 3. 1-21), in its use of the debating form, with questions and answers, and the picture of the reluctant lover haled into love, against his will but not unwillingly. Benedick like Berowne takes to sonnetting, though more unsuccessfully: but his physical transformation is not of the old fashion, to let himself appear distraught and ungartered; on the contrary, like Orlando, he goes point-devise and shaves himself, which may be a proof merely that he is ignorant of the rules. His wooing—and his sparring—is all conducted in russet yeas and honest kersey noes: the language of the play is in revolt against courtly decorum throughout.

Yet Beatrice's reaction to the news is given in ten rhymed lines of extreme formality:

> What fire is in mine eares? can this be true?
> Stand I condemned for pride and scorn so much?
> Contempt farewell, and maiden pride adew,
> No glory liues behind the back of such.
> And *Benedick*, loue on, I will requite thee,
> Taming my wild heart to thy louing hand:
> If thou dost loue, my kindenesse shall incite thee
> To binde our loues up in a holy band.
> For others say thou dost deserue, and I
> Believe it better then reportingly.
>
> (3. 1. 107–116.)

This cannot be carelessness, remains of an old play, or laziness: it is a most important moment in the story. Yet here is the verbal equivalent of the dummy villain. Beatrice is to be shown still preserving some of her defences until the climax of the church scene, her next encounter with Benedick, and therefore nothing personal enters into her confession because her feeling must be held back for the critical release. He, being given the wooer's role, can be allowed to speak his mind after the eavesdropping.

Both Benedick and Beatrice are comic without being ridiculous, and they provide the audience with the same kind of mirth that they are supposed to provide their friends. Their transparent attempts at disguising their feelings under the form of a toothache and a cold in the head, their slight peevishness and their extreme gullibility, Benedick's halting sonnet and February face, and Beatrice's extraordinary taciturnity, allow their friends to tease them, and the audience to indulge that particularly pleasing kind of superiority which arises when one's own predicaments are recognizably displayed in larger forms than life. If the two were not so admirable in all their more important actions—if Benedick were not so honest and soldierly, Beatrice so constant and loyal—there would be a good deal less pleasure in this identification. But to see characters in all other respects heroic reduced to such complete helplessness by Nature's ruthless device for ensuring that 'the world must be peopled' is exhilarating in the extreme. It was a form of entertainment which was to be exploited much more coarsely by Fletcher with his conquering heroes reduced to absolute imbecility, like Arbaces, and his heroines of a wide-eyed innocence verging on impropriety, like Ordella.[23] To an age brought up on the Platonic politenesses, such a display of Nature must have been doubly engaging. The frank bawdiness and the human inconsistencies of Benedick and Beatrice must be seen against the proprieties of Valentine and Silvia, the stately splendour of Belmont, to win their full value.

To make the human relationship between two lovers display itself through the wit-combat of courtly love, by the simple process of extending the role of 'unwilling' lover to the lady as well as the gentleman[24] was a stroke of genius which once achieved, takes on the appearance of the obvious. To quarrel was the stock recipe for comedy. Beatrice may indeed have owed something to the earlier Kate of *The Taming of the Shrew*, for her wit was certainly more forcible as well as more nimble than stage tradition would allow the court. Rosaline of *Love's Labour's Lost* is, like Beatrice, tilting against a professed enemy to her sex and is therefore justified of her tartness; Rosalind of *As You Like It* is speaking in the role of a pert page.[25] Beatrice is called on for a moment of clarity which all the merry wars, the evasions and dissemblings serve to throw into high relief—the moment when she is confronted and in her turn confronts Benedick with a choice. Like the choice of the caskets, it is perilous: Benedick hesitates. For he has 'to give and hazard' something which he weighs with the whole world.

Beatrice. I love you with so much of my heart, that none is left to protest.

Benedick. Come, bid me doe anything for thee.

Beatrice. Kill *Claudio.*

Benedick. Ha, not for the wide world.

Beatrice. You kill me to denie it, farewell. (4. 1. 291ff)

Beatrice's passion is no assertion of principle: it is blind, savage and generous, offering Benedick simply the testimony of character, the testimony of her unshakable faith in her cousin's innocence. This is weighed against the sworn ocular proof of his two closest friends.[26] His acceptance of the challenge is prosaic in manner as well as in form.

Enough, I am engagde, I will challenge him, I will kiss your hand and so leave you: by this hand Claudio shall render me a deere account: as you heare of me so thinke of me: goe comfort your cousin, I must say she is dead, and so farewell. (4. 1. 239ff)

These are the sort of old ends that were flouted by Claudio and Don Pedro; they are part of Benedick's soldierly plainness, and it is this quality—his readiness to act on his belief without hesitation and without requiring more conviction than Beatrice's oath and his own intuition—which gives him an easy lead among Shakespeare's heroes of comedy.

Claudio has on the other hand been the object of a good deal of critical venom. He has much larger stretches of flat dialogue to sustain but his part is developed from a courtly to a natural one in the course of his wooing. In contrast to Benedick and Beatrice, Claudio and Hero are silent lovers. Hero chatters to Beatrice and her women or under the protection of a mask (2. 1. 90–104): Claudio, 'Lord Lack beard', is similarly at ease with Benedick and the Prince, but he can only introduce Hero's name in his conversation by asking the Prince a question whose answer is already known to him (1. 1. 304–306). He and Hero have seen each other in public; but virtually all he knows of her is her looks. He has fallen in love with a pretty face and a modest manner. It is quite natural to him to think that the Prince must want Hero too.

Fancy is not bred altogether in his eyes, nor, though it has an interest, in his liver.

In the betrothal scene both the lovers are prompted by Beatrice:

> *Leonato.* . . . his grace hath made the match, and all grace say, Amen to it.
> *Beatrice.* Speake Count, tis your Qu.
> *Claudio.* Silence is the perfectest Herrault of Ioy, I were but little happy if I could say, how much? Lady, as you are mine, I am yours, I giue away myself for you and dote upon the exchange.
> *Beatrice.* Speake cosin . . .
>
> (2. 1. 316ff)

Like Bassanio Claudio is bereft of words; but when Pedro asks him to name the marriage day, his precipitate 'To-morrow, my lord' is as telling as the fact that he has not exchanged one word more with Hero nor she with him—except in his ear, to be interpreted by Beatrice to the company.

So the shock of the ocular proof which Don John offers has little but Hero's appearance to contradict it; and hence the agony of Claudio's dilemma. Claudio's idealization of Hero is shown by his first comment, 'Is it not a modest young lady?' He is horribly mocked, as he takes it, by the 'seeming' which she maintains under his accusations.

> Behold how like a maid she blushes here! . . .
> Would you not sweare
> All you that see her, that she were a maide,
> By these exterior shewes?
>
> (4. 1. 34-40.)

When he speaks of his own behaviour, 'like a brother to a sister', Hero asks:

> And seem'd I ever otherwise to you?

The word is match to tinder.

> Out on thee seeming, I will write against it,
> You seeme to me as Dian in her orb.

That is, she *still* 'seems' so. The speech looks back to Bassanio's comment on the caskets and the false seeming of gold; it looks forward to Hamlet's 'Seems, madam! nay, it is, I know not seemes'. The lament which follows, lovely in its rhythm—

> O *Hero*! what a *Hero* hadst thou beene
> If halfe thy outward graces had been placed
> About thy thoughts and counsels of thy heart?
> But fair thee well, most foul, most faire, farewell
> Thou pure impiety and impious purity—

has not the agonized force of his question to Leonato:

> Is this face *Hero's*? are our eyes our own?

So Troilus, looking at Cressid, was to exclaim, 'This is and is not Cressid' while Thersites commented, 'Wil he swagger himself out on's eyes?'

And Borachio, confessing his villainy to the Prince, says, 'I haue deceiued euen your verie eies'. It is the 'image of *Hero*' that then reappears to Claudio 'in the rare semblance that I lou'd it first'.

Hero has indeed nothing but her image, her appearance with which to defend herself. Like Desdemona, Hermione or Imogen she is too shocked at first even for a verbal denial. She is left with nothing but a bare protest when the Friar puts his gentle question to her (but be it noted, the question contains a trap). The Friar can read faces: he takes as sure testimony what to Claudio had been hideous 'seeming',[27] and what he proposes is that Claudio should be left with the memory of Hero's image which will in time work its conviction upon him also.

> The Idea of her life shall sweetly creep
> Into his study of imagination.
> And every lovely Organ of her life,
> Shall come apparel'd in more precious habite,
> More mouing delicate and full of life
> Into the eye and prospect of his soule
> Than when she liv'd indeed.
>
> (4. 1. 226–232.)

The relation of the men and women of the play depends upon such an attraction and such an imperfect knowledge: but they each know their own sex extremely well. Hero knows the surest way to catch Beatrice and sometimes explains her meaning to others:[28] Beatrice champions her cousin sooner than the girl's own father dares to do. Claudio, the Prince and Benedick are a sufficiently good set of messmates (princely aloofness a little slackened in the field) for Benedick's challenge to Claudio to extend as far as an indirect giving of the lie to Don Pedro as well:

> My lord, for your manie courtesies I thank you, I must discontinue your companie . . . you haue among you kill'd a sweet and innocent Ladie.
> (5. 1. 195ff)

Claudio's flippancy about the pitiful insults of Leonato and Antonio (though he behaved admirably in their presence) and his readiness to take a second bride in reparation for the killing the first create difficulties for the modern reader where they are not likely to have existed for an Elizabethan. Leonato's challenge in the presence of the Prince was a social outrage which would have landed the greatest nobleman in prison (Benedick draws Claudio aside to make his defiance). As for the marriage, it may rank with other fictions; by this time the audience and everyone but Claudio can see the happy conclusion, and to treat Claudio as an independent character at this point, and upbraid him for his failure to lodge an objection —like Bassanio when he was asked for the ring—is to abandon all sense of theatrical propriety and comic decorum for the sake of a psychological consistency which would defeat its own ends. Claudio cannot now be made into a tragic character or allowed more than a pretty lyric by way of remorse. In the church scene he had spoken out, and spoken the words which his earlier character warranted. There is no further role for him, or for Hero, save to make a pair in the final dance. They each sink back into the kind of formality which the plot allowed, and the conclusion belongs to Benedick and Beatrice. The full story was not to be told till Shakespeare wrote *Cymbeline*, and depicted remorse in Posthumus, with constancy in Imogen.

In both *Much Ado* and *The Merchant of Venice* the clowns are ingeniously but loosely attached to the main plot by a few lines of intrigue—Gobbo acts as go-between for Jessica, Dogberry serves to keep Borachio in safe custody till Act V. Their real function is to act as parody or, in musical analogy, as undersong; Lancelot's debate with the fiend about his leaving his master, 'who (God blesse the marke) is a kind of deuill', is a very pretty speech for the clown and reflects in a charmingly direct manner upon the brisk decision of Jessica, to leave her Hell. Dogberry and Verges are clearly reincarnations of Gobbo and his father, and their role of comic policeman was one of the oldest and most assured cards in popular comedy. But their parts are confined to scenes immediately preceding and following the church scene, where the relief of their broad comedy is most tellingly juxtaposed with the straightforward drama of the main plot. As interludes between the wit combats of Benedick and Beatrice they would have been unnecessary. The clowns of the later comedies were more closely woven into the main structure of the play, and indeed Feste is the central figure of *Twelfth Night*; but here the low comedy serves rather by contrast to strengthen the range and complexity of 'interchangeable variety'.

This variety, which, if it did not extend to hornpipes and funerals, extended to wedding festivity and mock-funerals, is marked by a strict control. Nothing could be further than the masterly shaping of Shakespeare's art from the wild incongruities of the Elizabethan hacks or the baroque eclecticism of the Jacobeans. The nearest analogue to the bold contrasts of these middle comedies is probably to be found in Chaucer, where the Canterbury Pilgrims tell their tales and conduct their debates in such a way as to bring out the individuality of each, whilst subordinating it to the whole pattern. Shakespeare, like Chaucer, drew largely from life, though both his heroic and his low characters were also recognized literary types. Shakespeare, like Chaucer, defined his characters largely in terms of their idiom, their own private speech. Both are given to raising moral issues, but not to pronouncing on them, except by implication. Both present a picture of the world which is above all wise and humane.

CHAPTER XI

COMICAL-HISTORICAL

'Part 1 Henry IV—II 'Part 2 Henry IV'—III 'Henry V'

TO consider *Henry IV Parts 1 and 2* and *Henry V* as a group
does not imply that they were so designed in advance
or even that the two parts of *Henry IV* constitute a single ten-act
play. In this matter, I am inclined to agree with the late
Aubrey Attwater and Professor Shaaber[1] that 2 *Henry IV* was
'a hastily written encore'. But whatever the truth of this
matter, it is generally conceded that *Henry IV* is the greatest
of Shakespeare's English histories, and that *Henry V* is a *coda* to
the preceding plays.

Yet it is only incidentally that the themes of the moral
history re-enter. By incidental reference back and forth
Shakespeare keeps the pot boiling, the links with *Richard II* and
with the Yorkist plays are there[2]; but these plays are about
human relationships and heroic acts, not about politics. If
in Prince Hal Shakespeare has drawn a Prodigal Prince and in
Henry V the perfect Governor, his particular position on the
Plantagenet family tree has not a great deal to do with either.
The Wars of the Roses are all but out of sight.

This is confirmed by the way in which Shakespeare has
broken away from the Chronicles. The Percy rebellion of
1403 and the Scrope rebellion of 1405 are but two episodes in
a very much longer reign: his parallel between Hal and
Hotspur makes them both of an age, whereas Percy was
actually older than Henry IV:[3] Hal is given the honour of
killing him in single combat, an honour which history does
not bestow: in *Henry V*, Shakespeare altered the style of
Henry's claim in order to furnish a parallel to a contemporary
campaign.[4] Not only are the facts of history juggled with

in order to point a moral or simply to adorn the tale: the
bulk of the play is taken up with figures who are not historical
at all. If the amount of space given to history in Part 2 of
Henry IV be compared with the amount given to it in Part 1,
it will be realized that Shakespeare had no alternative but to
kill Falstaff, for not only did he elbow royalty off the stage,
his folly proliferated, and gave birth to Shallow, Silence,
Pistol, Doll, and the ragged regiment.

In short, the model is no longer 'tragical–historical' but
'comical–historical' and the comic writer, as distinct from the
tragedian, was free to invent his material. In doing so Shakespeare fell back upon popular tradition, particularly the
tradition of the popular stage. There were a number of
comical–historical plays, such as *George-a-Greene*, *Friar Bacon
and Friar Bungay*, *Look About You*, (and the later *Shoemaker's
Holiday*, *Edward IV*, *Mayor of Quinborough* may be added to
the list).[5] In these the King, who was usually disguised, and
some particularly bold, jovial subject revelled together, in a
spirit of good fellowship. National solidarity was thereby
celebrated, and perhaps some local or trade patriotism gratified.
The prototype of the bold subject was Robin Hood, with
the legend of his meeting and standing a buffet with Richard
Coeur-de-Lion in Sherwood Forest. Robin Hood appears
in person in *George-a-Greene* and *Look About You*. The stories
came from popular ballads and such tales as those of Thomas
of Reading and Jack of Newbury. These plays have often no
relation to any known or chronicled history at all: nevertheless, the tone and atmosphere of revelry, horseplay, good
fellowship and patriotic fervour—with a dash of romantic
love, never allowed to become too prominent—constituted a
genuine comic tradition, if not one so clearly distinguishable
as that of the tragical–history, the Mirror for Princes. It might
be called the Mirror for Subjects, though the glass is a flatter-
ing one. Merry England, where the king revelled and reigned
as king of good fellows, was a theme which the groundlings
would applaud. Shakespeare added to it his study of the perfect
ruler, his New Machiavelli. In *Richard II* he had studied a

tragic division between Man and Office: here he presented the perfect coalescence of the two.

One or two episodes can be paralleled from the older plays. Pistol's compelled eating of the leek is modelled on Mannering's compelled eating of the seals in *George-a-Greene*, and the same incident is reproduced in the play of *Sir John Oldcastle* which the Admiral's Men put on to rival Shakespeare's successful trilogy.[6] Shoemakers in *George-a-Greene* force King Edward to 'vail staves' as he enters the city of Bradford in disguise, in much the manner in which Williams challenges King Henry V to fight.[7] The wooing of the King or the King's son is a frequent theme in these plays: in Heywood's *King Edward IV*—which was later than Shakespeare's plays— Hob, the Tanner of Tamworth, offers his daughter as a match to 'Ned, the King's butler' to whom he takes a great fancy. In *Edward IV* and *Sir John Oldcastle* may be seen a clear reflection of what those whose 'thoughts kept the highway' enjoyed in Shakespeare's comical-histories. The prologue to the play of the Admiral's Men virtuously disclaims any 'forg'd invention', but the disclaimer only refers to the person of Sir John Oldcastle himself.

> It is no pampered glutton we present,
> No aged Councellor to youthful sins

may apply aptly enough to the portrait of Oldcastle, the good Lord Cobham, and ancestor of the Elizabethan lord whose favour was certainly worth winning. But what's in a name? A certain fat priest, Sir John of Wrotham, who lives by taking purses on the King's highway, plays a prominent part and defends his vocation by a reminder that the good King Henry V had himself taken purses in his younger days. Sir John goes accompanied by a certain Doll, in defence of whose charms he quarrels with Oldcastle's serving man. Even quite minor figures, like two carriers, who appear with their razes of ginger and are shamelessly robbed, have a familiar air. Something is heard of the King's expedition to France, and when Cambridge, Scroope and Grey are arrested at Southampton,

Cambridge puts forward his claim to the throne in a long genealogical speech which he might almost have studied from the Bishop of Ely. If the lost second part of *Sir John Oldcastle* had survived, we should have had an even clearer picture of what features in Shakespeare's plays seemed to the rival house most worth the stealing. As it is, the historical sections of *Sir John Oldcastle* are brief compared with the comedy of the plain Lord Cobham (who has something of the character of Thomas of Woodstock) of Harpoole his man, of the comic rebels led by Murley the Brewer of Dunstable—a sort of Simon Eyre turned villain—and lastly of two comic Welshmen, Owen and Davy, who quarrel and defend their quarrelsomeness in the very accents of Fluellen. There can be no doubt that comedy was a getpenny, and the innumerable references to Falstaff which are listed in the *Shakespeare Allusion Book* represent the Elizabethan assessment of what Shakespeare really had to offer. Revels and fighting—*Hotspur* and *Falstaff*, as the Henry IV plays appear to have been called on occasion[8]—constituted the argument, with the life of the Perfect Governor as relish for the more judicious spectator. York and Lancaster's long jars come in a poor third.

The *Famous Victories of Henry V* (entered 1594: written much earlier) has been dismissed with contempt except by B. M. Ward, Sir Edmund Chambers and Professor Kittredge. Whether it is an abridgement of an earlier trilogy or an actors' reconstruction is irrelevant, for in either case it presented the salient features of the popular legend, the groundlings' *Henry IV* and *Henry V*. Shakespeare drew upon earlier stage tradition as indeed he was bound to do for certain scenes, characters and phrases. In *The Famous Victories* Hal's riotous youth and military glory have been compressed into a single play in a manner which implies that the audience must at least have known the story well enough to accept an eroded abridgement or token version of it.

The importance of *The Famous Victories* lies not so much in the possibility of Shakespeare working from it as a source play but that, in conjunction with *Sir John Oldcastle* it provides a check upon what constituted the popular requisites for a play on Henry V before, and after, the subject had been treated by Shakespeare.

As in *Sir John Oldcastle*, the robbery on Gadshill is the first and most prominent story in Hal's riotous youth. In *The Famous Victories* his striking of Justice Gascoigne—for which there is no basis in record—is directly related to the Gadshill robbery, since he comes into court in a swaggering attempt to get off one of the gang who is charged with the crime. (In Shakespeare where the incident is not shown, Bardolph is said to be the culprit.) The Hal of *The Famous Victories* is a rowdy young prodigal, not differing at all from *The London Prodigal* or Mattheo of *The Honest Whore* or any other of the roaring boys. He blusters into court with loud oaths of 'Gogswouns' and the like, fetches the Justice a box on the ear, and is committed to prison for the second time, since, as we learn, the Lord Mayor has already locked him up once for inciting a riot.[9] Hal's followers are all rowdy young men like himself, and Oldcastle, who appears among them, has only a minor part to play. Hal promises the office of the Lord Chief Justice to Ned, the original Poins, and forecasts a reign of misrule for himself not unlike that which in Shakespeare is prophesied by Falstaff.[10] In the rejection scene Ned not only accosts the newly-crowned king but also claims the office which he has been promised, whereupon the King publicly dismisses him and the others in words which are close to Shakespeare's, while differing from them most significantly:

I prithee Ned mend thy manners,
And be more moderate in thy tearmes . . .
Thou saist I am changed
So I am indeed, and so must thou be, and that quickly
Or else I must cause thee to be chaunged . . .
Ah, Tom, your former life greeves me,
And makes me to abandon and abolish you company for ever,
And therefore not upon pain of death to approach my presence
By ten miles' space, then if I hear well of you
It may be I will do somewhat for you

Otherwise look for no more favour at my hands
Than at any other man's. . . .[11]

The scene of repentance with his father and the subsequent
taking of the crown and final reconciliation are likewise
common to the *Famous Victories* and *Henry IV*. There is no
hint that Hal ever had an earlier thought of repentance,
indeed his language and manners make it impossible that such
should have been the intention. After he becomes Henry V,
the tennis-balls scene forms an interlude between the dis-
missing of the rioters and the reinstatement of Justice Gascoigne, who is made regent of the realm during the king's
absence. The famous victories themselves are very hastily
dealt with, and the play concludes with a fairly extensive
wooing of Katherine, in much the tone of rustic simplicity
adopted by Shakespeare's king.

The alternation of very simple jests and very simple moralizing is the recipe here propounded. Hal is genuinely riotous
and experiences instantaneous conversion. In *Sir John Oldcastle*, however, we see him only as Henry V, the good king:
faint echoes of his youthful pranks resound, but the riotous
followers have become a quite independent group, having no
relation with the king, or indeed with one another, except
when their paths cross by hazard. In both plays, however,
the history is much more a matter of humours than of morals.

Shakespeare united this comical material to the moral history
of the Chronicle, because his interest had expanded beyond
both to the contemplation of Man and his Nature. Falstaff,
Hotspur, Hal and Henry IV are 'four to a mess' in 1 *Henry IV*
and in their characters, seen in relationship to each other, and
issuing in action, lies the governing idea of the play. As a
play, it aims at nothing less than holding the mirror up to
Nature, or, in modern phrase, providing a slice of life. 'He
that thinks rationally must think morally', said Dr. Johnson,
and there is no doubt a moral configuration at the basis of the
play. But this is not 'a song of good life'. It is, with *Antony
and Cleopatra*, Shakespeare's most humane and universal

vision. Its key is inclusiveness, and its method what I have clumsily called 'multiple relations'.

Q's hint that the morality pattern has shaped the play— 'Why it might almost be called Contentio inter Vitium et Virtutem de Anima Principis'[12]—has recently found much favour. Falstaff becomes a morality vice, Riot personified: and those two stumbling-blocks, Prince Hal's first soliloquy ('I know you all. . . .') and the rejection scene, the points at which the Pilgrims' Song emerges above the Venusberg music.

The ancient models of the mid-Tudor morality are adduced in support. Our difficulty is that Hal is never in any danger of being seduced by Riot. Unlike the hero of the *Famous Victories* he is reformed from the beginning. His notorious first soliloquy does not proclaim his intention of having his fling and repenting at leisure: it announces a policy of moral disguise, akin to the physical disguise which the ruler so often assumes in Elizabethan drama, not only for the purposes of revelry, but also for the purpose of attaining knowledge, as in the case of the Duke of Vienna, Henry V before Agincourt, Edward IV at Bradford, and the whole class of characters akin to him.[13] Hal has a purpose:

I'll so offend to make offence a skill.

That is, 'my disguise of riotous living will become as potent a source of knowledge as magic could be'. He plans his emergence from the 'base contagious clouds' as his father had planned his appearances, 'seldom but sumptuous' in King Richard's time (3. 2. 39–85). This conception is Shakespeare's own, and in the eyes of some critics it made Prince Hal, in the opposite direction from that meant by Poins, 'a most princely hypocrite' (2 *Henry IV*, 2. 2. 60). His riots have been carefully toned down, from those which tradition warranted. Hal is not given to women, the Gadshill affair turns into a practical joke, the famous scene of his striking the judge is left out, and his promises for the future do not go beyond the office of hangman for Falstaff.[14]   At any moment in the course

of the revelry he may rap out a princely reprimand almost, as
in very different circumstances, Lear rounds on his all-licensed
fool with 'Take heed, sirrah! the whip'. Falstaff himself
gets a broken head for overstepping the bounds of decent
speech (2 *Henry IV*, 2. 1. 100–101). In the first repentance
scene Hal speaks of slanderers, and the king's chief accusation
is that he keeps base company and mixes too freely with
common men.

But the Renaissance ruler was encouraged to consort with
inferiors, that he might relax and refresh himself,[15] and such
condescension did not blemish his state. Hal always remains
aware of what he is doing. His merciless fooling of the drawer
ends in sheer nonsense of the kind with which Hamlet baits
Polonius:

> Why then you brown bastard is your only drinke? for look
> you Fraunces, your white canvas doublet will sulley. In Barbary
> sir, it cannot come to so much.[16]
>
> (1 *Henry IV*, 2. 4. 83–6.)

But he is equally ironic about the martial humours of Percy,
his own reputation in the eyes of such as Poins, and all the
claims of Sir John. His bestowal of the small page on the huge
Manningtree ox is like the Spanish royal taste for physical
freaks: and after the 'epitaph' on Falstaff at Shrewsbury:

> Poore Jacke farewell,
> I could have better sparde a better man,

with its cool series of puns, he has in effect, taken his leave of
the revels. 'The primary means to virtue is self-control.
The primary requisite of self-control is self-knowledge.'[17]
This according to Professor Babb is the motivating belief
behind Elizabethan theoretical literature on psychology. It
is at all events the motive behind Hal's self-tuition in applied
psychology.

Prince Hal has such complete self-control that he is presented
as one of those persons, very embarrassing to the more simple-
minded, who can have both an immediate and an ultimate
aim in one action, being naturally of a detached and ironic

temper. Dr. Tillyard has commented on Hal's possession of the princely grace which Castiglione called 'sprezzatura', but which is a particularly English quality.[18] It is that easy, gentlemanly unconcern for professional intensity which produces Montgomery's disregard for uniform, Nelson's disregard of naval etiquette, the hesitant manner and diffident phrase of the diplomat who knows perfectly well what he wants and how to get it. Understatement and a refusal to take desperate situations too seriously are prime virtues in soldier or statesman, and the Renaissance prince must be both. Hal's complete insulation against blandishments or flatteries is tested by the severest homoeopathic method. He is inoculated in Eastcheap, and thereafter he can rule as one who may say to all his subjects, 'I know you all'. To know the qualities of men was the first requisite for successful rule, and in his riotous living Hal put in hand his own very liberal education, as Warwick at the end quite clearly explains to the King (2 *Henry IV*, 4. 4. 67–78).[19] The fruits are seen in the fellowship of Agincourt.

As the hero in disguise—a sort of moral Scarlet Pimpernel—but with self-knowledge and self-control clearly established by the opening soliloquy, the prince becomes a hypocrite only if Falstaff's relationship with him is to be taken as a serious and personal one. It is the nature of the relation between the Prince and Falstaff which determines their characters. In Chapman's *Gentleman Usher* (1601), the young prince pretends to an affection for the foolish Gentleman Usher in order to get into touch with his mistress; his treatment suggests that a prince was allowed a wide latitude in cozening.

In Part 1, where Falstaff stands in close relationship to the Prince—he never appears in a single scene without him—his role is that of the Fool or jester, the Lord of Misrule and the high-water mark of his ascendancy is the scene in which he and Hal play the King. Dover Wilson has compared it to the antimasque of Mak the Sheepstealer in the Wakefield Second Shepherds play, preceding as it does the great scene of reconciliation which it so recklessly parodies. Falstaff usurps the seat of Hal's father, which is what, in the eyes of the world, he has done as the tutor to the young Prince's riots: he is *diabolus in loco parentis*.

This mockery of all moral history is given in terms of the old moral drama: Falstaff announces his intention to 'do it in King Cambyses' vein', (Cambyses killed his brother and his wife), and his rhetorical flowers of speech are choicely culled from Peele and Lyly. The prince puts the full case against Falstaff to his face: it is the equivalent in some sense of the play scene in *Hamlet*, but Falstaff, unlike Claudius, does not recognize the purport. Such brilliant double meanings are characteristic of the play: Empson would see a number of ironic correspondences in the Battle of Shrewsbury, where Falstaff[20] and Hotspur, the prince's two chief rivals, fall together. There is certainly an element of extreme irony, of sharp ruthlessness beneath the jesting and the parodies: Falstaff's macabre jests as he plays the hangman on Hotspur's corpse have the same kind of destructive force as the King's speech to him has upon his own pretensions at the end of Part 2. There is a sense in which, with his parody on Honour, his farcical sham death and insults to the corpse, Falstaff does 'kill' Hotspur. They are natural opposites. In the feast of fools, clerks played at dice on the cathedral altar. At this point in the play, where Prince Hal has proved his chivalry by the conquest of the greatest soldier of his realm, Falstaff apes the whole thing. He is the stage clown, with a bottle of sack in his holster for Hal to throw at him, but he is also a medieval grotesque, a cathedral gargoyle, as Professor Willard Farnham has pointed out in a penetrating article on 'The Medieval Comic Spirit in the English Renaissance'.[21]

To examine the question of his cowardice as if he were a man like other men is to miss the point of his role.[22] The whole structure of the play makes such questions irrelevant. Cowardice can only exist when standards of honour exist to be violated: and Falstaff is the ape of honour, whose views on the subjects are known. This does not mean that he is open to moral condemnation. The fool who exists to mock greatness has no existence apart from the greatness which he mocks. Falstaff exists as part of the play and not in any other sense. He is no liar, because his lies are so open, gross, palpable, that none of them are ever believed. They are pure blarney. He deceives nobody—in the first part of the play. He is the Flesh, our brother the Ass, as well as the Devil or Vice, the Ape of goodness. The numberless layers which go to build up his character, from the classical Braggart Soldier, to that faint reflection of the old harlotry player who let his affections stray out of his station and was charmingly jilted by his noble friend,[23] make it as irrelevant to defend Falstaff as to condemn him. He does not belong to the realm of moral judgments.

II

Such at all events was the Falstaff of Part 1. The Falstaff of Part 2 is, I think, a rather different creature. Here he takes up much more of the action, but he is kept apart from Prince Hal. The Prince indeed appears only twice before the scene of his father's death, and in one of these scenes he is not with Falstaff. Instead of being contrasted with Chivalry and the forward child Understanding in the persons of Hotspur and Hal, Falstaff has a train of attendants who are his dupes and hangers-on: Pistol, Doll Tearsheet, Justice Shallow, Silence and the ragged regiment are provided for him to exercise his wits upon. In Part 2 he has a number of soliloquies—those on the page, on Shallow and on John of Lancaster—in which he speaks with a new tone, one of shrewd analysis, cool calculation and detached satiric observation.[24] He speaks in the accents of Prince Hal's satiric portrait of Hotspur in Part 1. The Prince has indeed misled his old companion and infected him with the spirit of 'policy'. In Part 1 Falstaff's charm lies largely in his unpremeditated and extempore sallies, his brilliant improvising. He 'does it all natural'. But in Part 2, where he is no longer revelling with the Prince, but playing his dupes, like any coney-catcher, or meditating upon his next move, Falstaff becomes less of the clown and medieval grotesque, more of an observer and commentator. The narrative connexion between his wanderings and Prince John's mopping-up operation does not carry any significance. He is roving at large and, until the last scene, is given a large tether.

Nevertheless Hotspur being dead and Prince Hal kept off the stage, Falstaff has the scene to himself, except for his encounter with the Lord Chief Justice, who plainly tells him 'The king hath severed you and Prince Harry' (1. 2. 231–232). Yet Falstaff is as confident as ever: he boasts to the Lord Chief Justice that he has 'checked' the young prince for mis-behaving in court—as if he would dare!—he gives an extreme-ly cool little sketch of Hal and Poins to Doll Tearsheet, and in soliloquy for the first time he is shown calculating the effect of his mirth upon the prince:

O I will divise matter enough out of this Shallow to keep prince Harry in continuall laughter, the wearing out of sixe fashions . . . O, it is much that a lie, with a slight oathe, and a jest, with a sad browe, will doe with a fellow that never had the ach in his shoulders.
(5. 1. 86–93.)

This is Falstaff's own version of 'I know you all'. The Prince may think he has been making use of Falstaff: Falstaff thinks he has been making use of the Prince.

Whereas in Part 1 the relation of Falstaff and the Prince had been kept to revelry, parody and unembittered mirth, and had been counterweighted with the relations of each of them to Hotspur and to Bolingbroke, in Part 2 things are very different. The Prologue is spoken by Rumour, 'Painted full of tongues', or as we might say, the Fairy Wish-Fulfilment, who sets the tone not only for the following scene but for the whole play. Hesitation, uncertainty and deception are the themes of the Second Part. It is in fact more symbolic than Part 1: instead of the quartet of fully-drawn characters, we have an open antagonism between Falstaff and the Law. The gorgeous figure of Justice in scarlet and ermine appears. We never see Hal opposed to Gascoigne as we see him opposed to Hotspur, and as a character the Lord Chief Justice cannot compare with the representative of Chivalry: he is symbol, not man. Yet though he and Falstaff part with sparring honours easy, the mere appearance of Justice in robes of office, and the sound of that cold legal voice which we realize Prince Henry had already once obeyed is a very *memento mori* to Sir John. When King Henry V openly adopts this unbending embodiment of Law—whose noble defence of his office has been cunningly reserved to this point—as 'the Father to my youth' (5. 2. 118), the symbolic significance is plain. Justitia is in loco parentis. Falstaff's place is filled. Henry takes up the burden of Office, and Gascoigne symbolizes Office as well as the Rule of Law. It is in the next scene that Sir John, hearing of the old King's decease, cried: 'The laws of England are at my commandment. Happy are they who have been my friends and woe unto my Lord Chief Justice' (5. 3. 143). Perhaps some of the audience would remember that among the crimes charged against Richard II at his deposition was that he had said the laws of England were whatever he declared them to be. The subjection of the King to the Rule of Law, which had been one of the main constitutional issues of the later Middle Ages, was perhaps a topic not to be handled other than circumspectly under the Tudors: the Stewarts however were to receive a lesson on the subject in the course of the next century.

The final rejection of Falstaff has caused many qualms for the manner in which King Henry speaks. It has been defended on the grounds that the King and Falstaff have both travelled a long way since the revels in Part 1. From one point of view Falstaff is here the cheater cheated. Throughout Part 2 he has been shown engaged in a series of confidence tricks, such as the ordinary coney-catcher of the time was accustomed to use: the last of his dupes is with him as the booty he hopes for—all but the thousand pounds—is snatched from under his nose. As Falstaff said to the Lord Chief Justice, it is 'tit for tat'.

But this is also the clash of two distinct and differing worlds. Professor Willard Farnham has spoken of the religious overtones of King Henry's words beginning:

I know thee not old man, fall to thy praiers.

(5. 5. 52.)

An anointed King was *persona mixta*, who had some of the functions of an ecclesiastic and when Professor Farnham compares this scene, the rejection of the world of the tavern with rejection of profane love at the end of *Troilus and Criseyde*, he seems to me to have hit on a particularly happy analogy. Chaucer was no more turning into a misogynist and a Desert Father than Hal is turning into a precisian. 'Like Hal, Shakespeare can accept Falstaff and even love him but at the same time keep him in his place ... Shakespeare never for a moment shows the irritation of the reformer-satirist that the world can produce such a creature as Falstaff. Nor does Shakespeare ever suggest in a modern fashion that Falstaff, by never allowing any of his desires to be repressed, really has a good answer to life'.[25]

I have said that Falstaff does not belong to a world in which moral judgments apply. Hence when he comes into contact with the world of morality, which is the real world, there is a direct clash. We have a creature of one sort of world, the hero of one literary 'kind', coming up against another. Hal and Falstaff had revelled together, but, as in real life, the world of the Boar's Head—that emblem of Christmas misrule—had joined what the world outside would put asunder.[26] A kindly dismissal in private such as Bradley would have wished for would be quite impossible; for when Henry says:

Conceive not that I am the thing I was

he means it quite literally. Conversion, transformation, the power of holy oil, or what you will—man and office were now inseparably conjoined and even to his brothers, Henry is The King.[27] It may even be that, in spite of the fact that he dominates Part 2 and that his rogueries seem to be the main reason for its existence, Falstaff's rejection was overshadowed for an Elizabethan audience by the scene of reconciliation with the Lord Chief Justice, and treated as a kind of antimasque. Certainly, if his fall had to be shown, the more steep and grievous it could be made, the better; and I doubt if the high social standing of the Fleet Prison would provide much mitigation.

On the simplest level, the last act gives the audience the pleasure of a transformation scene, long anticipated, in which disguises are thrown off. The stage transformation of Henry's appearance in robes, crown and sceptre is one of the soundest dramatic cards to play; and Henry himself recalls the opening soliloquy of Part 1 in showing:

> th' incredulous world
> The noble change that I have purposed.
>
> (4. 5. 152–153.)

when he proclaims that he lives

> To mocke the expectation of the world,
> To frustrate prophecies, and to race out
> Rotten opinion, who hath writ me downe
> After my seeming.
>
> (5. 2. 126–129.)

Rumour, 'rotten opinion', those who judge by the view are to be confounded: the disguise, or seeming,[28] is triumphantly cast off, as in the older plays the King would cast off his physical disguise.

Though Henry may be allowed the final act, the previous ones have been Falstaff's. In terms of contemporary reference, he was more popular than any other character. It is Falstaff and Justice Shallow whose names fill pages of the Shakespeare Allusion Book: it is Hotspur's part that the stage-struck prentice quotes in *The Knight of the Burning Pestle*. Prince Hal, the student in the art of reading men, may have pleased the judicious, Bolingbroke provided some continuity with the themes of the moral history,[29] but Hotspur and Falstaff, the

Prince's two factors, outshone everyone else in popular esteem.

Hal robs Percy in the end, as he robs his own factors at Gadshill in the older account.[30] He engrosses the glory by slaying his rival at Shrewsbury. But in the early part of the play Percy is the embodiment of military virtue and of all the more endearing military weaknesses. He is cheated by the politician Worcester, deserted by his friends, but his sheer courage carries the fight almost to a successful conclusion. Choler, recklessness and ungovernable persistence in his humour are his weaknesses, in which he seems almost a first study for Coriolanus: yet his mocking scepticism of Glendower's claims, his banter of the charming Kate, and his scorn of the mincing lord who met him at Holmedon are as shrewdly observed as they are mercilessly indulged. The magnificent praise of him in King Henry's second comparison of the two young men, added to the praise of Hal, and his heroic disregard of the odds against him make him a true shadow of the hero of Agincourt: so that when the Prince again insists that he will absorb all Percy's honours:

> Two stars keep not their motion in one sphere,
>   Nor can one England brooke a double raigne
> Of Harry Percy and the Prince of Wales
>
> (5. 4. 65–67.)

Percy is seen like one of the men whom King Henry has 'marching in his coats', as Hal's understudy and deputy, a symbol of greatness to come.

Shakespeare may have felt a particular warmth for the Percy family through his connexion with Sir Charles Percy, Essex's friend. A letter of Sir Charles, written in 1600 from his home in Gloucestershire, and comparing himself with Justice Shallow, shows a most lively appreciation of the fun, and it was Sir Charles who ordered the notorious performance of *Richard II* on the eve of the Essex rising.[31]

At all events Hotspur does far more than is required of the conventional rebel leader, and his character, which is perhaps an amplification of the Bastard Falconbridge, as well as an anticipation of Coriolanus, is Shakespeare's own invention. With such a pair to set him off, Prince Henry is in some danger of being overshadowed. His principal moment is the scene with his father in which the King compares his son with *Richard II* and Percy with himself. The tragic echoes back and forth are sounded less for their political implications than to give depth and resonance to the deep personal emotion that wells up between father and son. The King's tears of 'foolish tenderness', the deep tones of his distress, and the personal nature of his appeal call out in Prince Hal as moved a response:

> Do not thinke so, you shal not find it so. . . .
> . . . and in the closing of some glorious day
> Be bold to tell you that I am your sonne. . . .

The estrangement between Prince Henry and his father is one between two whose likeness is so strong, and whose feelings are so deep-seated that only at such a moment do they betray themselves. This scene is anticipatory of the one at the end of 2 *Henry IV*, and really forestalls it. For a reconciliation at this level cannot be undone, and it gives implicit but sufficient measure of the relation between the Prince and Falstaff.

The construction of 1 *Henry IV* is therefore built on a fourfold contrast, the four 'species' represented by the King, the Prince, Falstaff and Hotspur, and the relationships between them. The method is that of shadowing or parody, and of contrasts and opposition: heroics and clowning, robbing in sport and rebelling in earnest, the King of Misrule versus the King of England, Harry Hotspur versus Harry Monmouth.

Part 2 is constructed rather differently. Rebellion, a desperate venture even with Hotspur, dwindles and diminishes and splutters out without a fight. Lancaster's merciless duping of the miserable remnant by something akin to a legal quibble is a mere episode in the story, and the end of the great Northumberland is told in half a dozen lines by a messenger (2 *Henry IV*, 4. 4. 94–99). The chief effect of the wars is to furnish Falstaff with opportunities for recruiting.

Prince Hal, having nothing to do but hang about in the wings waiting for the end of the play, and being kept carefully away from his father and Falstaff, makes but a single appearance at the Boar's Head, where, however, the interest is less in his duel of wits with Falstaff than in the humours of Mistress Quickly, Doll Tearsheet and Pistol. The whole of the political theme is kept 'marking time'. It is true that Shakespeare tidied up the odds and ends left over from Part 1, but such an occupation cannot counterbalance the effect of Falstaff and his rout of gulls and disreputables. The counterbalance is left to the emblematic figures and the emblematic moments: to Rumour, the Lord Chief Justice, the taking of the crown by Hal and his final appearance as King. The low comedy on the other hand is more realistic, more directly a painting of contemporary manners than it was in Part 1. Justice Shallow and Mrs. Quickly are 'humours' of the Dickensian sort: portraits, with notes of pathos such as are not heard in the comic revels of Part 1,[32] but with a good deal of realistic writing in the 'low style'.

Except for the last act, Part 2 is Falstaff's play; and the play of a Falstaff who was almost as unlikely as the hero of *The Merry Wives of Windsor* to die of a heart fracted and corroborate, but who had gained in malice, shrewdness and calculation. In *Henry IV*, Part 1, the delights of the characters were dolphinlike and showed above the element of revelry in which they lived and moved. The uncongealed flow of life sustained them. In Part 2 the characters have particular humours and whimsies, observances to be noted. They are more Jonsonian. The most penetrating annotation is King Henry's account of his son, given to the Duke of Clarence.

III

In *Henry V* Shakespeare was fulfilling a promise to his audience. It is a celebration, a pageant, and a public display. Everything about it, every character in it is—in a perfectly satisfactory sense—stagey. There has been general agreement among the critics that the deeper levels are not sounded. King Henry, the centre of the play, loses his ironic detachment when he attains the crown: like his opposite, *Richard III*, he finds little opportunity for wit. In his speech before Harfleur, where he recommends 'putting a good face on it' to his soldiers, he is virtually asking them all for the kind of good acting that produces confidence by auto-suggestion; the duty of the perfect ruler and the commander-in-chief. At the only moment when we see him alone and plain man, in the only really sympathetic speech of the play, he prays that God will take from his soldiers the sense of reckoning, that they may not realize the odds against them.[33] The old traditional scene of the wooing of Katherine, which Shakespeare could not have afforded to leave out, for it was the natural climax, all would expect it, and he had promised to give it, becomes an opportunity for a sleight-of-hand. Here is the rustic 'king of good fellows' to delight the groundlings with his plain speech; and here too is the son of Henry Bolingbroke— 'off goes his bonnet to an oyster wench'—putting on an act to ease a very difficult situation. When the diplomat is confronted with a nervous and potentially hostile young woman who is to be thrown in as makeweight to a treaty, what does he do? The alliance is necessary for his claims, although he is not going to allow the other side to use it as a lever.[34] Nothing more reassuring could be devised than a simulation of some little soldierly plainness. Henry's tact is the converse of Bertram's rudeness and Claudio's gaucherie.

The comradeship of Agincourt—

> He to-day that sheds his blood by mine
> Shall be my brother, Be he neer so base.
>
> (4. 3. 61–62.)

is the comradeship of the mess: but we have already seen Henry's condemnation of the three traitors at Southampton, the men whom he claims to have reposed his trust in. Though he pardons them in his own particular, he dooms them as commander-in-chief. This is a distinction which can command respect and assent, though at one time it was attacked as another of Henry's hypocrisies. The depth of feeling in the lines spoken to Lord Scroop, as Dr. Tillyard has noted,[35] almost anticipates the tragedies, and is quite foreign to the character of Henry as presented in the play.

> May it be possible that foreign hire
> Could out of thee extract one spark of evil
> That might annoy my finger? tis so strange
> That though the truth of it stands off as gross
> As black from white, mine eye will scarcely see it.
>
> (2. 2. 100–104.)

For this Henry, unlike Richard II, does not taste grief or need friends. His protest to the soldiers that the king's affections stoop with like wing to those of common men is qualified by the addition that 'they are higher than ours'. Henry may live with bread or smell the violet: he is so regally in control of all his faculties that he can be friendly to all, treat all as his brothers, because all are his subjects; and like a certain New England family, the only person he can really speak to without reservation is God, King of Kings and Supreme Commander-in-Chief upon this occasion.

The quality of the rhetoric is the perfect vehicle for the exposition of Henry's state. A clear bold surface, with no subdued undertones and no transient modulations, it reflects the pageantry of arms and also the necessary violence of war. Henry tells Harfleur what happens when troops get out of hand: and his order to kill the prisoners when the enemy counter-attacks is too true to the facts of war for some of his editors to stomach. The common soldiers endure long periods of watching, waiting and quarrelling in the mess, enlivened by short bouts of hand-to-hand fighting and the opportunity to loot.

This is a great advance on the old Chronicle play, yet clearly based on the old tradition. Shakespeare may also have had in mind when he wrote *Henry V* the most remarkable and successful of earlier attempts at a like theme, the pseudo-Shakespearean *Edward III*.[36] This play is divided into two parts; the earlier half is concerned with Edward's conquest of his feelings for the Countess of Salisbury, in order to prosecute the French war. In the second half he is shown again exercising almost inhuman self-control in withholding support from his son in order that the Prince may 'win his spurs', and finally he conquers his natural resentment against the Burghers of Calais. The unity of theme in *Edward III* and its similarity to that of *Henry V* does not seem to have been recognized; it is generally in the first half that Shakespearean echoes are detected,[37] but the fight against odds with the double battle (Creçy-Poitiers) corresponding to the double battle of Harfleur-Agincourt contains some close parallels with Shakespeare's work. Consider the picture of the two invading fleets:

> The proud Armado of King Edwards ships:
> Which at the first, far off where I did ken,
> Seemd as it were a grove of withered pines;
> But drawing neere, their glorious bright aspect,
> Their streaming Ensignes, wrought of coloured silke,
> Like to a meddowe full of sundry flowers,
> Adornes the naked bosome of the earth:
> Maiesticall the order of their course,
> Figuring the horned Circle of the Moone. . . .
> Thus titely carried with a merry gale,
> They plough the Ocean hitherwards amain.
>
> (3. 1. 64-78.)

> his brave fleet
> With silken streamers the young Phoebus fanning:
> Play with your fancies, and in them behold
> Upon the hempen tackle shipboys climbing;
> Hear the shrill whistle which doth order give
> To sounds confused; behold the threaden sails
> Borne with the invisible and creeping wind,
> Draw the huge bottoms through the furrowed sea . . .
> A city on the inconstant billows dancing;
> For so appears this fleet majestical,
> Holding due course to Harfleur.
>
> (Act II, Chorus, 5-17.)

In the conduct of Poitiers the odds are so heavy that the French, as in *Henry V*, send various taunting messages to the English, and thereby provide the Black Prince, like Henry, with the opportunity for a few telling retorts when the victory is won.[38] In Shakespeare's play the Black Prince's victories against odds are recalled on three several occasions,[39] and the speech of old Audley on death—he is the Sir Thomas Erpingham of the earlier play—foreshadows Henry's own contempt of death before Agincourt:

> To die is all as common as to liue:
> The one inch-wise, the other holds in chase;
> For from the instant we begin to liue,
> We do pursue and hunt the time to die:
> First bud we, then we blow and after seed,
> Then, presently we fall; and as a shade
> Follows the bodie, soe we follow death
> *(Edward III,* 4. 4. 133–139.)

The eve of battle is a moment so dramatically potent that Shakespeare returns to it again and again: Bosworth, Shrewsbury, Philippi, Actium, each has its moment of highest emotional tension immediately *preceding* the fight. Here too, at this point, in the scenes on the night of Agincourt, Shakespeare allows the common soldiers and the King to speak as men.

In *Henry V*, as in *Henry VI*, the one scene that lives fully, with the depths of Shakespeare's art, is the tableau of the King set against representatives of his people, and left to meditate on the price of greatness. Henry V at Agincourt looks back to Henry VI at Towton. The difference in dramatic and poetic power between the formal speech of the father who had killed his son and Williams' description of the common soldier, thinking of his children's chance to be 'rawly left', by his own chance of a bloody death, is the measure of Shakespeare's development. The likeness between the lament of the pitiful son of Henry V and his father's sterner musings is a proof of the continuity underlying it.

Tis not the balm, the sceptre, and the ball . . .
The farced title running fore the King . . .
The throne he sits on, nor the tide of pomp
That beats upon the high shores of the world
No, not all these, thrice-gorgeous Ceremonie,
Not all these laid in bed majesticall
Can sleep so soundly as the wretched slave,
Who with a body filled and vacant mind,
Gets him to rest, crammed with distressful bread . . .
And follows so the ever-running year
With profitable labour to his grave;
And but for ceremony, such a wretch,
Winding up days with toil and nights with sleep,
Had the forehand and vantage of a king.

(4. 1. 280–300.)

CHAPTER XII

COMICAL–FANTASTIC

'Love's Labour's Lost'—II 'As You Like It'—III
'Twelfth Night'

THE elegance and wit of Shakespeare's courtly comedy is nowhere so polished as in *Love's Labour's Lost*. Although the relation of this play with *As You Like It* would seem sufficiently obvious, the earlier drama has not enjoyed the same popularity until quite recently, when Granville Barker's study and a number of stage performances have shown how much life remains in the most fantastic scenes.

Whether or not the play had a particular topical significance, as has often been asserted, it appears to have been written for an audience of wits, perhaps for the young gallants of the Inns of Court,[1] the 'Third University' of the kingdom, who would particularly enjoy an attack on book-learning, and such skilful use of the technique of the debate.

The play is as near as Shakespeare ever came to writing satire; and yet there is more than a spice of panegyric behind the ridicule of fine manners. After seeing such a comedy, no one would be ashamed to continue in the use of taffeta phrases, silken terms precise, although they might be a little moderated. The sport is intended for the ears of friends, and like the banter of the 'mocking wenches' it is even a subtle way of establishing good relations. For *Love's Labour's Lost* implies a clever audience. It is a bout of verbal fencing, carried out before experts.

The action is slighter than even the slightest of musical comedies. Gone are the elaborate disguises and mistaking of earlier courtly dramatists like Lyly and Peele. Two masques, a number of songs and a quantity of sonnets fill out the spaces between the wit-combats, the clowning and the passionate soliloquies of Berowne. If some of the actors were indeed young noblemen or gentlemen, the atmosphere of charade would be strong, and the double use of masquers for 'plays within the play' would heighten the sense of a mirror-image, the reflection of the spectators in the glass of comedy.

The lack of action is compensated for by elaborate and intricate style. Many speeches are in the nature of a verbal *tour de force*: quibbling and innuendo flourish. Nowhere else does Shakespeare display so consistent a linguistic interest as here. The varieties of speech set off each other, and are more sharply differentiated than elsewhere: style is a garment indeed, and each character dresses in his own fashion. The play, like Lyly's, largely depends on the control of rhythm, the contrasts in vocabulary, and the use of 'figures': it is an artificial consort of voices. The light cut-and-thrust of the courtiers is broad enough in its matter, and far from Petrarchan:

Boyet.	My Lady goes to kill hornes; but if thou marrie,
	Hang me by the necke, if that yeare hornes miscarrie
	Finely put on.
Rosaline.	Well, then, I am the shooter.
Boyet.	And who is your Deare?
	If we choose by the hornes yourself come not neare
	Finely put on, indeede
Princess.	You still wrangle with her, *Boyet*, and she strikes at the brow.
Boyet.	But she herselfe is hit lower: have I hit her now?
Rosaline.	Shall I come upon thee with an old saying, that was a man when King *Pippin* of *France* was a little boy, as touching the hit it
Boyet.	So may I answere thee with one as old, that was a woman when Queen *Guinever* of *Brittainne* was a little wench, as touching the hit it.
Rosaline.	Thou canst not hit it, hit it, hit it,
	Thou canst not hit it my good-man.
Boyet.	[An] I cannot, cannot cannot:
	An I cannot, another can.

(4. 1. 114–132.)

The mixture of couplet, prose and popular song is like a bravura passage in opera; it is completely assured, and as far from the elegant monotony of the *Two Gentlemen of Verona* as is the exuberant outburst from Costard that follows. The lovers in the *commedia dell' arte* spoke Tuscan whilst the masks (Braggadoccio, Zanni and the rest) spoke in dialect. So the fantastical speech of the 'masks' of this play[2] is deliberately set against the lovers' wit, Berowne's rhetoric, and the patterned grouping of the figures upon the stage. The 'magnificent Armado' puffing out his 'smoke of rhetoric' is somewhat old-fashioned. His two letters with their elaborate rehearsal of logical predicaments, copious variation of epithets and the splendid superscription to the King go beyond anything which he actually delivers by way of dialogue: but such a conjuration as *'Artsman preambulat*, we will be singled from the barbarous' is set off against Costard's 'And I had but one penny in the world, thou shouldst have it to buy Gingerbread' as he rewards Moth for a telling retort; and on the other side Holofernes, in his earnest applause of Moth's master—'The *posterior* of the day, most generous sir, is liable, congruous and measurable, for the afternoon: the word is well-culd, chose, sweet and apt I doe assure you, I doe assure' (5. 1. 75–102). Applause for such linguistic feats is common: 'a quick venew of wit', 'a set of wit well played' or, *sotto voce* from Moth, 'They have beene at a great feast of language and stolne the scraps'. Costard loves big words, especially Latin: only the constable is dumb. All leads up to the moment when Berowne renounces, in highly elegant phrases, the elegance of a courtly wooing; penned speeches, rhymes, hyperboles and figures pedantical. Nevertheless, he runs a manage, or career at tilt against Boyet, immediately afterwards, in his invective; and when Boyet admits he is touched, breaks off with

> Loe, he is tilting straight. Peace, I have done.
>
> (5. 2. 484.)

The characters are defined by their individual accent and

idiom: Jacquenetta's set of catchphrases ('With that face?' and 'Lord, how wise you are' and the rest) are inherited from Lyly's country wenches,[3] and Moth is descended from his pert pages; the tone and imagery of their speech constitutes the characters. The contrast of different characters in terms of their different idiom, played off or chiming in together, constitutes the 'form' of the comedy. In tragedy a recurrent image binds the play together and is the embodiment of the moral, the 'objective correlative' to use Mr. Eliot's perhaps too famous phrase; in comedy the consort of voices is, in itself, the definition of those characters, and the sum of these definitions makes up the play.

Some characters, of course, have more than one voice. Berowne, who is both guilty of courtly artifice and critical of it, plays a double game with language throughout; the same game that the author himself is playing. He runs with the hare and hunts with the hounds. When at the beginning he mocks the set pedantries of the little academe, the King's private university, it is in the same figure that Speed the page uses to Valentine.

'You were wont, when you laughed, to crow like a cocke: when you walk'd, to walke like one of the lions: when you fasted, it was presently after dinner: when you looked sadly, it was for want of money.

Two Gentlemen of Verona   (2. 1. 28–35).

Come on then, I will swear to studie so,
To know the thing I am forbid to know:
As thus, to study where I well may dine,
When I to dine expressly am forbid.
Or study where to meet some Mistresse fine,
When Mistresses from common sense are hid.
Or having sworne too hard a keeping oth
Studie to breake it and not breake my troth.   (1. 1. 59–66.)

Lovers' perjuries were always held excusable, and it is precisely 'some salve for perjurie' that Berowne is called upon to minister at the end of the discovery scene. His great speech in praise of the art of living is based on logical form and sustains the paradox (4. 3. 290 ff.):

> O we haue made a vow to studie, Lords,
> And in that vow we have forsworne our Bookes.

It is decorated with 'all kinds of figures that do be rhetorical' and its word-play is fantastic, yet the praise of Love with which it concludes is a frank hymn to the senses recalling, perhaps not unconsciously, the climax of *Hero and Leander*:

> For Valour, is not Love a *Hercules*?
> Still climbing trees in the *Hesperides*.

Berowne has become, like Leander, a 'sophister' of love's school: echoes of Spenser's *Hymn to Beautie* are ironic.

The King applauds with a triumphant but strictly courtly salute:

> St. *Cupid* then, and Souldiers to the field

and the warfare between the lords and their mistresses is conducted in the approved manner, with the ladies easy victors.

Poetry is seen as an occupational disease of lovers; all the gentlemen break into sonnetting. The King's sonnet, unlike those of his gentlemen, did not appear in any collection of the period, and it is certainly the nearest to burlesque of them all. Berowne 'jeers' his lines:

> Thou shinest in every tear that I doe weepe,
> No drop but as a Coach doth carry thee:
> So ridest thou triumphing in my woe.

with his

> Your eyes doe make no coaches in your teares.
> There is no certain Princesse that appears (4. 3. 155-6).

but all Shakespeare's lovers are bad poets, except Hellen of Narbonne, who writes a sonnet-letter to the Countess when she steals away from Roussillon. Holofernes can improvise on the letter in an old-fashioned mid-Tudor manner which he probably learnt at the University:

> This is a gift that I haue, simple: simple, a foolish extravagant spirit, full of formes, figures, shapes, objects, Ideas, apprehensions, motions, resolutions. (4. 2. 67 ff.)

Even Armado talks of composing:

Assist me some extemporall god of Rime for I am sure I shall turn Sonnet. Devise Wit, write Pen for I am for whole volumes in folio.   (I. 2. 192-4.)

The letter which he writes to Jacquenetta is in exactly the vein of the letter he writes to the King, and it is plain that Armado has only one style, the loftiest. Berowne can sing both high and low: in spite of his difficulty in turning a plain phrase for Rosaline:

> And to begin Wench, so God helpe me law,
> My love to thee is sound *sans* crack or flaw.

he ended his soliloquy of reluctant submission to love with a learned figure and a homely proverb bound up together in one couplet:

> Well, I will love, write, sigh, pray, shue, grone,
> Some men must love my Lady and some Jone.

Berowne rails against Rosaline; she is neither beautiful nor of a chaste quality. He says all that Shakespeare says in his anti-Petrarchan sonnet.[4] But his loud outcries against Cupid, the lady, and himself when he finds himself infected with the 'plague' are also in the courtly tradition. The constrained lover, fighting manfully against overwhelming odds, was a recognized variant upon the entirely submissive lover who had made unconditional surrender. Sidney was of the first kind and Spenser of the second. Shakespeare himself played both parts in his sonnets, according as he wished to entertain or move to pity. Drayton's most famous sonnet:

> Since there's no help, come let us kiss and part

is a more serious modification of the fundamentally comic situation of the lover who attempts to make his getaway and does not succeed.

Love's Labour's Lost is a play about courtship which turns out to be a play about love, and an attack on fine speech which is consistently full of fine speeches. Even the attack on learning becomes rather paradoxical when the unusually full use of the *trivium* is considered. It is the most artificial of all Shakespeare's comedies and comes nearer than any other to containing a manifesto against artifice. The acting is exceptionally formal, with no less than four pairs of lovers—the usual allowance was two—and the symmetry of the discovery scene is heightened in the grouping of the dances and shows that fill up the fifth act. Masque and antimasque—the Russians and the Nine Worthies—underline the artifice and give a dramatic perspective to the last scene with its rapid alternations of farce, gravity, lyric pleading and for conclusion the simple, traditional song, old and plain; a medieval debate between Winter and Spring, the Owl and the Cuckoo, which dissolves all the foregoing wit into the simplest country humour, such as even Antony Dull could appreciate. Spring in the meadows and Christmas in the hall are in such a different world from anything else in the play that they carry the listener forward to the more complex world and the richer harmonies of *As You Like It*.[5]

Love's Labour's Lost is unsurpassed for sheer virtuosity of language; language which is always designed for the stage, for finely-turned dramatic speaking. Changing of pace, 'interchangeable variety' of couplet, stanza, blank verse, and prose, the consort of voices is conducted with a masterful ease amounting almost to showmanship. The manage in which an expert horseman displayed his skill, in fencing matches or in hazards of Real Tennis might to its contemporaries best reflect its intricacies. Yet it is completely different from the genuine court poetry of the time by reason of that extra-heightening, that element of make-up which the stage requires. Shakespeare in this play, at least, never wanted Arte. He improved Nature just enough to flatter her. He dispraised the speech of his young nobles, but 'in a kind of praise'. His tribute to love was railing, and his tribute to rhetoric a flout. It stands half-way between the comedy of Lyly, where the court is reflected uncritically but elegantly by a member of the Revels Office, and the bitterness of Ben Jonson in *Cynthia's*

Revels, where current abuses are pilloried in the figures of the court ladies Philautia (Self-Love), Phantaste (Light Wittiness), and Argurion (Money); their gallants have such names as Hedon, the Voluptuous, Anaides the Impudent and Amorphus, the boasting traveller. These courtiers practise behaviour, rehearse jests, and play games till they are all severely chidden at the end by Cynthia herself, and by her poet, the stern and upright Crites, whose features are not without resemblance to those of the author. There is, for example, a duel in courtship between Amorphus and Mercury, which is conducted with all the outward form of a fight, introduced with a flourish of trumpets, criticized in all the phrases of swordsmanship and lost by 'playing too open'. The lady who stood to be courted by the combatants grew tired and was relieved by another. Amorphus thinks he has his opponent 'put to the Dor' and, after motioning Mercury to begin, he stops the combat.

Amorphus.	The common mistress, you see, sir, is changed.
Mercury.	Right, sir.
Amorphus.	But you have still in your hat the former colours.
Mercury.	You lie, sir, I have none: 1 have pulled them out. I meant to play discoloured.
Crites.	The Dor, the Dor, the Dor, the Dor, the Dor, the palpable Dor!
Anaides.	Heart of my blood, Amorphus, what have you done? stuck a disgrace upon us all and at your last weapon!

Such a scene recalls rather the foppery of Osric (who appeared at approximately the same time) than the wit-combats of Navarre, and his court.

II

The increase in delicacy and complexity that marks *As You Like It* should not disguise its relationship with *Love's Labour's Lost*. The absurd Armado has been replaced by the sardonic Jaques, the curate and schoolmaster shrunk to a mere Sir

Oliver Martext, the lovers developed out of all recognition: only the stolid country folk remain much as they were before. Yet *As You Like It* is also a literary play, even a literary satire of a particularly light and airy kind. It is not without nipping airs as Professor Campbell has shown.[6] It is certainly not the dish of melting sweetness that is sometimes served up to the modern audience; or the pretty picture that is so often presented as safe reading to the upper forms of our schools. The bawdry can be overlooked by those who are willing to do so, or whose knowledge of the Elizabethan *nuances* is rather limited: the literary parody will not be distinguishable without a reasonable knowledge of the background; and the artifice will be avoided by those intent on nature. A romping Rosalind and picnicking Duke are creatures of modern misunderstanding. The play is a most subtle blend of the personal and the conventional; it is shot-taffeta of pastoral, satire, courtesy literature and the plays of Robin Hood. Whereas in *Love's Labour's Lost*, the consort of voices made up a harmony dependent on each of the characters being more or less a Mask, simplified and symmetrical, in *As You Like It* the variations work at a much deeper level, and produce rather a consort or blending of many different literary 'species'. Each is represented by one or more characters, and each character is in itself a blend of many different roles. In Lodge's novel, the source of the play, there was also the personal equation with his own elder brother as Oliver.

Rosalind's wit was born of the pages, her theatrical ancestors of the one side—Halfpenny, Risio and Moth.[7] But the role of pert page is one which the Princess herself has consciously taken up; she delights to play the sprightly springcock, and in her jests with Orlando she uses this simpler role like a mask for the face, to enable her to dispense with strict modesty. Her two great scenes with him, the first and second encounter in the forest, are full of lively satire upon lovers; the forlorn state of the 'unfortunate he' and the capriccios of the weathercock she are mercilessly mocked. But the ridicule itself by its very vivacity demonstrates Love's power.

No, faith, die by Attorney. . . . *Leander*, he would haue liv'd
manie a faire yeare though *Hero* had turn'd Nun; if it had not bien
for a hot Midsomer-night, for (good youth) he went but forth to
wash him in the Hellespont, and being taken with the crampe,
was droun'd, and the foolish Chroniclers of that age, found it was
Hero of Cestos. But these are all lies, men haue died from time to
time and wormes haue eaten them, but not for loue.

(4. 1. 97–112.)

The Asteismus or Merry Scoffe as Puttenham would call
it is the method by which Rosalind relieves her feelings. She
flouts all the patterns of true love because she is so firm a
believer in the religion of love that she can afford to jest with
it: indeed, if she is not to be overwhelmed, she must jest.
When her professed heresies lead Celia to a mock scolding,
she yields with an exclamation:

O coz, coz, coz: my pretty little coz, that thou didst know how
many fathoms deepe I am in love:

only to turn it off with a 'disabling comparison':

but it cannot be sounded: my affection hath an unknowne bottome,
like the Bay of Portugal. (4. 1. 217 ff.)

Rosalind is rhetorically deflating the rhetoric of lovers, as
Berowne and Rosaline had done: but whereas in that play
the sincerity of passion had been allowed to appear only
obliquely through the soliloquies of Berowne, here it flows
through the very matter of the satire, 'like roses overspread
with lawn'.

The sharpness of Rosalind's wit varies with her company.
To Phoebe she is merciless—the doubts that Berowne breathes
to himself about his dark beauty are hurled in this poor girl's
face. To Jaques also she is tart, and countermines below his
satire.

In Rosalind, and to a lesser degree in Orlando, Shakespeare
has drawn the heroine and hero full into the circle of the
comedy. In earlier plays the lovers had either been heroic
or absurd; the general rule for courtly comedy was that jests
belonged to the clowns and lyric passions to the lovers, as

they do in *The Two Gentlemen of Verona*. The courtly lovers of Navarre and Athens are made ridiculous: but in so far as they are ridiculous, laughably inconsistent or affected in speech, they become detached from the audience's sympathy. Here the lovers are allowed to be both absurd and fully human: the attitude is one of sympathetic amusement. This may sound commonplace enough, but very little Elizabethan laughter was sympathetic. The Broad Flout, the Fleering Frump, the Dry Mocke and the Bitter Taunt were the expected figures for comedy. Sidney has described comedy as an imitation of the common errors of our life 'which the poet representeth in the most ridiculous and scornful sort that may be'.[8] If the vagaries of the lover did not provide such sport as Armado's, they tended to be as serious as Valentine's, or Bassanio's. Here the lovers are self-deceived and glory in their own follies:

> Love is meerely a madnesse, and I tel you, deserves as wel a darke house and a whip, as madmen do: and the reason why they are not so punish'd and cur'd is that the Lunacie is so ordinarie, that the whippers are in love too.
>
> (3. 2. 426–430.)

This is perhaps meant to include the audience, for the Epilogue conjures all the women by the love they bear the men and all the men by the love they bear the women that 'between you and the women, the play may please'.

With no suggestion of a division between the sympathy and the raillery, the audience is invited to share them both, and to apply to itself the same truths.

> I charge you (O men) for the love you beare to women (as I perceive by your simpring, none of you hates them) . . .

The lovers are entirely and wholly comic and at the same time entirely and wholly delightful.[9] It needs only a glance at *The Gentleman Usher*, *The Shoemakers Holiday*, and *Bartholomew Fair*, or any other widely assorted group of Elizabethan comedies, to see how firmly the 'leading juveniles' are kept segregated from any breath of ridicule. In Chapman's plays, for example, the lovers' complicated intrigues and disguisings carry the structural weight of the comedy, whilst the gulls and knaves provide its 'humours'.

In Rosalind her wit reveals a mind

'like a planet moving several ways'

—it is a perspective picture which 'beheld awry' shows a clear depth of feeling that directly appears only at the end of the play.

To you I give my selfe, for I am yours.

Rosalind knows some of the truth about herself which she does not confess, but she does know all of it. Her impatience when Celia comes in with the news that she has seen Orlando is like her first encounter with Orlando, a piece of self-betrayal. Orlando, being constrained at times to behave in a correct Petrarchan manner, is altogether less enlightened. But the delicate play between mock-wooing and real wooing is left deliberately ambiguous.

It is Rosalind of course who takes the initiative. The role of the wooer was defined by convention, but that of the lady had not been developed. Petrarchan poetry was masculine poetry. The woman's part was seen from the outside; either as the fair warrior who inflicted cruel wounds, the saint to be worshipped, the divinity to be appeased or finally the relenting mistress to be hymned. Though Shakespeare is careful to keep his women's parts within the compass of the boy actors, he makes a virtue of the restrictions which this imposed upon him. The absolutely natural impulse towards disguise, evasion, even flight—Beatrice's

beleeve me not, and yet I lie not, I confesse nothing, nor I deny nothing, I am sorry for my cousin—

is given scope by the disguise, and Rosalind can both yield to it and overcome it in the form of Ganymede. As she is woman, she is free to betray her feeling to Celia, to appear as tetchy and changeable as she had painted woman's mind to Orlando. Above all, by the rapid transitions from one mood to another, from one level of jesting-in-earnest to another level of dissembling-earnest-by-jest, and by a self-mockery which both guards and betrays her feelings, Rosalind enchants by an infinite variety.

The lesser characters of *As You Like It* are varying parody upon simpler modes. Silvius and Phoebe, the shepherd and shepherdess of pastoral, have all the marks of courtly love upon them. They come straight from Lodge's *Rosalynde*, where however they are not different either in manners or speech from the noble lovers. Silvius's description of Phoebe as a 'murderess' is in the old style of compliment, and Rosalind by her mere presence does as much as by her quipping taunts in the role of Ganymede to 'place' the fashion. It is Silvius who defines the true lover and leads the Lovers' Madrigal (5. 2): it is Phoebe who exhibits most truly the weathercock mind of her sex. The Lovers' Madrigal, a figured quartet, recalls again the style of Lodge.[10] (His Rosalynde and Rosader conduct their wooing in a song which they sing together in the manner of musical comedy and he has other lyrical passages in which his story is carried forward, with no sense of incongruity when it lapses again into his Euphuistic prose.) Our lovers' repetitions:

Silvius.	It is to be made all of sighes and teares
	And so am I for *Phebe*
Phebe.	And I for *Ganymede*
Orlando.	And I for *Rosalind*
Rosalind.	And I for no woman

(5. 2. 91–95.)

is as formal as anything in *Love's Labour's Lost*, but it is abruptly broken off by Rosalind.

Pray you no more of this, tis like the howling of Irish Wolues against the Moone.

She then drops into the kind of riddling prophecy which befits the wizard's child she claims to be, and which recalls such wise figures as Lyly's old Mother Bombie; she promises apparently incompatible things which are to ensure everyone's happiness.

In this scene, and still more in the formal Masque of Hymen which concludes the play, the sense of the theatre is deliberately invoked. Jaques's

> Nay then God buy you, and you talke in blanke verse

is an even bolder invitation to the audience to see the scene which follows, the most natural and charming of love-encounters between Rosalind and Orlando, as something on the stage—if not of the Globe, then of the world.

Jaques's speech on The Seven Ages of Man[11] uses the familiar metaphor of 'The World's a stage' to place all humanity in a series of roles, at once absurd and passionate. From the mewling babe to the mere oblivion of age, the stagey types are strictly faithful to their decorum, yet each is absorbed and engaged in the passion proper to his role. Their character is achieved through assuming the habit of the appropriate type. This artificial pageant of man is the 'cause' or germ of the play's construction. It acts like a play within the play, reflecting back upon all that has gone before and forecasting all that is to follow. While Jaques speaks, all humanity becomes puppets before us. He has the artist's eye which transforms the spectacle of the sobbing deer into an emblem.[12] Jaques is expected to comment upon all occasions, but he does not always choose to do it. 'He is too disputable for my company', he says of the duke: 'I think of as many matters as he, but I give Heauen thankes, and make no boast of them'. Yet he cannot but anatomize the world, as Touchstone, his complement and *alter ego*, cannot but ape it. Jacques is ambitious for motley because he would prove a 'bitter fool': Touchstone is 'a sweet fool' whose parodies of court manners are dependent on an acceptance of fixed codes. His most courtly speech, describing the quarrel upon the seventh cause, relies on Italianate codes of the duello as set forth for contemporary instruction by Saviolo:[13] but to flout a quarrel by the book, as to flout death for love, except by attorney, is witty only if the true claims of courtliness and love bear an unchallenged sway. Touchstone also parodies courtly love, in his improvement of Orlando's verses, his account of the wooing of Jane Smile, and his final insistence on pressing in among the couples coming to the Ark. He plays the sententious philosopher to Jaques, the condoling amorist to Silvius and Phoebe. Whilst Jaques dissects the world, Touchstone parodies it, like the true court fool that he is, and he receives his 'lot' from Jaques, who plays Fortune in the Masque of Hymen[14]

> thy loving voyage
> Is but for two moneths victuall'd.

Touchstone's nearest approach to an oration is his speech on the Horn; and though but a faint echo of Chapman's gigantic Praise of the Horn in *All Fools*, it is almost his only piece of pure satire in the Elizabethan sense.

Jaques is not only a satirist, but is also satirized himself. As Professor Campbell says, he is the satirist's portrait of the disillusioned traveller, melancholy, captious and not without a first-hand knowledge of the newest modern vices.[15] He is such a character as Marston drew in *The Scourge of Villanie*. But Marston's portrait was savage, direct invective, modelled upon the Roman satirists—or what the Elizabethan took the Roman satirists to be. Shakespeare's Jaques is but an element in a comedy whose main tone is a subtle blend of mockery and delight. He is allowed the virtues of his kind—wit, and a somewhat old-fashioned strain of moralizing. His seven ages of man were familiar but not quite of the newest cut: his emblem of the deer was Spenserian, and belonged to the same period as the pastoral amours of Silvius and Phoebe.

There is one more species which contributes its flavour to the *cuvée:* the Robin Hood pastoral of the Duke and his followers and the homely humours of William, Audrey and Corin.

Robin Hood stories represented an idyllic folk tradition which was the popular equivalent of the courtly pastoral. The King fraternized with his subjects in the greenwood, and all were good fellows together.[16] Lovemaking and deer-stalking were the main occupations and jests were broad, but friendly. The note struck by the Duke is indeed graver at times:

> Are not these woods
> More free from perill then the envious Court?   (2. 1. 3–4.)

is in the tradition of the greenwood, but the greenwood is not altogether idyllic in its climate:

> the Icie phange
> And churlish chiding of the winters winde,
> Which when it bites and blows upon my body
> Euen till I shrink with colde, I smile and say
> This is no flattery: these are counsellors
> That feelingly persuade me what I am.   (2. 1. 6–11.)

Such observation contrasts with the lively songs, the quite unrealistic life of the Pages and Amiens, as the set pastoral of Silvius and Phoebe contrasts with the 'low style' of Corin, his hands greasy from handling his ewes, and his wit stocked with ancient threepennyworths:

> No more, but that I know the more one sickens, the worse at ease he is; and that he that wants money, meanes and content, is without three good friends. That the propertie of raine is to wet and fire is to burne: That good pasture makes fat sheep.
>
> (3. 2. 24 ff.)

'Such a one', replies Touchstone gravely, 'is a naturall Philosopher', but the quirks which he breaks upon Corin do not disturb the shepherd's unassailable simplicity.

Speech guarded with old ends of proverbs had been used in Lyly's plays for his countryfolk:

Silena. I cannot help you at this time, I pray you come again to-morrow.

Accius. You need not be so lustye, you are not so honest,

Silena. I cry you mercy, I tooke you for a ioynd stoole . . .

Accius. I am taken with a fit of loue: haue you anie minde of marriage?

Silena. I had thought to have asked you.

Accius. Upon what acquaintance?

Silena. Who would have thought it?

Accius. Much in my gascoins, more in my round hose: all my
fathers are as white as daisies, as an egge full of meate.

(*Mother Bombie,* 4. 2.)

This is the speech of Jaquenetta and of Audrey and William:
it belongs with the wintry aspect of the Forest of Arden and
with the deflationary jests of Rosalind. Yet the idyllic scene is
not destroyed by its interlude in the low style; the songs and
the pretty artifices of the lovers counterbalance it.

The play is then a compound of many simples—Rosalind's
gay variety, Orlando's polite Petrarchanism and ability in
slaying lions, the conceited prettiness of Phoebe, the biting
epigrams of Jaques and the nimble parodies of Touchstone.
The brilliance of the individual figures depends on the contrasts which they make with each other. Some characters
exist for shadow-work, such as Oliver, whose lightning
conversion and lightning wooing are a piece of sheer recklessness designed to underline the artificiality of the story: to
remind the audience that all the world is a stage, and that even
the gravest crimes are not hanging matters here. The sophisticated nature of the courtly games of pastoral and sonnetting is
as vital an ingredient as the native strength and sweetness
which is contrasted with it. An appreciation of *As You Like It*
might be called the last reward of Elizabethan studies, for
though the play is for all time, it is likewise of its age.

III

If *As You Like It* depends upon unity within variety and its
'cause' or germ is the interdependence of the natural and the
artificial, the human and the literary, *Twelfth Night* is a subtler
and more delicate exposition of variety within unity. The
tone and 'keeping' of this play is absolutely consistent. It is
pure holiday, as the title implies: Twelfth Night, the end of
the Christmas Revels, was the occasion for the King of the

Bean to hold his court of Misrule, for all the gaiety to reach its climax. In this play Shakespeare seems to gather up all that he has achieved in comedy.[17] Viola loves as hopelessly and serves as devotedly as Hellen: she goes a-wooing for her master like Julia, and converts the lady unexpectedly, like Rosalind. Antonio reappears from *The Merchant of Venice*, in the guise of a sea captain but otherwise unchanged in his devotion. Sir Toby has some traits of Sir John, though the likeness does not amount to identity. Aguecheek is Slender called by another name, whilst the twins reappear from *The Comedy of Errors*.

The fooling of the clown is the chief solvent. His songs and jests reflect whatever company he is in—true love or a catch come equally readily.

This is a Practice,
As full of Labour as a Wise Mans Art.

The elusive spirit of *Twelfth Night* inhabits the fool's lively jests and melancholy songs, Olivia's mourning and Orsino's elegant despair, Viola's silences and her paradox of telling her love, under guise of the 'daughter of her father's house', who never told hers. The combination of delicacy and penetration in *Twelfth Night* is finer than the magnificence of *Much Ado* or the comprehensive variety of *As You Like It*. Bitter-sweet Feste blends Touchstone and Jaques. It is the end of the revels: the fooling is absurder than ever because the comedy is no longer a young man's comedy. Viola, the Duke, Sebastian and Olivia are seen as at the end of a long perspective, their sentiments are dream-like, without the stab and sparkle of life at first hand. None of them ever speaks directly to their love as Rosalind to Orlando or Benedick to Beatrice; all their wooing is oblique, rarefied, and their love an 'enchantment' as Olivia terms it.

There is little profit in dissecting *Twelfth Night*, since its strength lies precisely in its even unity of tone. It is a little enclosed world, with few links reaching to the world of the day. There is no direct source for the play, as for its predecessor, where the story had a topical significance, since as

Professor Sisson has shown, Lodge depicted his own wrongs in the character of Orlando and what he considered the perfidy of his elder brother in the behaviour of Oliver. If Lodge and his friends really went to see the dramatic version and 'led the applause and the groans' at the appropriate moments,[18] then the fun in places must have been broad. But *Twelfth Night* was possibly designed for private performance at the Revels of the Inns of Court: its humour is decorous with no sallets to make the matter savoury;[19] and the use of the twins very naturally recalled to Manningham, who recorded an early performance, the classical comedies of Plautus and the Italian plays deriving from them.

In Sir Toby, the fool, Maria and Fabian there is something approaching the Masks, translated into an entirely different idiom. Structurally they provide the *lazzi;* all their business is to devise sport. In this way too they resemble the Falstaff-group of 2 *Henry IV.* But Sir Toby does not cheat his own followers and dependants as Falstaff does, or flatter his rich young relative; he is an impossible old man for Olivia to have as an uncle, but he has an assured place in the household, in spite of the threats which Malvolio uses, and which Malvolio's station in life makes it most improper for him to use. Therefore Sir Toby's plots, being confined to fleecing his good friend Sir Andrew, are less serious and without any moral shadow of old father antic the law to darken them; Sir Andrew is getting his money's worth in experience. In all his reworking of his own earlier material to form this smooth and harmonious play, Shakespeare has slightly modified the tone and colouring to bring it into relation with a new theme. This is the delicate illusions of lovers, the false images created by Olivia, Orsino, more grossly by Malvolio, and dispelled by the conjuring trick of 'One face, one voice, one habit and two persons, A naturall Perspective that is and is not'.

The difference can be seen by comparing Viola's use of her page's part with Rosalind's: she is no pert little brother of Moth and Risio, but through all her sympathetic tenderness to Orsino and her shrewd undermining of Olivia's disdain shows a purely feminine habit of mind. Her banter of Olivia is subtler than Rosalind's banter of Phoebe, mixed with genuine admiration of beauty and with a pretty gravity and pathos. Her picture of how she would play the Petrarchan lover:

> Make me a willow Cabine at your gate
> And call upon my soule within the house,
> Write loyall Cantons of contemned love,
> And sing them loud euen in the dead of night:
> Hallow your name to the reverberate hilles
> And make the babling Gossip of the aire
> Cry out *Olivia*
>
> (I. 5. 289–295.)

transforms without mockery the old worn conceits so that the melancholy quite overshadows the object of it. This is a picture of exquisite sensibility, meant for the ear of sympathy, and not a sonnet addressed to a lady for public declamation.

Yet each and all of the characters are mocked: the Duke for his over-fastidious humour of melancholy, Olivia for her humour of grief and quick tumble into doting; the whole pattern is made artificial by the use of Sebastian as Olivia's lover, a more drastic 'shadowing' even than the wooing of Oliver and Celia. Above all the duel with Sir Andrew Ague-cheeke subjects Viola to the severe test of farce; Rosalind is never called on to show her swashing and martial outside in action.

A great deal of sympathy has been wasted on Malvolio. The self-opinionated and self-satisfied have always been legitimate butts: and the jest of Sir Toby was not half as unpleasant for the victim as the majority of jests which were practised in London taverns. When Sir Walter Ralegh sealed up Charles Chester's mouth with hot wax, or Marlowe drew his dagger in a playful manner, the incident might remain imprinted not only on the victim's memory but on his person. Sir Toby has the same sort of humour as Squire Western;[20] he is prepared to plot a hoax elaborately, in a manner indeed which has not yet died out among such remnants of his class as remain. The hoaxing of Malvolio was the most notable thing in the play in the eyes of the contemporary John Manningham; he described it as 'a good practice'—a clever trick.

In Chapman's *Gentleman Usher*, Bassiolo, the character equivalent to Malvolio, is seized upon by Vincentio the Duke's son, and adopted as his 'ingle'.[21] Vincentio fools the poor wretch to the top of his bent, and having persuaded him that he is the object of a princely infatuation of the most doubtful kind, proceeds to make use of him as go-between, to arrange letters and interviews with his mistress. Such a duping, ending in the quite casual and brutal repulse of the confident Usher before the whole assembled court was evidently not expected to provoke any sense of injustice in the audience. Malvolio's presumption, and his precise formality make him a natural target: his self-conceit is a standing temptation and worst of all perhaps is his cold sneer at the entertainment of the fool:

> Look you now, he's out of his gard already, unless you laugh
> and minister occasion to him, he is gag'd.   (I. 5. 91–93.)

Such a remark would perhaps justify his discomfiture in the eyes of a company of players, and even of their chief playwright: it is at all events recalled to Malvolio by the fool in the very last scene of the play, which gives it the air of being the 'cause' of his undoing.

The fool is himself something of a dramatic improvisor, as Viola observes:

> This fellow is wise enough to play the fool,
> And to do that well craues a kind of wit:
> He must obserue their mood on whom he iests,
> The quality of persons, and the time:
> And like the Haggard check at every Feather
> That comes before his eye.   (3. 1. 68–73.)

With a little modification, this would serve well enough as the definition of a 'chameleon poet'.[22] It is also a definition of the dramatist's use of decorum; each of the characters must be seen in their inner mood and quality before they can be bodied forth in 'lively images'.

In this play Shakespeare takes his farewell of comedy. It is over the border of the new century; and its atmosphere, clear, rarefied and, in spite of the fooling, a little fey, has a touch of the enchantments of Prospero's island or the golden world that in *Cymbeline* is called Brittaine.

APPENDIX

Significant Costume

It has been said in dispraise of some of Marlowe's descriptions that they recall Benvenuto Cellini's salt-cellars. This would perhaps not have seemed such great dispraise to an Elizabethan: for like the other decorative arts, that of the goldsmith was closely related to the common emblematic techniques, as the name of Nicholas Hilliard alone is enough to imply. Emblematic jewels might inspire poetry, or a poem might provide the device for a jewel.

The medicinal and moral value of jewels meant that they were sometimes worn for protection as well as for adornment. The sapphire was supposed to staunch blood and ward off poisons, and jewels inscribed with Kabbalistic signs had of course a special value. Among Queen Elizabeth's jewels there are many representing animals including a golden frog (*Frog* was her nickname for Alençon). Sir John Harington is said to have sent the news of her death to James by means of a jewel in the form of a dark antern, signifying that the queen's life was extinct. One of the most splendid emblematic jewels in existence, the Darnley Jewel, now at Windsor, was made for the Countess of Lennox, mother-in-law of Mary, Queen of Scots. It contains a figure of Queen Elizabeth, a great many mottoes—most of them anagrams—and symbols, signifying the Countess's fidelity to her husband's memory, and upholding his claim to the throne.[1]

Mary, Queen of Scots, had an Agnus Dei 'de crystal de roche, ayant dedans un Neptune'. The two were evidently not thought incongruous. The most splendid jewels formed part of the insignia of knightly orders, and the symbolism of jewels was linked with heraldry. The tincture sanguine, for instance, was related to the sardonyx: the virtue of the sardonyx was the protection of chastity: in Chapman's *Hero and Leander*, the bride wears a red veil for modesty.

There is a charming poem on an emblematic jewel by Sir Robert Ayton.[2]

Upon a Diamond cut in the form of a heart, set with a crown above
and a bloody dart piercing it, Sent in a New Year's Gift.

> Thou sent to me a heart was crowned,
> I thought it had been thine:
> But when I saw it had a wound,
> I knew the heart was mine. . . .

In the *Arcadia*, when Musidorus first catches sight of the Amazon
Zelmane, she is wearing a jewel that tells him 'she' is really his
cousin Pyrocles, in disguise for love of Philoclea.

Over all this she wore a certain mantle made in such a manner that
coming under her right arm and covering most of that side, it had no fasten-
ing on the left side, but only on the top of the shoulder, where the two
ends met and were closed together with a very rich jewel: the device
whereof, as he afterwards saw, was this: a Heracles made in little form,
but set with a distaff in his hand as he once was by Omphale's commandment, with a word in Greek but thus to be interpreted, *Never more valiant*.[3]

In *Ovid's Banquet of Sense*, Julia dresses her hair in the form of a
heart:

> and then with Jewels of devise it graced:
> One was a sunn graven at his evens depart,
> And under that, a man's huge shadow placed
> Wherein was writ, in sable charactery,
> *Decrescente nobilitate, crescunt obscuri.*
>
> Another was an eye in sapphire set
> And close upon it a fresh laurel spray,
> The skilful posie was, *Medio caret*,
> To show not eyes but means must truth display.
> A third was an Apollo with his team
> About a Dial and a world in way.
> The Motto was *teipsum et orbem*,
> Graven in the Dial: these exceeding rare
> And other like accomplements she ware.[4]

In Daniel's *Complaint of Fair Rosamund* the king sends his mistress
a casket on which the riotous loves of the gods were carved, as
they were painted on the walls of Venus's temple in *Hero and Leander*.
There was

> Amymone, how she with Neptune strove.
> Amymone, old Neptune's fairest daughter,
> As she was fetching water all alone
> At *Lenna*: whereas Neptune came and caught her,
> From whence she strived and strugled to be gone.

> But all in vain, with him sh' is forced to go.
> 'Tis shame that men should use poor maidens so.

Amymone's further despair and tears of crystal only make her more beautiful:

> To show that nothing ill becomes the fair,
> But cruelty that yields unto no prayer.

This device had an obvious moral for Rosamund: but on another square of the casket she found 'transformed Io':

> Turned to a heifer, kept with jealous eyes,
> Always in danger of her hateful spies.

The casket was a love-token, but Rosamund later sees that Providence had figured on it the wrath of Eleanor and her own death.

> These precedents presented to my view
> Wherein the presage of my fall was shown,
> Might have forewarned me what would ensure
> And others' harms have made me shun my own.[5]

Sometimes clothes were symbolically embroidered,[6] as the 'wondrous scarf' of Hero in Chapman's part of the story, which had figures emblematic of her fate upon it, the costume of Drayston' Phoebe, or that of Mercy in Fletcher's *Christ's Victory in Heaven*, which takes nine stanzas to describe. Mercy's upper garment had the whole world embroidered upon it, and all its inhabitants; whilst her head-dress represented the heavens.

> About her head a cypress heaven she wore,
> Spread like a veil, upheld with silver wire,
> In which the starres so burnt in golden ore
> As seem'd the azure web was all on fire:
> But hastily to quench the sparkling ire
> A flood of milk came rowling up the shore,
> That on his curded waves swift Argus bore,
> And the immortal swan, that did her life deplore.

Still later, Chalkhill's *Thealma and Clearchus*[7] depicts some very elaborate symbolic costumes, for the shepherdess Thealma and the votaress Florimel (or Clarinda). There is another symbolic costume embroidered with turtle doves, eagles, lions, and jewels of device:

> an Amethyst,
> Made like a heart with wings: the motto this,
> *Love gives me wings.*

This poem also has an elaborate witches' grotto, with a roof carved in vines, and walls painted with pictures from 'lascivious Ovid'. Such symbolism was not confined to courtly literature, for in Ralph Johnson's *Pleasant History of Tom-a-Lincoln*, there is a magnificent group, of the Black Knight, his mother, and a negro bond-slave who clearly stands for Base Desire; all are symbolically clad.

And in this manner departed they the land: the Black Knight wore on his helmet for a scutcheon a black raven feeding on dead men's flesh, his caparisons were all of black velvet embroidered which most lively figured forth the blacke furie lodged in his princely bosome. Anglitora his mother had the attire of an Amazon made all of the best Arabian silk: coloured like the changeable hue of the rainbow: about her neck was a jewel of a wonderful value which was a diamond cut in the form of a heart split asunder with a Turkish scimitar: betokening a doubt she had of her knight's loyalty. The slavish Moor that attended them, went all naked, except for a shadow of greene taffeta that covered his privy parts, upon his feet a Morisho shoe, which is nothing but a soule made of an asses' hide, buckled with small leathers to his insteps, upon his head he ware a wreath of cypress gilded with pure gold, and a plate of brass about his neck close locked with the word BOND-SLAVE engraved about it.[8]

This gorgeous group might have come from a masque: and the fantastic costumes of the masque no doubt inspired some of the poetic descriptions. So perhaps did tourneys (see Chapter iv).

The languages of colours and flowers were likewise used in courtship: blue stood for fidelity, yellow was symbolic of jealousy, green was the colour of lovers. A red petticoat was the badge of a harlot as unequivocally as a blue coat of a serving man. Symbolism of colour was of particular importance in the drama (see M. Channing Linthicum, *Costume and Drama in the Age of Shakespeare*, Oxford 1936). The white, red, black banners of Tamburlaine were so famous that Nashe could use them to symbolize Christ's attitude toward Jerusalem (*Christ's Tears*, ed. McKerrow, *Works*, vol. ii. p. 20). In *The Arraignement of Paris*, the costumes of the three goddesses, as they are depicted or wrought by Flora, are symbolical both in the colours and in the flowers themselves.

Flora. First, stately Juno eith her port and grace,
    Her robes, her lawns, her crownets and her mace,
    Would make thee muse this picture to behold,
    Of yellow oxlips bright as burnished gold.

Pomona.	A rare device: and Flora well, perdie,
	Did paint her yellow for her jealousy.
Flora.	Pallas in flowers of hue and colour red:
	Her plumes, her helm, her lance, her gorgon's head . . .
Pomona.	Good Flora, by my flock, 'twere very good
	To dight her all in red resembling blood.
Flora.	Fair Venus of sweet violets all in blue,
	With other flowers infixed for change of hue:
	Her plumes, her pendents, her bracelets and her rings,
	Her dainty fan and twenty other things,
	Her lusty mantle waving in the wind,
	And every part in colour and in kind.
Pomona.	A dainty draught to lay her down in blue,
	The colour commonly betokening true.

(I. I. 76 ff.)

The most splendid development of the symbolic costume for gods and goddesses as they were actually presented is that of the Jonsonian masque.[9] There is a pleasant little poem called *A Nosegay* in *A Handful of Pleasant Delights* in which the lover tells over the significance of all the flowers in the nosegay he has given to his mistress. The song is recalled in the scene of Ophelia's madness. Drummond of Hawthornden has a poem addressed to the Countess of Perth, painted with a pansy in her hand, in which he asks why the painter depicted 'that flower of purple hue that follows on the planet of the year'. Was it to show her as another Sun? or that she subdues the mind as the sun does the pansy? or would he compare her to the flower in her constancy to virtue? or to Clytie? Rather he has given her this mourning flower in memory of the end of some faithful lover, 'to grace his grave', instead of a cypress wreath.

To-day, the natural impulse would be simply to accept the pansy on its merits, but for an Elizabethan this was almost unthinkable. When, in another poem, Drummond says of his lady, 'A hyacinth I wished me in her hand', his choice is again not dictated merely by alliteration.

At the end of *The Merry Wives of Windsor* Shakespeare evokes the splendours of the Order of the Garter in a floral setting, as Falstaff is being tormented under the oak.

And nightly, meadow fairies, look you sing
Like to the Garter's compass, in a ring. . . .

And *honi soit qui mal y pense* write
In emerald tufts, flowers purple, blue and white,
Like sapphire, pearl and rich embroidery
Buckled below fair knighthood's bending knee. . . .

(5. 5. 71–78.)

The magnificent procession of Cleopatra's barge upon the river Cydnus is the greatest of Shakespeare's pageants, but it depends partly at least upon the symbolic costume of her attendants, the mermaids and cupids who represent all the power of witchery and desire that royal Egypt commands. And when at the end Cleopatra says:

Give me my robe, put on my crown:

she adorns herself again, as Mary, Queen of Scots, in real life had adorned herself to die in a manner fitting for a Princess. The interplay of drama and life was constant but no scene in the theatre of the time approaches that on the scaffold at Fotheringay, when Mary put off her mourning gown of black velvet and faced the headsman clad all in scarlet to meet what she held to be a martyr's death.

NOTES

List of Abbreviations used

A.M.S.   J. Q. *Adams Memorial Studies*, ed. J. McManaway and others (Folger Library, Washington, 1948).
J.H.I.   *Journal of the History of Ideas.*
J.W.C.I.   *Journal of the Warburg and Courtauld Institutes.*
M.P.   *Modern Philology.*
P.M.L.A.   *Publications of the Modern Language Association of America.*
R.E.S.   *Review of English Studies.*

Chapter I

[1] See his *Elizabethan World Picture* (London 1943), p. 5.

[2] See J. C. F. Hood, *Icelandic Church Saga* (London 1946).

[3] See J. M. Manly, 'Chaucer and the Rhetoricians' (*Proceedings of the British Academy* 1926), p. 97. The question is also dealt with by C. S. Lewis in *The Allegory of Love* (Oxford 1936). The work of Nevill Coghill, S. B. James and others who followed the lead of R. W. Chambers in their studies of Langland has passed into general currency.

[4] W. B. Yeats, 'Ego Dominus Tuus' *Collected Poems* (London 1933), p. 180.

[5] J. Huitzinga, *The Waning of the Middle Ages* (London 1924).

[6] E.g. the kind of manners depicted in *The Paston Letters*, where a mother beats her daughter black and blue, or the savage case of murder recorded in *Chaucer's World* (ed. E. Rickerts, New York, 1948, p. 74), where a stranger attempting to pacify a domestic brawl was stabbed and killed.

[7] See Beryl Smalley, *The Study of the Bible in the Middle Ages* (Oxford 1934), for a full treatment of this subject.

[8] The story of Bethsabe became an allegory of Christ's love for the Church, who saw her washing herself from her sins, and took her away from the world (Uriah) to whom she was wedded. Conversely many of the merry tales of the *Gesta Romanorum* could be given a moral interpretation and used in their sermons by expert preachers, such as Chaucer's Pardoner.

[9] A. O. Lovejoy, *The Great Chain of Being* (Cambridge, Mass., 1936), p. 101: 'It was an ideally classical universe . . . indeed the most classical thing about the Middle Ages may be said to have been the universe'. Cf. also p. 10: 'There is the organismic or flower-in-the-crannied-wall motive, the habit of assuming that . . . no element . . . can be understood, or, indeed, be what it is apart from its relation to all the other components of the system to which it belongs'.

For *Ovid Moralisé* see D. Bush, *Mythology and the Renaissance Literary Tradition* (Minneapolis 1932), p. 17.

[10] E.g. the she-bear licking her whelps into shape was said to typify action of the Holy Spirit in shaping the souls of those reborn of the Spirit.

[11] Cf. the moral (but not specifically doctrinal) interpretation given by Pico to the story of Circe as quoted below, p. 13. The older interpretation of the behaviour of animals was dropped at the Renaissance but men continued to be compared with the animal kingdom in respect of their temperaments: see, e.g., the pictures from G. B. Porta's *De Humana Physiognomania* (1586) reproduced by Lily B. Campbell in *Shakespeare's Tragic Heroes* (Cambridge 1936).

[12] E.g. in *The Book of St. Albans,* Juliana Berners related the nine tinctures (or colours) of heraldry to the nine hierarchies of the angels. The correspondences between the signs of the zodiac and the different parts of man's body which they governed is represented frequently. Mention is made of it as late as *Twelfth Night* where Sir Andrew thinks to be born under Taurus signifies predominance of 'sides and heart' but Sir Toby corrects it to 'legs and thighs'.

[13] See E. W. Tristram, in *The Month*, new series, vol. i, no. 6, and vol. ii, no. 1, 'The Wilton Dyptych'. The symbolic nature of the cathedral, building, vestments and ordinances was set forth in the twelfth-century *Rationale Divinorum Officiorum*. The *Biblia Pauperum* and *Speculum Hominis Salvationis* expanded the iconographic aspect. An account of the significance of the different parts of a cathedral is given by H. O. Taylor, *The Medieval Mind* (London 1914), vol. ii, pp. 106 ff., but the most complete account is to be found in the works of Émile Mâle. For a limited treatment of an English field of study, see E. S. Prior and A. Gardner, *Medieval Sculpture in England* (Cambridge 1912): 'The persons and scenes of medieval carving were the same as appeared in the wall paintings and the glass paintings of the windows, as well as in the metal enamels, in the embroideries and the tapestries and in the manuscript illustrations. . . . Each character had its traditional type and its recognized attributes and moreover each subject had a definite arrangement for its figures. Attributes and arrangements were universally known and accepted, so that even the most unlettered and ignorant could read the meaning' (pp. 24–25).

[14] See Hilda F. Dunbar, *Medieval Symbolism and its Consummation in Dante* (New Haven 1929)—a most valuable survey—p. 21. 'The question is never one of "either-or" but always of all the meanings as true at once. The meaning on each higher level both includes and illuminates the lower, but never in any sense falsifies them. All the meanings are necessary to an understanding of a fact in its universal implications. The essence of this method was the recognition of the simultaneous validity of different levels of interpretation which by their correction of each other might ever more exactly express the truth'.

R

[15] Quoted by L. S. Stebbing, *A Modern Introduction to Logic* (London 1933), p. 251.

[16] A. O. Lovejoy, op. cit., p. 107.

[17] See Hardin Craig, *The Enchanted Glass* (Oxford 1936), pp. 110–112, for a discussion of the use of medieval modes of exegesis in Bacon and Cornelius Agrippa.

[18] See E. H. Gombrich, 'Botticelli's Mythology' *J.W.C.I.*., vol. viii (1945). In an earlier article (vol. i, 1937) he had traced how the grouping usual for a figure of Charity with her babes had been transferred to secular subjects and survived in modern poster art.

[19] Cornelius Agrippa and Paracelsus also held this view. The connexion between magic and the Neo-Platonic doctrines appears to have been maintained in England by such figures as the 'Wizard Earl' of Northumberland, the friend of Ralegh.

[20] In 1536 the Logician, Ramus, set up his thesis on the doors of the Collège de Navarre at the Sorbonne, which might be rendered, 'Aristotle is all wrong'. Ramus was famous in Elizabethan England and studied by the generation of Sidney and Marlowe. Marlowe, indeed, introduces him into *The Massacre at Paris*—he was a Huguenot and perished in the Bartholomew—making him beg his murderers for a moment's respite, which he uses to make a dying speech proclaiming that Aristotle was not *all* wrong.

[21] For a more detailed account of this see below, chapter iv. The 'Spenserians', Drayton, Drummond, Brown, are the chief poetic exponents of this view in English. Henry Reynolds's *Mythomystes* is probably the most complete statement of the doctrine. On the other hand even Bacon, in *The Wisdom of the Ancients*, tried to re-interpret classic myth in terms of modern knowledge, so that Cupid becomes Democritus' atom. On other occasions he would give an interpretation in terms of modern statecraft.

[22] Quoted by E. H. Gombrich (see note 18) from Ficino, *Opera Omnia* (Basle, 1576).

[23] Pico della Mirandola, *De Hominis Dignitate*, translated by E. Forbes, *J.H.I.*, vol iii (1942), pp. 347–354. God seems at this point to preach Pelagianism!

[24] In this paragraph I have drawn on the work of Ernst Cassirer, 'Giovanni Pico della Mirandola', *J.H.I.*, vol. iii (1942), pp. 123–144, 319–346. I have not seen the study which he mentions, Avery Dulles, *Princeps Concordiae* (Cambridge, Mass., 1941), in which the connexions between Pico and medieval philosophy are developed. Cassirer says Dulles sees in Pico only a medieval realist (op. cit., p. 123).

[25] The absolute conviction that truth must prevail, and that man could truly know led to such extraordinary situations as are described below, chapter VI, p. 97. See Hardin Craig, op. cit., p. 18, 'Those into whose ears the truth passed had no choice. . . . They who heard the established

truth and did not thereupon profess it, were condemned upon the doctrine of persuasion as children of the devil. It was just and right that such persons should be led to the stake and burned'.

[26] Pico della Mirandola, from a letter translated by Sir Thomas More (*English Works of Sir Thomas More*, ed. Campbell and Reed (London, 1931), vol. i, p. 10.

[27] See F. J. Shirley, *Richard Hooker and Contemporary Political Thought* (London 1949), chapter i. I am also indebted to this work for observations on Hooker's view of law as compared with the medieval view.

[28] See Lawrence Stone, 'The Anatomy of the Elizabethan Aristocracy' (*Economic History Review*, vol. xviii (1948), no. 1) for a most interesting account of the finances of Elizabethan courtly life.

[29] 'Ideas were held together by tension and no longer by the interlocking of a system', as Miss R. Freeman observes in *The English Emblem Books* (London 1946), p. 20. This work provides a significant illustration of the transition from medieval to modern thought and style in those regions which lie between literature and the decorative arts.

[30] See below, Chapter ii, p. 18.

[31] Carleton Brown, *English Lyrics of the Thirteenth Century* (Oxford 1932), p. 29.

[32] John Donne, *Songs and Sonets*, 'Upon the Primrose, being at Montgomery Castle' (composed *c.* 1590?).

Chapter II

[1] In her royal capacity she was Gloriana, in her private person Belphoebe. Elsewhere she is Elissa, Queen of Shepherds, Cynthia, Goddess of Ocean, Una (pure religion, in contrast with Duessa), Mercilla or Mercy, and perhaps the mysterious Fair One whom Calidore sees in the Sixth Book under the figure of Ariadne's Crown. For the last suggestion and for ideas in the rest of this paragraph I am indebted to Miss Frances Yates, 'Queen Elizabeth as Astraea', *J.W.C.I.*, vol. x (1947).

[2] Miss Yates reproduces a number of pictures showing the Queen with these attributes. In the well-known picture by Hans Eworth at Hampton Court she is shown taking the golden apple in the Judgment of Paris, exactly as she is represented as doing in Peele's play, *The Arraignement of Paris*.

[3] B. Griffin, *Fidessa* (1596). In *Gli Eroici Furori*, Giordano Bruno, Sidney's friend, cites the Canticle as parallel to his own work. It was of course used by the medieval love-poets, just as the medieval religious poets would borrow the language of earthly love to blend with that of the Canticle, as in the celebrated *Quia Amore Langueo*.

⁴ This line comes from Chapman's *Coronet for his Mistress Philosophy*. He was one of the Platonists, who interpreted classical myth in terms of such handbooks as Natales Comes, or Boccaccio's *Geneologia Deorum;* and apparently Roman history also.

⁵ Poor Chapman was most unfairly credited with *The Amorous Zodiac,* an improper little catalogue of a lady's charms, in which the learned correspondences between the signs of the zodiac and the parts of the body is used for a very extended piece of description. The fleshly poets sometimes took refuge in elaborate allegorical explanations when their work went too far for the censor. Marston explained his *Metamorphosis of Pygmalion's Image* (1598) as a satiric parody of the Ovidian Romance.

⁶ See E. Greenlaw, *Studies in Spenser's Historical Allegory* (Baltimore, 1932), ch i. Leicester was her Bear, on account of his cognisance, the bear and ragged staff, Alençon her frog, Hatton her 'mutton', Simier, the French Ambassador, her ape. Simier in turn had an elaborate code which he used in his correspondence with the French King.

⁷ The beast fable could be savagely satiric and had a long medieval tradition behind it, culminating in Skelton: but it is one of the 'species' that unexpectedly dies out.

⁸ The significance of the *Mirror for Magistrates* as the great exemplum for Princes was strengthened by its connexion with the medieval tradition of Lydgate's *Fall of Princes.* See chapter viii for its influence on early Tragedy. When therefore the condemned Buckingham appeared to take his farewell and explicitly recalled the fate of his father, the audience would pick up the cue almost instinctively. This was Winter. With Elizabeth came Spring.

⁹ Vergil's *Fourth Eclogue,* the 'Messianic Eclogue', was a poem of such outstanding significance that the echoes of it in this passage could not fail to give an added splendour and sanctity to the occasion. Christian and Pagan prophecy here join hands. For the sense of the importance of this whole passage I am indebted to Professor Peter Alexander, who first pointed it out to me.

¹⁰ *Titus Andronicus,* 4. 3. 4. I cannot agree with Miss Yates that this phrase refers to Elizabeth as Astraea. Titus is rather imitating the accents of old Hieronimo, who goes down to hell in search of Justice, but not finding her, seeks Revenge instead (*Spanish Tragedy,* 3. 12. 6–8: 3. 13. 108–113).

¹¹ The last pages of Castiglione's *Courtier* (written in 1508, translated in 1561 by Sir Thomas Hoby). Love is 'a certain coveting to enjoy beauty' and because longing cannot proceed but by knowledge, beauty is known either to sense (which we share with beasts) by election or choice, which is proper to man or by understanding, which is shared by the angels, and issues in the will. Beauty is 'an influence of the heavenly bountifulness, the which for all it stretcheth over all things that be created . . . yet when it finds

NOTES 245

out a face well proportioned . . . thereinto it distilleth itself and appeareth most well favoured and decketh out and lyghtenth the subject where it shyneth with a marveylous grace and glistering'. Of the three kinds of love, Heavenly love is of the understanding alone. 'Thus the Soule, kindled in the most holy fire of love, fleeth to couple herself with the nature of Angelles, and not only cleane forsaketh sense, but hath no more need of the discourse of reason, for being changed into an Angell, she understandeth all things. . . without anie veile or cloude she seeth the meine sea of the pure heavenly bewtye and receiveth it into her, and enjoyeth that sovereigne happinesse, that cannot be comprehended of the senses'.

[12] Miss Yates suggests in 'The Emblematic Conceit in *De Gli Eroici Furori* and in the Elizabethan Sonnet Sequences', *J.W.C.I.*, vi (1943), pp. 101–121, that the new Petrarchan poets were using the old conceits not simply as descriptive material but as 'more like the medieval allegory of the Song of Songs to which Bruno compares his own works which were *emblematic* or symbolic; and not intended to be read in their surface meaning only'. Medieval allegories could be translated into Hermetic hieroglyphs (p. 105).

[13] The Heavenly Beauty of Spenser's *Fourth Hymn* may be compared with Drayton's Phoebe, and with his Idea, with the beauty celebrated in *Ovid's Banquet of Sense* by Chapman and perhaps even with Donne's Elizabeth Drury.

[14] Symbolic costume is discussed in the Appendix. It was important both in life and in literature. Miss Freeman has something to say on the subject in her book on emblems (see above, chapter i, note 29) for costume could become emblematic. See especially pp. 98 ff.

[15] See below, p. 24, for the significance of Mutability in Spenser and chapter iv, pp. 52–4, for Mutability as the subject of Ovidian Romance.

[16] An interesting argument is given by Chapman in the Epistle 'To the most honoured now living instance of the Achillean Virtues Eternized by Divine Homer, The Earl of Essex, Earl Marshal, etc.' prefixed to his *Seven Books of the Iliads* (1598). The soul, 'her substance being too pure and illustrate to be discerned with ignorant and barbarous sense and the matter whereon she works too passive and drossy . . . she hath devised another . . . receptacle to receive her image with unspeakable profit, comfort and life to all posterity: and that is this poor scribbling, this toy. . . .' In other words, Homer had in fact depicted the *real* Essex, in the figure of Achilles, more truly than he could ever be made manifest after the flesh.

[17] *Twelfth Night*, I. I. 33–39.

[18] *Astrophel and Stella*, x. The case for love however can still be proved by reason—but only after conversion.

[19] This letter is quoted in Michael Roberts, *Elizabethan Prose* (London 1933), p. 161.

[20] The debt of Yeats to the Neo-Platonists and to Plotinus in particular

has been sufficiently acknowledged in his works, and is of course behind the 'philosophy' of *A Vision*, but I do not know how much the taste was implanted by his early study of Spenser.

[21] *The Faerie Queene*, 4. 11. xlv. The rhythmic power of *The Faerie Queene* was perhaps Spenser's greatest contribution to the development of English poetry. The mere capacity to sustain such a lengthy work was an achievement without whch the flowering of the nineties could not have taken place. The effort required to drag English out of the awful pit into which it had been thrown by the loss of the older verse rhythms (Chaucer could not be read metrically at all owing to the loss of final *e*, and other modifications)—this effort is sometimes so visible in Spenser's verse that it reads like one trying to turn over heavy clay soil with a branch broken from a hedge:

> At last yled with far reported praise
> Which flying Fame throughout the world had spread
> Of doughty knights whom Faery land did raise,
> That noble order hight of maidenhead,
> Forthwith to court of Gloriane I sped,
> Of Gloriane, great queene of glory bright,
> Whose kingdom's seat Cleopolis is red:
> There to obtain some such redoubted knight
> That parents dear from tyrants power deliver might.
>
> (1. 7. xlvi.)

[22] This tapestry technique is discussed below, chapters iv and vii.

It is a favourite one of Spenser. Compare the amours of Jove which are painted on the walls of the House of Busyrane, where Britomart, the Knight of Chastity, overcomes the forces of Cupid. These paintings also include a Leda:

> Then was he turned to a snowy swan
> To win fair Leda to his lovely trade:
> O wondrous skill! and sweet wit of the man
> That her in daffadillies sleeping made
> From scorching limbs her daintie limbs to shade,
> Whiles the proud bird, ruffling his feathers wide
> And brushing her fair breast, did her invade:
> She slept, yet twixt her eyelids closely spied,
> How towards her he rushed and smiled at his pride.
>
> (3. 11. xxxii.)

Perhaps it is Spenser or perhaps the picture of Leonardo which has made Leda a favourite symbol of modern poets. See the lovely poem by Yeats (*Collected Poems*, p. 241), and the skittish one by Oliver St. John Gogarty (*Others to Adorn*, London 1938, p. 156).

[23] Cf. below, chapter iv, p. 64, for a more subtle use of the association of whiteness.

²⁴ The convention which presents woman under the similitude of a bird in a love poem was not new in Chaucer's day. See J. M. Manly, Studien zur. Eng. Phil. (L. Morsbach Festscrift), pp. 279 ff.: and E. Rickerts, *M.P.*, vol. xviii (1921).

²⁵ Donne's poem on Mistress Elizabeth Drury was justified by him as depicting 'the Idea of a woman' when Ben Jonson accused him of flattery. Ben Jonson's inability to understand the Platonic convention is very revealing. 'If it had been written of the Virgin Mary', he said, 'it would have been something'.

²⁶ Very little has been written upon this lyric. J. Middleton Murry acclaimed it in *The Problem of Style* (Oxford 1922), pp. 147–148, and G. H. W. Rylands has a short passage on it in his article 'Shakespeare and Poetry' in *A Companion to Shakespeare Studies* (Cambridge 1933), p. 111. The studies of B. H. Newdigate which tended to identify the Phoenix with Lucy, Countess of Bedford, were summarized in his edition (Blackwell 1937).

Chapter III

¹ Jonson, *Works*, ed. Herford and Simpson, vol. viii (Oxford 1948), p. 41. Like = please, as in 'An it like you'.

² Chapman, Preface to *The Revenge of Bussy d'Ambois*.

³ Puttenham, *Elizabethan Critical Essays*, ed. G. G. Smith (Oxford 1904), vol. ii, p. 5. The excellent edition of Puttenham's *Arte of Poetry*, by G. Willcock and A. Walker (Cambridge 1936), gives the full text, whereas Smith prints only extracts: but I have cited the former for convenience of comparison with Sidney whose *Apologie* is reprinted in the same collection. Puttenham's latest editors would date his work as having been started in 1569, revised about 1585, when Puttenham—a nephew of Sir Thomas Wiat—was about fifty-five years old, and when he would have read Sidney. The work thus represents successive stages of Elizabethan critical thought, the last book being in the nature of an addition, or rewriting.

⁴ Sidney, *Elizabethan Critical Essays*, vol. i, pp. 156–157. Cf. G. Bickersteth's *Golden World of King Lear* (British Academy Annual Shakespeare Lecture, 1943), for an exposition of this view as applied to tragedy.

⁵ Puttenham, book iii, chapter xxv (ed. cit. p. 188). It is worth noting that H. S. Wilson, in *J.H.I.*, vol. 2 (1941) distinguishes no less than 35 different senses for 'Nature' at this time!

⁶ See note 16 to chapter ii above. The idea was a commonplace.

⁷ The argument was originally Plato's (book x of the *Republic*) and it is the usual plea of the Puritan detractor such as Gosson. The argument from 'abuse' was an easy one to answer and Sidney in his reply to Gosson does not waste much time on it. He finds some difficulty however, in

spite of his own delightful humour, in defending comedy. Puttenham thinks poetry should be frivolous on occasion, not vicious.

[8] Harington, *In Praise of Ariosto* (1591) reprinted in *Elizabethan Critical Essays*, vol. ii, p. 214.
Compare Marston's defence of *Pygmalion's Image* cited in note 5 to chapter ii above.

[9] Sidney, *Apology*, ed. cit., p. 161. He compares poetry with the craft of a saddler and the skill of a soldier, as having both an immediate and a further end: Cf. K. O. Myrick, *Sir Philip Sidney as a Literary Craftsman* (Harvard, 1935).

[10] The phrase is Bacon's.

[11] Puttenham, book iii, chapters v and vi.

[12] In this paragraph and indeed throughout this chapter I am indebted to the work of Miss Rosemund Tuve, *Elizabethan and Metaphysical Imagery* (Chicago 1947). Miss Tuve has notably enriched our understanding of Elizabethan poetry and even where I dissent from her views, it is often under the stimulus of her writing that I do so. I feel that her case rests on theory and that there is something to be said, particularly in the field of drama, for the achievement of the unlearned poet. Moreover the low style of Nashe, Donne, and the rest may have been as conventional as the high style of Spenser and Sidney but the fact that the low style came in and the high style went out is symptomatic of an important shift of interest. For the particular simile of 'Style as a garment', see Puttenham, ed. cit., pp. 142–143.

[13] Ibid, pp. 153–155.

[14] *Works*, ed. Herford and Simpson, vol. viii, p. 585.

[15] E.g., E. E. Stoll, *John Webster* (Harvard 1905), A. H. Thorndike, 'The relation of Hamlet to Contemporary Revenge Plays' (*P.M.L.A.*, xvii, 1902), which are pioneer works: L. B. Campbell, 'Theories of Revenge in Renaissance England' (*M.P.*, xxviii, 1931), Percy Simpson, 'The theme of Revenge in Elizabethan Tragedy' (British Academy Annual Shakespeare Lecture, 1936), F. T. Bowers, *Elizabethan Revenge Tragedy* (Princeton 1940).

[16] This imagery derived from the Vergilian Journey to the Underworld, and was perhaps mediated through the Induction to the *Mirror for Magistrates* (see note 8 to chapter ii above. It is discussed at more length in chapter viii below, pp. 132–3).

[17] The satiric comedy of Marston, *The Malcontent*, first uses some of the Revenge material in a play that is written with a Jonsonian accent, full of epigrammatic metaphor directed against the corruption of court life. Webster echoes the style in the satiric parts of *The White Divel*, and he too was clearly endebted to Jonson.

[18] Webster, *The White Divel*, 5. 2. The debt of later revenge plays to Lucian was first pointed out by W. Sherwood Fox (*Philological Quarterly II*, 1923).

[19] This passage does not appear to have been noticed by writers on the Revenge convention. For use of the Revenge conventions in domestic drama see *Bateman's Tragedy*, reprinted in W. Bang, *Materialien*. An interesting example of a late use is provided in the anonymous *Second Maiden's Tragedy*.

[20] A list of these plays is provided in the introduction to *Mulleasses The Turk* in Bang's *Materialien*. There were about forty such plays and they go on from the early days to the very close of the theatres. The villain had a set of maxims by which he can be identified. There is an example of these maxims in the first scene of *Alphonsus of Germany*, attributed to Chapman and printed in T. M. Parrott's edition of the tragedies. From *Selimus Emperor of the Turks* to *The Rebellion* with its twin villains, Raymond the Moor 'who wears the devil's livery' and 'the Count Matchevil', the plays of the villainous tyrant show very little modification. Aaron in *Titus Andronicus* is related to these villainous characters (see chapter vii, p. 107).

[21] See below, chapter vi, p. 98. Interest in Elizabethan comedy has tended to be one-sided, and apart from the greater figures of Shakespeare and Jonson, has stressed the popular comedy of Middleton, Dekker and Heywood. The intellectual comedy of Lyly, Chapman, Day, forms a distinct species which deserves a full-length study.

[22] *Mother Bombie*, 3. 4. This is much the most developed of Lyly's plays. It has something in common with the fairy-tale atmosphere of Peele's *Old Wives' Tale*.

[23] See below, chapter v, p. 89. Chapman excuses the fact that his plays had to be put on the common stages (Preface to *Revenge of Bussy d'Ambois*), and Jonson revised his works for the press, cutting out collaborators' work and suppressing some plays (or so it would seem) which he did not consider worthy of his reputation. Note that Sidney, in condemning the other arts compared with poetry calls them 'Actors and Players, as it were, of what Nature will have set forth' (ed. cit., p. 155). To be an actor or player was to be servilely dependent on copying others' invention. The poet is above nature and therefore cannot be compared with these hirelings.

[24] Duke Theseus on the Poet's Eye, a few phrases in *As You Like It*, the instruction to the players in *Hamlet*, the Induction to *Timon of Athens*; and some of the Sonnets, especially xxxviii, lxxviii, lxxxv, cxxx.

[25] As Sidney had expressed it, and as Chapman was more forcibly to claim for his kind of divine poesy, when in the preface to *Ovid's Banquet of Sense* he compares the 'poets of Nature' to those unfortunate Pierides who with their natural talents challenged the nine Muses, and for punishment were turned into magpies who could only chatter senselessly.

[26] This is the point I would wish to make in distinction to the thesis of Miss Tuve. See below, chapter v, p. 82. The arrival of parody is clearly connected with the transition from a predominantly courtly to a predominantly popular mode of writing.

Nashe's orator occurs in McKerrow's edition of the *Works*, vol. ii, pp. 247–249.

[27] In the notorious preface to *Ovid's Banquet of Sense*, already quoted, Chapman makes a plea for the 'difficult' subject as such:

'That *Enargia* or clearness of representation requird in absolute Poems is not the perspicuous deliuery of a lowe invention: but high, and harty invention expressed in most significant and unaffected phrase.... Obscuritie in affectation of words and indigested conceit is pedanticall and childish: but where it shroudeth it selfe in the hart of the subject, vttered with fitnes of figure and expressive Epithetes: with that darknes wil I stil labour to be shaddowed....'

[28] Pedants of language range from Holofernes to Osric: Mercutio mocks pedants of the duello, and Touchstone pedants of the quarrel: the orthodoxies of consolation are offered to Constance in her bereavement, Bolingbroke at his banishment, and Hamlet at his first appearance in court, only to be brusquely rejected. Polonius gave model parental advice, though hardly a model parent; lovers who speak by the book include Prince Lewis in *King John*, who is mocked by Falconbridge, and the gulls Master Silence and Andrew Aguecheek.

Chapter IV

[1] Giordano Bruno was interested in Lucretius' philosophic doctrine, i.e. the more shocking and atheistic aspect of the poem. I do not mean to imply that Spenser was introduced to Lucretius by Bruno. We do not know how he became acquainted with Lucretius' work.

[2] The one poem Spenser *mentions* in the *Mutabilitie Cantoes* is Chaucer's 'Fowls' Parley'. I am not sufficiently well read in the classics, philosophy or Spenserian studies to speak with any authority on the much disputed question of Spenser's debt to Lucretius. That he did know *De Rerum Natura* I think the passage from *The Faerie Queene* makes clear. When Professor Greenlaw published his article 'Spenser and Lucretius' (*University of N. Carolina Studies in Philology*, xvii (1920), 439–464), he provoked a storm of controversy: rival claims were put forward for Bruno, Empedocles, and Boethius. Professor Greenlaw replied and the honours seem to me to rest with him. The whole controversy is summarized in *The Variorum Spenser*, ed. Greenlaw, Osgood, Padelford and Heffner (Baltimore and Oxford), vol. vi (1938), in so far as it relates to the Mutabilitie Cantoes. Here Professor Greenlaw would claim that the personifications and the pictorial qualities as well as some of the episodes come from Ovid, and while there is some debt to the *Metamorphoses* 15 (the Pythagorean sections) Lucretius has furnished particulars for the masque, the whole conception

of the gods as mortal and earth-born, and the conception of mortality as distinct from protean transformation. Certainly there can be no question of 'either-or'.

³ Chaucer was here indebted to the *Filostrato*, but Boccaccio himself was drawing on older traditions.

⁴ For a discussion of the whole topic see D. Bush, *Mythology and the Renaissance Literary Tradition* (Minneapolis 1932). This view of the Gods is the classic Epicurean view.

⁵ *Metamorphoses*, book ii, pp. 457 ff. It includes also elements from the stories of Actaeon (book iii, p. 173. ff) and Alpheus and Arethusa (book v, p. 572 ff.). Boccaccio had adapted Ovid's stories to fit local topographical features in his *Ninfale Fiesolano*, and the Italian myth of locality *may* have influenced Spenser (see W. W. Greg, *Pastoral Poetry and Pastoral Drama* London 1906, pp. 36–37, 137).

⁶ I am indebted for this remark to an unpublished Cambridge thesis on translations from Ovid and Vergil during the Renaissance, by Miss Sylvia Clark.

⁷ The use of *Arcadia* by the writers of textbooks on rhetoric and logic, who produced from it so many examples to illustrate their case, would imply, I think, that the study of its technique must have been widespread among writers of all kinds. It was the technical modes provided by Sidney and Spenser which won them such especial gratitude from the *writers* of their time. K. O. Myrick, *op. cit*, thinks *Arcadia* was planned as a Heroic Poem and the *Apology* as a Classic Oration.

⁸ E.g. the Tournament at Whitehall in 1581, in which he appeared as one of the Four Children of Desire 'with armour part blue and all the rest gilt and engraven' his horses and pages dressed in cloth of gold and pearl, or cloth of silver laid with gold lace: thirty gentlemen and yeomen and four trumpeters in yellow velvet laid with silver lace: all with white buskins and white feathers in their caps, and all wearing silver scarfs embroidered with the posie, '*Sic nos non nobis*'. The account is given in Holinshed. The encounter of Phalantus and Amphialus is from Book iii of the *Arcadia* (ed. E. A. Baker, London n.d.), p. 348. Cf. the 'ostrich' caparison in Nashe's *Unfortunate Traveller* (*Works*, ed. McKerrow, vol. 2, p. 272).

⁹ This is the year of entry in the Stationers' Register, and also the year of Marlowe's death. It was published by Blunt in June 1598, and reprinted shortly after with Chapman's poem. The original issue did not divide the poem. Since the great outburst of Ovidian poetry in the years 1593–98 is clearly influenced by Marlowe, his poem must have been known almost from the date of entry, at least to the literati of the capital.

¹⁰ Cf. below, p. 65. Miss R. Tuve has an interesting passage on the image of the horse and one also on the use of Neptune as a personification of the sea (*Elizabethan and Metaphysical Imagery*, p. 103, p. 157).

¹¹ D. Bush, *Mythology and the Renaissance Literary Tradition*, p. 131.

[12] *Works of Sir Thomas Malory*, ed. E. Vinaver (Oxford 1948), vol. i, p. lxxv. Just as the allegorical mode of interpretation allowed a medieval preacher to introduce witty and sometimes improper stories into his sermons, and excite his audience's attention by the brilliant *tour de force* of his explanation, so a story traditionally comic might be modified to suit the decorum of a particular literary kind. Shakespeare's rejection of the traditional happy ending to *King Lear* (which moreover was chronicled, therefore *true*) must have appeared to his contemporaries an innovation of this kind, for they were accustomed to the older version. I can remember from my childhood a poem called 'Kate Barlass', which told the story of how Katherine Douglas barred the door against the murderers of James I by thrusting her arm through the staple—but it omitted the end of the story, in which James was dragged from the hiding place which Katherine's heroic act had given him time to discover, and stabbed to death.

[13] Some of his arguments are Aristotelian and the whole has a flavour of the medieval *suasio*. This medieval commonplace was inherited by the Elizabethans who played strange tricks with it. Parolles's attack on Virginity in *All's Well* is that of a bold sharp sophister, too, but it has been taken as serious evidence against him, and even against Hellen as his auditory. The culmination of the whole series is Comus's speech to the Lady.

[14] Rosalind and Orlando quote *Hero and Leander* (*A.Y.L.I.*, 4. 1. 103–112): so does Phoebe (3. 5. 81–82). Dover Wilson would place the first draft of this play in 1593, the year in which *Hero and Leander* was 'entered'.

[15] Particularly of course sonnets i–xix: but also xli: xlvi–xlvii for typical conceits of 'eye' and 'heart' at war: lvii, xcv, xcvi may be compared with Venus's 'doting' submission to Adonis's whims.

[16] Coleridge cites this stanza and discusses it at length in *Biographia Literaria*, chapter xv. A commentary on Coleridge is to be found in I. A. Richards's *Coleridge on the Imagination* (Kegan Paul, 1934), pp. 77–80. For a general discussion see H. T. Price, 'Functions of Imagery in Venus and Adonis' (*Papers of the Michigan Academy of Science, Arts and Letters*, xxxi (1945).

[17] See below, chapter viii, note 27. The symbol seems to be a regular one: There is a splendid emblematic example in Chapman's *Biron's Conspiracy*, 2. 2. 66–81.

[18] Statius gives it on Vergil, *Eclogue* viii, 30: also on the *Aeneid*, i. 651. It is also found in Boccaccio, *De Genealogia Deorum*, book v.

[19] D. Bush, op. cit., p. 126, quotes Abraham Fraunce in support of the torch of Hero signifying lust, and the waves in which Leander was drowned, the cold of old age, but says the interpretation is as old as Fulgentius. Teras wears a scarf of purple and black (mourning colours) (5. 68–69): the stars are yellow for jealousy (5. 171–173): the sun rises as a saffron mirror Hymen's colour) on the wedding morning (5. 407). The five torches of

the wedding procession are explained by a theory taken from Plutarch (see F. L. Schoell, *Études sur l'Humanisme continental en Angleterre* (Paris 1926), pp. 225-227): the number three is used in the last verse of the Epithalamion: Hero and Leander also theorize about numbers (4. 356-360: cf. 1. 255-258).

[20] See the passages on the torches referred to above in the text: Leander is compared with the sun (5. 17-19), so is the torch (6. 159-162): Hero's ominous scarf has a double-tongued flame on it (4. 37-111): Hymen is compared with the sun (5. 95-96, 309-310) and the nymphs with the stars (5. 171-186): Eucharis goes to church surrounded by a virgin firmament of nymphs, and looks like flame (5. 314-315).

Hero complains of her own lack of harmony (3. 199-280) yet she is aware of concord between herself and Leander: her body is harmonious and a concord (4. 26-30). Hymen's beauty has concord in it (5. 107) and he puts his 'beauties rare musick' 'with maids in concord' when he disguises himself as a maid (5. 129-130).

[21] Drayton is also of course indebted more particularly to Du Bartas, and his *Uranie*. See the notes to the *Collected Works*, ed. J. W. Hebel, K. Tillotson and B. Newdigate (Oxford 1941, vol. v, pp. 19-20).

[22] Milton must have surely known this poem. It contains the lovely word *imparadized* which he used for his Adam and Eve 'imparadized in one another's arms'.

[23] In *Christ's Victory on Earth*, part of *Christ's Victory and Triumph* (1610) Christ is not only given the conventional catalogue of lovers' charms, but presented as Ganymede or Orpheus: the Virgin weeping at the tomb is compared with Philomel, a comparison only less surprising to modern taste than that which links the Assumption with James I. Correggio has replaced Titian. Christ is depicted thus:

> His hair was black and in small curls did twine,
> As though it were the shadow of some light. . . .
> His cheeks as smooth as roses sopt in wine
> Had their red roses quenched with lilies white.
>   (*Christ's Victory on Earth*, lxv.)

[24] J. E. Spingairn, *Critical Essays of the Seventeenth Century* (Oxford 1908), vol. 2, pp. 88-89. Cowley's *Preface* to his *Poems* (1656).

Chapter V

[1] Professor T. W. Baldwin in *Shakespeare's Five Act Structure* (Urbana, 1947), and Professor Leslie Hotson in *The Dating of Shakespeare's Sonnets* (London, 1949), both wish to push back the date of composition of certain works into the eighties. But apart from the difficulty of squaring this with the

publication of e.g. *Venus and Adonis* and *The Rape of Lucrece* in 1593 and 1594 respectively (when I think they must have been newly composed) the whole feeling of poetry of the late 'eighties is such that it would be extremely difficult to imagine Shakespeare producing his work at that time, even without the added difficulty of relating this early date with the known dates in his career. I have therefore retained the traditional chronology.

² *The Laws of Ecclesiastical Polity*, i. xvi. 8.

³ By Professor Alfred Harbage, *As They Liked It* (New York, 1947), p. xi, cf. pp. 8–13.

⁴ See Edwin Muir, 'Politics and King Lear' in *Essays on Literature and Society* (London, 1949), and compare R. C. Bald, 'Edmund and Renaissance Free Thought' (*A.M.S.*, p. 337): E. C. Pettet, 'Timon of Athens, the Disruption of Feudal Morality' (*R.E.S.*, vol. xxiii, 1947, pp. 321–336) and his essay on *The Merchant of Venice* in *Essays and Studies of the English Association*, vol. xxxi, 1945. The article by Lawrence Stone cited in note 28 of chapter i above is relevant here.

⁵ See the passages quoted in note 21 to chapter ii above. The best brief account of this development of the language from the barrenness of the mid-Tudor period is that in Miss Willcock and Miss Walker's Preface to their edition of Puttenham, *Arte of Poesie*.

⁶ See below, chapter viii, for an account of this early style of Shakespeare.

⁷ It is hardly necessary to mention such works as Baldwin's *Small Latin and Less Greeke* (Illinois, 1944): Rosemund Tuve, *Elizabethan and Metaphysical Imagery* (Chicago 1947), Karl Warren, *Bacon on Communication and Rhetoric* (Chapel Hill 1943), the edition of books of rhetoric such as Hoskyns, *Directions for Speech and Style* (ed. H. H. Hudson, Princeton 1935), and the work of Professor Hardin Craig, of Professor Hereward T. Price and of Sister Miriam Joseph.

⁸ I am indebted for these examples to G. H. McKnight, *Modern English in the Making* (New York, 1928).

⁹ In 'Shakespeare and the Diction of Common Life' (British Academy Annual Shakespeare Lecture, 1941).

¹⁰ From 'The Preface to *Troilus and Cressida* containing the Grounds of Criticism in Tragedy'. The relation of the Restoration improvements of Shakespeare to their originals is a subject that repays detailed study, illustrating as it does the extraordinary decline in the richness and complexity of vocabulary (all the emendations are in the direction of a simplified, translatable, explicit statement), and the structural alterations, which provide a mathematical symmetry, and a quantity of what Dryden called 'the mechanic beauties' prove equally clearly that the older way of writing had become completely alien, and was no longer understood.

Chapter VI

[1] W. B. Yeats, 'Three Moments', *The Winding Stair* (*Collected Poems*, London 1933, p. 271).

[2] The first and best of such studies was Lily B. Campbell's *Shakespeare's Tragic Heroes, Slaves of Passion* (Cambridge, 1930).

[3] Particularly Louise C. Turner Forrest, 'A Caveat for Critics against Invoking Elizabethan Psychology', *P.M.L.A.*, lxi (1946): Lawrence Babb, 'On the Nature of Elizabethan Psychological Literature', *A.M.S.*, 509-522. Professor Babb points out that there is no agreement about such fundamental matters as the classification of the passions, or the number of spirits in the body: that the Elizabethan dramatists apply psychological concepts only intermittently to their characters: and, one might add that the newer psychological interpretation may often be imposed upon an older stage character type, with little regard for consistency.

[4] Keats, *Letters*, ed. M. Buxton Forman (Oxford 1931), vol. i, p. 77.

[5] Preface to Lewis Lavater, *Of Ghosts and Spirits Walking by Night*, edited by M. Yardley (Oxford 1929).

[6] John Leslie, *De Origine Moribus et Rebus Gestis Scotorum Libri Decem*, (Rome 1578), p. 257. Quoted by Henry Paul, 'The Imperial Theme in *Macbeth*', *A.M.S.*, p. 261.

[7] Hardin Craig, 'Trends in Modern Shakespeare Scholarship', *Shakespeare Survey II* (Cambridge, 1949), pp. 113-114.

[8] Hamlet shares this mysteriousness with Falstaff and Cleopatra: but in Hamlet alone does the contemplation of the mystery form part of the presentation of the character.

[9] See Charles Williams, *The Figure of Beatrice* (London 1943).

[10] *The Revenger's Tragedy*, (2. 2. 163-166).

[11] This subject has been discussed by S. L. Bethell, *Shakespeare and The Popular Dramatic Tradition* (Staples Press, 1944).

[12] See E. H. Gombrich, 'Botticelli's Mythology', *J.W.C.I.*, vol. viii (1945), p. 32, note 1. See also the list of authorities quoted there on the role of the spectator in painting.

[13] A medieval legend emphasized this by telling of the rood which came to life, when the figure of Christ bent forward and kissed the good knight who knelt before it. A parallel story about the stage describes how at a certain performance an unknown 'super' appeared among the devils and at the end carried off one of the players to hell.

[14] The relation between play and induction in *James IV* and the prologue to *Alphonsus of Arragon*.

[15] These figures are discussed below, chapter viii, p. 127.

[16] J. M. Stewart, *Character and Motive in Shakespeare* (Longmans, 1949) especially chapters iv and v.

[17] Cordelia is so treated in John Danby's *Shakespeare's Doctrine of Nature* (London 1949), Hermione in various works, beginning with those of Wilson Knight, and little Macduff in Roy Walker's *The Time is Free* (London 1949).

[18] This perpetually recurring habit is too widespread to require particular citation. It should be noticed that the only contemporary evidence we have of a personal reflection—the 'purge' which Shakespeare is said to have ministered to Ben Jonson—was so cunningly disguised that if it survives, it cannot be identified with any certainty. Suggestions range from Jacques to Nym.

[19] Stewart, op. cit.. p. 108.

[20] Babb, loc. cit., makes this point.

[21] I owe this example to Professor Hardin Craig, *The Enchanted Glass*, p. 17.

[22] See K. L. Lea, *Italian Popular Comedy* (Oxford 1934), vol. ii, chapter vi.

[23] The title, *A lamentable tragedy mixed full of pleasant mirth, conteining the life of Cambises King of Persia . . .* recalls *A tedious brief scene of young Pyramus and his love Thisbe: very tragical mirth.* The prologue, who tells all, speaks in the fourteener, and mentions how

But he, when sisters three had wrought to shear his vital thread,
As heir due to take up the crown Camyses did proceed

Compare:

O sisters three, come, come to me with hands as pale as milk:
Lay them in gore, since you have shore with shears his thread of silk.

And the Mother's lament over her slain child—

Is this the joy of thee I reap?
O king of tiger's brood!
O tiger's whelp, hadst thou the heart
To see this child's heart-blood?
Nature enforceth me, alas!
In this wise to deplore;
To wring my hands O wel-away,
That I should see this hour!
Thy mother yet will kiss thy lips,
Silk-soft and pleasant-white . . .

is in the manner of Thisbe lamenting over Pyramus's 'lilylips', 'cherry nose', and 'yellow cowslip cheeks'. *Cambises* is reprinted in volume iv of Hazlitt's edition of *Dodsley's Old English Plays*.

[24] Keats, *Letters*, ed. cit., vol. i, p. 72.

[25] Compare for a modern instance in real life, Katherine Mansfield, *Letters*, vol. ii, pp. 131–332:

'It seems to me that there is a great change come over the world since people like us believed in God, God is now gone for all of us. Yet we must believe and not only that, we must carry our weakness and our sin and our devilishness to somebody. I don't mean in a bad abasing way. But we must feel that we are *known*, that our hearts are known as God knew us. Therefore love to-day between lovers has to be not only human, but divine. They love each other for everything and through everything, and their love is their religion.'

The sequel is found on p. 260:

'The world as I know it is no joy to me, and I am useless in it. People are almost non-existent. This world to me is a dream and the people in it are sleepers. . . . What is important is to try to live—really live—and in relation to everything—not isolated.'

[26] See an article by the present writer, 'Marvell and the Poetry of Rural Solitude', *R.E.S.* 1941 (xvii).

[27] *The Spanish Tragedy*, 3. 3. 127: 3 *Henry VI*, 5. 6. 86: *Richard III*, 5. 3. 184.

[28] *Preface to Shakespeare* (Raleigh, *Johnson on Shakespeare*, Oxford 1908, p. 18).

[29] J. I. M. Stewart, op. cit., pp. 121–122.

[30] The facts and quotations in this paragraph are taken from G. E. Bentley, *Shakespeare and Jonson. Their reputation in the seventeenth century compared* (Cambridge and Chicago 1945, 2 vols.).

Chapter VII

[1] Ben Jonson, Induction to *Bartholomew Fair*: Gabriel Harvey, MS note in his copy of Chaucer (see *Shakespeare Allusion Book*, vol. i., p. 247 and p. 56 respectively).

[2] There are three references to the Lucrece story in *Titus Andronicus*, 2. 1. 108: 4. 1. 64: 4. 1. 91: both have in common references to Philomel. Other parallels are *Titus*, 5. 3. 171, *Lucrece*, l. 577, 2. 3. 25–26, ll. 579–580, 3. 1. 37–42, ll. 592–4, 4. 3. 45, ll. 664–665. Cf. also *Titus*, 2. 4. 36–37 and *Venus and Adonis*, ll. 330–334—a striking echo, though the phrase is perhaps proverbial.

[3] See Howard Baker, *Induction to Tragedy* (Louisiana, 1939). This book has an excellent survey of the relations of Shakespeare's early work to Sackville and Kyd. See also William Farnham, *The Medieval Heritage of Elizabethan Tragedy* (California 1936), upon which Baker draws.

[4] See below, chapter viii, p. 125.

[5] *Lust's Dominion* is reprinted in Hazlitt's Dodsley, volume XIV, from the Quarto of 1657. It was at one time attributed to Marlowe, perhaps because of the superficial likeness of the villain-hero to Marlowe's Machiavel and some echoes of Marlowe's style. It is fairly representative of the mediocre tragedy of the earlier period, violent, headlong and quite infantile in its taste for blood.

⁶ Cf. 'I count religion but a childish toy' (*Jew of Malta*, Prologue): 'My policy hath framed religion: Religion, O Diabole!' (*Massacre at Paris*, scene 2): 'So that religion of itself a bauble, was only framed to make men peacable' (*Selimus*, ll. 244–245): 'Religion is the fool's bridle, worn by policy. As horse wears trappings, to seem fair in show' (*Mulleasses the Turk*, ll. 427–428): 'Tush, mere policy, A trick, a cheat to keep the world in awe' (*The Jew's Tragedy*, 2. 2. 96–97:) 'Conscience . . . a fear they tie up fools in, Nature's coward' (*The Bloody Brother*, 4. 1).

⁷ See below, chapter viii, p. 132.

⁸ See above, chapter iv, p. 64.

⁹ *King John*, 3. 1. 43–59, 3. 4. 93–98. Cf. *Richard III*, 4. 4. 118–122.

¹⁰ Andrew Borde, *Introduction of Knowledge* (1542) Early English Text Society Pub. Extra Series 10, p. 116.

¹¹ See Appendix for the negro bond-slave of *Tom-a-Lincoln*. In spite of his faithful service this slave is buried in the earth up to the arm-pits and left to starve.

¹² The point has often been recognized by editors of *Titus Andronicus*, not so often by editors of *King Lear*.

¹³ A mark of abatement was a dishonourable sign added to the arms for some base action. It seems to have existed only in the fancy of heralds and writers on heraldry: derived perhaps from the bend sinister which was really a means of enabling nobles' bastards to bear arms. Shakespeare's knowledge of heraldry was considerable: see G. C. Rothery, *The Heraldry of Shakespeare* (London 1930). *Lucrece* contains an unusually large number of such terms: the decription of Pyrrhus in the first player's speech in *Hamlet* is also full of heraldic technicalities, e.g. 'trick'd' in the sense of blazonry. Heraldry was of course a popular subject of study among fashionable young gentlemen: Earle's undergraduate (in the *Characters*) divides his time between books of heraldry and playing tennis.

¹⁴ This parallel is also commonly noted by editors of *Lucrece*, not by editors of *Macbeth*.

¹⁵ *Lucrece*, ll. 83–84, 1219–1225, 1338–1344, 1590–1596, 1604–1608, 1716–1718, 1779–1792. The alternation of long passions and complaints with these moments of dumbness occurs also in *Titus Andronicus*.

¹⁶ *Venus and Adonis*, ll. 1063–1068. *Lucrece*, ll. 449–462.

¹⁷ I am indebted for this point to H. B. Charlton, *Shakespearean Tragedy* (Cambridge 1947).

¹⁸ *Epithalamion* was entered in November 1594 and published next year 'written not long since' according to the title page. But the envoy suggests that Spenser had been long engaged on the composition, and we have no clear record of the occasion of his second marriage: the poem tells us it was on St. Barnabas' Day.

Chapter VIII

[1] J. Dover Wilson, *The Fortunes of Falstaff* (Cambridge 1943): E. M. W. Tillyard, *Shakespeare's History Plays* (London 1944): Lily B. Campbell, *Shakespeare's Tragic Heroes* (Cambridge 1930), and *Shakespeare's Histories, Mirrors of Elizabethan Policy* (San Marino, Cal. 1947): Theodore Spencer, *Shakespeare and the Nature of Man* (Cambridge 1943): W. G. Zeeveld Articles in *E.L.H.* (1936, ii), *P.M.L.A.*, (1940, lv).

Pioneers were C. L. Kingsford, *Prejudice and Promise in Fifteenth Century England* (1928), E. Greenlaw, *Studies in Spenser's Historical Allegory* (1930) and Alfred Hart, *Shakespeare and the Homilies* (1934).

[2] Alfred Hart clearly demonstrated Shakespeare's debt to the Homilies, especially the second and the tenth, which was added after the Northern Rebellion of 1569—the only serious rising of Elizabeth's reign, which occurred in Shakespeare's childhood.

[3] A. P. Rossiter, *Woodstock, a Moral Play* (London 1946), introduction, p. 4.

[4] I think there is a real risk of applying the concepts derived from a study of Shakespeare's sources and his contemporaries too directly to the interpretation of his achievement, as distinct even from his own intentions. Nothing is clearer than that Shakespeare sometimes found out what he wanted to do in the course of doing it. The relation of his work to Marlowe's is to be discussed by Professor F. P. Wilson in his forthcoming Clark Lectures: perhaps Professor Wilson will redress the balance.

[5] See F. J. Shirley, *Richard Hooker and Contemporary Political Thought* (London 1949).

[6] 'Shakespeare's most impressive speech' is of course Ulysses' speech on degree (*Troilus and Cressida*, I. 3. 78-136), a speech which has been so much quoted as expressing the author's final views on the subject that it ought to be given a rest, or taken only in conjunction with that thoroughgoing counterblast, the King's speech in *All's Well that Ends Well* (2. 3. 124-151).

[7] *3 Henry VI*, I. 4: 2. 5: 3, 2. 124-195. A molehill was used as a kind of parody for a throne in *3 Henry VI*, I. 4. where Margaret stands the captive York upon a molehill and crowns him with a paper crown.

[8] H. T. Price, *A.M.S.*, pp. 101-114.

[9] Schemes or figures of words depend on balance and repetition of sounds, letters or clauses—alliteration, antithesis, anaphora, etc. Tropes, or images, are figures of thought. 'Pattern' I use to describe the effect of either or both these figures.

[10] *The Tree of Commonwealth* is a most interesting treatise on government. There is a modern edition by D. M. Brodie (Cambridge 1948)

The Five Alls, familiar from wood-cuts, and sometimes used as inn-signs, were: the king who rules all, the knight who fights for all, the priest who prays for all, the lawyer who judges for all and the peasant who works for all. Late forms sometimes substituted for the lawyer, an usurer who ruins all.

[11] The symbolic order of titles to the various reigns is quoted by Tillyard, loc. cit. p. 43.

[12] They also anticipate the procession which appears later between the figure of Banquo's ghost and that of Macbeth, prophesying the eventual triumph of one and ruin of the other.

[13] Anne's curse 1. 2. 1–32 recalled 4. 1. 70–86: Buckingham's 2. 1. 32–40 recalled 5. 1. 3–10. Stanley's dream 3. 2. recalled 3. 4. 79–91. Margaret's curse 1. 3. 196–233 recalled 3. 3. 14–18, 3. 4. 91–92, 4. 4. 61–78. York's curse, 3 *Henry VI* 1. 4. 111–149, recalled *Richard III* 1. 3. 174–181. His mother's curse on Richard, 4. 4. 184–196: the Ghosts' curses 5. 3. 119–177.

[14] 3 *Henry VI*, 5. 6 (Henry's prophecy and Richard's speech): *Richard III*, 1. 1. 1–40, 1. 3. 229–232, 2. 4. 16–30, 4. 4. 166–196.

[15] 1. 3. 241–301, 2. 1. 132–134, 3. 4. 102–104, 4. 2. 94–96, 1. 1. 39–40, 54–61.

[16] 1. 3., 2. 2., 4. 1., 4. 4.

[17] See F. S. Boas, *The Works of Thomas Kyd* (Oxford 1901), introduction, pp. lxxviii–lxxxiii, for a list of quotations in Shakespeare's works. The use of schemata and patterned speech was not typical of Marlowe or Greene but highly developed in Kyd (see F. G. Hubbard, 'Repetition and Parallelism in Early Elizabethan Drama', *P.M.L.A.* 20, 1905). Senecal rhetoric in Shakespeare's early histories has also been most comprehensively dealt with in two recent articles, F. R. Johnson, 'Shakespearean Imagery and Senecan Imitation' and Hardin Craig, 'Shakespeare and the History Play', both in *A.M.S.* (pp. 33–54 and 55–64 respectively).

[18] *Spanish Tragedy*, 1. 5. 79–89: *Richard III*, 1. 2. 68–80. A detailed comparison of the use of schemes in these two plays would yield many more parallels.

[19] *Spanish Tragedy*, 3. 13. 29: *Richard III*, 4. 4. 29. The only direct quotation of the earlier play by Shakespeare on this occasion.

[20] The influence of Marlowe is discussed in Hubbard's article (see note 17).

[21] 1. 1. 88–102, 1. 3. 47–53, 138–142, 310–315 (soldierly bluntness): 2. 1. 52–73, 3. 7. 103–245 (piety—which would be an added proof of his diabolic origins: for here is the devil's well-known accomplishment of transforming himself into an angel of light).

[22] 2. 2. 107–111: 1. 3. 234–240: 4. 4. 155–179. The Machiavellian villain was traditionally impervious, e.g. the unfilial Selimus.

[23] Una Ellis-Fermor, *Shakespeare the Dramatist* (*Proceedings of the British Academy*, vol. xxxiv, 1948, p. 7). Also published separately by Cumberlege, 1940.

[24] The phrase is Andrew Marvell's (*Nunappleton House*, xli); *Richard II*, 3. 2. 4–26, 3. 3. 160–169, 5.1. 76–80, 5. 2. 46–47, 5. 6. 45–46 and 1 *Henry IV*, 1. 1. 5–9.

[25] See R. D. Altick, 'Symphonic Imagery in *Richard II*', *P.M.L.A.* 1947, lxii.

[26] Cf. 3. 3. 62–67, 4. 1. 221, 260–262 and for the Boar in *Richard III*, 1. 2. 103, 1. 3. 228, 3. 2. 10–11, 28–30, 72–73, 4. 5. 2–3, 5. 2. 7–11.

[27] See e.g. Philip Sidney's description of horsemanship at the beginning of the *Defence of Poetry*, his Sonnet xlix: Chapman's Byron 'on his brave Pastrana' (*Byrons Conspiracy*, 2. 2. 66–81), which Miss R. Freeman compares with an emblem (*English Emblem Books*, London 1948, p. 6): Antonio's horsemanship as described in *The Duchess of Malfi* (1. 1. 141–146) and compare the revolt of Adonis's horse in Shakespeare's *Venus and Adonis*. Prince Hal's 'manage' is perfect (1 *Henry IV*, 4. 1. 97 ff.: *Henry V*, 5. 2. 141–147).

[28] The use of the stage crown symbolically is very prominent, e.g. in *Tamburlaine*: M. D. Anderson, *The Medieval Carver*, pp. 71–73, describes how a medieval Empress retained her crown even when she was in disguise! The Mirror for Princes, for Subjects, for London, was a common phrase: Richard takes the old phrase and by using it literally gives a strange depth to the scene. Cf. Hamlet to his mother, 'You go not, till I set you up a glass/Where you may see the inmost part of you' (3. 4. 19–20).

[29] See J. Dover Wilson's edition of the play (Cambridge, 1939), pp. xxxviii–lxxvi and the article by M. W. Black (*A.M.S.*, pp. 199–216), 'The sources of *Richard II*".

[30] Daniel's *Civil Wars* (1595) is generally recognized as one of the sources of *Richard II* and the relevant passages are printed by J. Dover Wilson, ed. cit., pp. 99–106. The popularity of narrative historical poems at this time was very great. Drayton's *Piers Gaveston* which is dated 1593–94 is a 'Mirror' poem in which the ghost of Edward II's favourite recounts his career, with, however, very little moral emphasis. It is rather a sensuous celebration of the pleasures of kingly favours, with a few perfunctory moralizings thrown in here and there. The year after the first recorded appearance of *Richard II*, 1596, Drayton issued his *Mortimeriados*, which shows the influence of *Richard II* as well as of Marlowe's *Edward II*, according to Drayton's latest editors (*Works of Drayton*, ed. H. Hebel and K. Tillotson, vol. v, p. 41). All these works on historical characters strongly emphasize what would now be called the human interest at the expense of the dynastic and moral patterns used by the chroniclers, and they appear so closely together (there are other complaints and epistles by both Daniel and Drayton which might be cited) that it seems clear that the years 1594–96 showed a particularly large crop of dramatic and non-dramatic historical poetry.

Chapter IX

[1] On the conventions of the sonnet see L. C. John, *The Elizabethan Sonnet Sequences* (New York, 1938).

[2] The fashion is continued to the present day in such ballads as 'There's No A.M.O. About Love', with the additional complication that the lady may now also have military jargon at her command, e.g. 'Oh Mary, this W.A.A.F. is a Wonderful Life':

'. . . He'd twenty E.A.s to his credit already,
So one little Waaf couldn't make him unsteady'.

[3] This sonnet has been discussed by Miss Tuve, op. cit. p. 325–326. Such equivoque is likely to appear in the most respectable writers: compare the riddles in Chapman, *Bussy d'Ambois*, 3. 2. 257, and *Byron's Tragedy*, 2. 1. 88.

[4] See Ruth Hughey, 'The Harington Manuscript at Arundel Castle', *The Library*, xv (1935).

[5] See Miss John, op. cit., pp. 126–134: and Sir Sidney Lee, *Elizabethan Sonnets* (Constable 1904), vol. i, p. lv. *cf.* note 16 to chapter ii.

[6] Though they are all part of the one persuasion to marriage, and the chief argument is the perpetuation of beauty, yet the fear of Time and 'love-devouring death' is akin to the ominous fears in *Romeo and Juliet*, the sense that beauty is vulnerable in proportion to its excellence.

[7] See Miss John, op. cit., pp. 92–102. Shakespeare uses conceits of the eye and the heart in Sonnets xxii, xxiv, xliii, xlvi, xlvii. The sleeplessness of lovers is another common theme which Shakespeare repeats. In cxiii, cxiv there is a set of conceits upon the eye and the mind, similar to those on the eye and the heart. In the sonnets to the dark lady, cxxxii and cxxxiii, cxxxix, cxli all make use of conceits on the eye and the heart.

[8] The folio text, the only authority, is apparently an assembled test, made up of actors parts and the 'plat' or scenario, The question of revision has also exercised commentators rather more I feel than is probable for a play which was evidently not very popular or very often mentioned even in early days.

[9] The 'cause' is the theme of the play, the subject *plus* the artist's intention in choosing such a subject. Dryden's discussion of the moral in his Preface to *Troilus and Cressida* is a significant misunderstanding, amounting to complete parody (see chapter iv, above). Restoration improvements of Shakespeare and other Elizabethans often have this enlightening distortion of older ways of thought and expression.

[10] See Ruth Kelso, *The Doctrine of the English Gentleman* (Urbana 1929), chap. v, 'The Moral Code'. The virtues of the courtier are discussed at length in Sir Thomas Elyot's *Book of the Governour*, being based on the Aristotelian moral virtues.

[11] This curious relic of the ancient code of courtly love is echoed even in Drayton's *Endimion and Phoebe*, where the shepherd, wooed in the most elevated and spiritual terms, 'vows secrecie, the crown of a true Lover'— not knowing as yet however that his nymph is a goddess. It is this last vow which moves Phoebe to disclose herself.

[12] Miss Kelso, loc. cit.

[13] *Politic moral and martiall discourses*, trs. Golding (1595), 2. viii. I owe this reference to Miss Kelso.

[14] See below, chapter xii, p. 219.

[15] In *Satiromastix* by Thomas Dekker (1602) and one of the plays of the Poets' War. Jonson appears at the court of William Rufus in his Roman character of Horace, the role he had assigned to himself in *Poetaster*! Heywood's *Rape of Lucrece* belongs to the next year, 1603, and is probably the worst piece of indecorum in the critical sense that the Elizabethans were ever guilty of.

[16] See F. Sidgwick, *Sources and Analogues of A Midsummer Night's Dream* (London 1908) for the connexions with *The Knight's Tale*. The general idea of juxtaposing clowns and nobles seems to me a much more significant debt than anything in the form of the plot. Bottom is surely not unrelated to Harry Bailly.

[17] This play, by Henry Porter, dates from 1598. It is reprinted in Hazlitt's *Dodsley*, vol. vii.

[18] E. Welsford, *The Court Masque* (Cambridge 1927), p. 331.

[19] E. Sharpham, *The Fleire* (1607). See *Shakespeare Allusion Book*, vol. i, p. 174.

[20] See above, chapter iii. Dr. Fian, the leader of the North Berwick Coven, wishing to bewitch a young girl to love him, tried to obtain some of her hair to make a charm, but was given instead the hairs taken from a heifer, who followed him amorously round in consequence. Compare Falstaff's 'metamorphosis' at the end of *The Merry Wives of Windsor*.

[21] E.g. the charming little 'nation of faies' in Ben Jonson's *Oberon the Fairy Prince* (1611), were acted by little girls, with the young Prince Charles in their midst.

[22] It is always said that to give the speech about Queen Mab to Mercutio is an example of dramatic incongruity, allowable because of the charm of the speech. It seems to me that a free-tongued, lively young scoffer such as Mercutio is just the kind of man likeliest to have such an innocent and imaginative fancy. Translate him into modern terms: he becomes the public-school type.

[23] *Venus and Adonis*, ll. 913–924: *Midsummer Night's Dream*, 4. 1. 125–132.

[24] There is possibly some recollection of the Sixth Eclogue, I feel, though it is not a case of parallel passages.

[25] The connexion between these two speeches has been noted by G. H. W.

Rylands, in the article 'Shakespeare the Poet', in *A Companion to Shakespeare Studies*, ed. Granville Barker and G. B. Harrison (Cambridge 1934), p. 93. Prospero's speech is of course based on Ovid (see above, chapter vi).

[26] This beautiful and interesting play, with its scraps of folk-custom, its masque-like figures and its songs was written in 1594, a year or two before Shakespeare's.

Chapter X

[1] In the following pages I have summarized my article 'Virtue is the true Nobility' *R.E.S.*, N.S., vol. I, 4 (1950). Those who are interested will find there a more extended account of the background of courtesy literature, and in particular the relation of civil nobility to Christian nobility as it is treated by the writers of courtesy books, and books of nobility.

[2] Her name is so spelt throughout the folio text. There is only one occasion on which the metre requires Helena. Shakespeare evidently took great care over his proper names; consider the way in which the diminutives Harry and Kate are used (like Jan ˑ Austen, he seems to think only the best people worthy to be called Henry): the beauty of his new forms, Desdemona and Cordelia. James Joyce erected a considerable biographic speculation upon Shakespeare's aversion from the name Richard.

[3] E.g. 4. 2. 14–30 where Diana rebukes him: 4. 3. 1–30 where the young Lords criticize him. Parolles's sonnet to Diana, 'Dian, the Count's a fool', contains some nasty hometruths. In the last scene the King and Lafeu are quite uncompromising. Bertram's word is no longer of the slightest value (5. 3. 183–185).

[4] The Countess is convinced of Hellen's virtue in the first scene (1. 1. 47–50), but not so fully of Bertram's. She loves Hellen as her own child (1. 3. 98, 143–144) and after Bertram's flight disclaims him for her son and takes Hellen as her only child (3. 2. 68–69). Lafeu's view of Bertram is never very high (2. 3. 105–108). In 4. 5. he and the Countess unite in praise of Hellen's memory and at the beginning of 5. 3. the king laments her and accuses Bertram's 'mad folly' in which he is heartily seconded by Lafeu, who joins his condemnation with still more praise of Hellen.

[5] E.g. the Countess (2. 2. 90–92), Hellen (1. 1. 112–115), Parolles is meant to be representative of the evils of the court, which are much stressed in the opening scenes. It is no longer the fount of good manners, exclusively, as it had been in *Two Gentlemen of Verona*.

[6] The formal couplets in which Hellen, after making ready to retire, suddenly returns and announces herself as a minister of Heaven mark the portentousness of the occasion. See Hardin Craig, *Shakespeare's Bad Poetry* (*Shakespeare Survey*, I; Cambridge, 1948). The automatic writing

down of such passages as 'first draft fossils' is not justified. Hellen's 'miracle' is discussed at length by Lafeu (2. 3. 1–44), it is 'a shewing of a heavenly effect in an earthly actor', as Hellen confirms (2. 3. 69) to the court.

⁷ For those younger sons of the nobility who were obliged to take to the professions, Law was considered the noblest study: the profession of arms was of course the oldest and most honourable, but it notoriously failed to supply means of livelihood. The physician was concerned with base matters, and approximated too nearly to the barber-surgeon and the apothecary to receive much honour.

⁸ John E. Mason, *Gentlefolk in the Making* (Philadelphia 1935), p. 8. This book is the most comprehensive account known to me of the doctrine of gentility.

⁹ Parolles, it should be noted, is a character entirely of Shakespeare's own invention. His alterations of his source (ultimately Boccaccio, *Il Decamerone*, 3. 9), are highly significant, tending to greater humility, and dependence on Hellen's part—in the original she has a fortune—and greater perfidy, weakness and youthfulness on Bertram's. I do not wish to suggest that *All's Well* is a morality disguised, but it is a moral play which, like *The Merchant of Venice*, depends on a central theme of ethical significance.

¹⁰ *Measure for Measure* has in common the rejection of a devoted bride for insufficiency, and a marriage compelled by the ruler: the substitution of one woman for another: the false self-accusation of the chaste woman followed by denial from the culprit and culminating in his exposure through the arrival of an absent person. The similarity between the themes is also noticeable: both plays deal with what Bacon called 'Great Place', the problems of authority, and both are moral plays; that is to say, they are concerned with general truths explicitly handled, though handled in human terms. But *Measure for Measure* seems to me to belong to a much later period: the close resemblances in plot, far from suggesting that the two plays were written close together, imply that Shakespeare returned to his earlier material when he returned to a similar theme.

¹¹ Hellen's three great speeches (1. 1. 91–110, 1. 4. 199–225, 3. 3. 102–132) have a number of parallels with the sonnets. The picture of her as a canny fortune-hunter is entirely twentieth-century, and may lead critics so far as to see in her careful disclaimer of any ambition to match with the 'royal blood of France' a vulgar foresight, rather than a due sense of rank. Elizabeth's sense of what constituted suitable matches was extremely strict: the Earl of Essex was considered to have committed a shocking impropriety by marrying the widow of Philip Sidney.

¹² See E. C. Pettit, 'The Merchant of Venice and the Problem of Usury' *Essays and Studies of the English Association*, xxxi (1945).

¹³ The point has been made by Nevil Coghill, who examines the play from this point of view in 'The Governing Idea, essays in the Interpretation of Shakespeare',—*Shakespeare Quarterly*, vol. i (1948).

[14] Not only Margaret but Tamora in *Titus Andronicus* is called a tiger on a good many occasions. The use of symbolism from animals in *King Lear* has often been commented on, e.g. by Miss Spurgeon and Wilson Knight. The relation of the 'wolf' in this speech to the execution of Lopez the Jewish physician—if such a reference were intended—does not seem to me in any way to preclude the larger significance being there as well.

[15] This momentous choice, so happy in the event, recalls that other 'lottery' in which the nobles of France stood for Hellen's choice. The words with which she gives herself to Bertram seem to have a far-off echo of the divine Portia's. The two plays are linked by a common seriousness of theme. The choice of Claudio in *Much Ado*, and the choice which Beatrice offers Benedick, are moments of great dramatic intensity in that play. The most extended discussion of the nature of choice is of course that in *Troilus and Cressida*, 2. 2.

[16] Compare the speech of Claudio to Hero below, p. 185. By exchange of sovereignties, Portia and Bassanio have reached that happy state depicted in the sonnets under the figure of exchanged hearts (see above, chapter ix).

[17] Kenneth Muir and S. O'Loughlin, in *The Voyage to Illyria*, have dealt with this subject tactfully and sensitively. The comparison of Bassanio with Bertram is I think an extremely interesting one.

[18] Gerrard de Malynes, *St. George for England, allegorically described* (1601). Those who regard Portia as the economic motive personified would do well to study this extraordinary little work. The Virgin who is the King's Treasure is threatened by a horrible dragon called Foenus Politicum, whose two wings are Usura palliata and Usura explicata, and rescued by St. George, who is the king's authority. The praise of the Virgin begins in accents that are not unfamiliar: 'Hide, *Absalon*, thy clear gilt tresses, and you *Hester*, your meekness and beauty, giving place to the Virgin and noble creature: neither you, *Lucrece* and *Polyxene*, *Dido*, *Laodamia* or *Tisbe*, that have bought your love so dear. . . .' Later it takes another strain: 'She is the rose of the field and the lily of the valley. . . .'

[19] It is clear that Don John has been fighting his brother and that this has been the subject of the recent wars: Don John hates Claudio because he won glory in the wars by Don John's overthrow (1. 3. 67–71): Don John is virtually a released prisoner of war. This might have been made plain in the staging. His bastardy, which explains his malignity, is not revealed till Act 5, but it should be clear from the way he is treated that he is not really thr heir of Arragon.

[20] Borachio says that they shall hear him call Margaret Hero and hear Margaret term him Claudio (2. 2. 44–45). It would not help the plot to hear Margaret call him Claudio: but it suggests that she will wear her mistress's clothes and use her name in the kind of court game that is familiar from courtesy books and other plays (e.g. *Cynthia's Revels*), i.e. she will

assume a character as a kind of masquerade (that of the bride of to-morrow)
in order to be courted with a more highflown set of compliments by her
sweetheart. If this is the explanation, Leonato seems to be right in dropping
his first view that Margaret was an accomplice (5. 1. 309–312) and accepting
that she was in fault against her will (5. 4. 4–6). But the whole point is left
extremely vague.

²¹ In his book on Shakespeare in the Home University Library series.

²² See below, chapter xii, for an example from Lyly of sparring between
rustic lovers.

²³ Arbaces is the hero of *A King and No King*, Ordella the heroine of
Thierry and Theodoret.

²⁴ The unwilling lover had been studied already in Berowne: see below,
chapter xii.

²⁵ See below, chapter xii.

²⁶ At first 'attired in wonder', Benedick is apparently convinced by the
Friar, as the first words of his colloquy with Beatrice show, that Hero is
innocent: it follows, as Beatrice convinces him, that Claudio must have
wronged her.

²⁷ See below, chapter xi, note 28, for other examples of 'seeming'.
Claudio like Posthumus is to be converted simply by the beauty of Hero as
it survives in his memory, and his conversion will depend on the strength
of his first impressions conquering his 'knowledge'. Compare Othello as
he looks at the sleeping Desdemona:

> Be thus when thou art dead, and I will kill thee
> And loue thee after.

²⁸ E.g. 1. 1. 35–36. It is Hero who convicts Beatrice in the end by producing the poem stolen from her pocket, containing her affection unto
Benedick.

Chapter XI

¹ See 'Shakespeare's Sources' in *A Companion to Shakespeare Studies*
(Cambridge 1934), and 'the Unity of *Henry IV*', *A.M.S.*, pp. 199–216
respectively. Cf. Tillyard, *Shakespeare's History Plays*, p. 237, for a statement
of the opposite case. Dr. Tillyard feels that because in 2 *Henry IV* Shakespeare quotes 'from the history play before last' (i.e. *Richard II*), this implies
that 'Shakespeare knew what he was doing from the beginning and
deliberately planned this stylistic contrast' between *Richard II* and *Henry IV*.
It seems to me that to 'keep in touch' with earlier work is not at all incompatible with change of plan, improvising, changes of interest even:
and to turn Shakespeare into a deliberate planner like Ben Jonson or
Chapman seems contrary to what testimony of the nature of his composition we have. As I have said above, I think Shakespeare found out what

he wanted to do in the course of doing it. These links I take to be in the nature of the connecting thread in a necklace rather than pillars of the structure.

[2] Henry IV's soliloquy, 2 Henry IV, 3. 1. 1–31, looks back to Henry VI and forward to Henry V on the cares of kingship: 1 Henry IV, 3. 2. 39–85, recalls Richard II: 1 Henry IV, 1. 1. 1–18, 2 Henry IV, 3. 1. 78–79, 4. 5. 132–136, 182–197, lament the usurpation and look back to Richard's prophecy in the deposition scene.

[3] His first appearance in battle occurred in 1378, when Bolingbroke was eleven years old.

[4] See the edition of J. D. Wilson (Cambridge 1947) pp. XX–XIV. Henry, like Essex in the Chorus to Act V, conquers usurping rebels.

[5] The use of a historical setting for the serious plot in plays like Fair Em or Satiromastix is quite different, and has no real bearing on the course of the play. But in the plays mentioned, the national feeling is very much alive. A full study of the comical history is long overdue.

[6] George-a-Greene (Works of Robert Greene, vol. i), 1. 2. Cf. Henry V, 5. 1., Sir John Oldcastle, 2.1.

[7] George-a-Greene, 5. 1. Cf. Henry V, 4. 1.

[8] E. K. Chambers, Elizabethan Stage, vol. ii, p. 217: vol. iv, p. 180.

[9] Famous Victories, ed. W. C. Hazlitt (Shakespeare's Library, 1875), vol. v, p. 335. Dover Wilson makes a slip (Fortunes of Falstaff, p. 138, note 20), in saying that the scene where Hal strikes the justice does not occur.

[10] Ed. cit., p. 339.

[11] Ed. cit., p. 349. The religious overtones are entirely lacking (see below).

[12] A. Quiller Couch, Shakespeare's Workmanship (Cambridge 1918), p. 148.

[13] See V. O. Freeburg, Disguise Plots in Elizabethan Drama. (New York, 1915.)

[14] 1 Henry IV, 1. 2. 67–77: Falstaff thinks at first the Prince means the Chief Justice's place, it may be noted, but the prince quickly disabuses him.

[15] See R. Kelso, The Doctrine of the English Gentleman (Urbana 1929), p. 87, quoting Guazzo.

[16] It is this continual ironic detachment and baiting of his companions which suggests that the opening soliloquy should not be read entirely as if it were a Senecan prologue, which shed no light on the real character of the Prince, but was purely expository like the opening speech of Richard III. For the speech leaves a very strong impression. It is the only occasion when we are allowed to see into the mind of Prince Hal, until his soliloquy on the battlefield at Shrewsbury.

[17] Lawrence Babb, 'On the Nature of Elizabethan Psychological Literature', A.M.S., p. 514.

[18] Tillyard, Shakespeare's History Plays, p. 278. The connexion of

Prince Hal with the books on courtesy need working out—such books as Castiglione's and Guazzo's, and Sir T. Elyot's *Book of the Gouernour*, where he is cited as an example of Placability (book ii, chap. vi), for submitting to Gascoigne.

[19] In this Prince Hal is following the dictates of Berowne in his famous speech, 'Have at you then, affection's men at arms' (*Love's Labour's Lost*, 4. 3. 290–364) in which he preaches the advantages of learning from experience rather than by precept.

[20] William Empson, *Some Versions of Pastoral* (London, 1935), pp. 43–46.

[21] *A.M.S.*, p. 429–438. Incidentally one of the best later reincarnations of Riot is Ben Jonson's Comus in his masque, *Pleasures Reconciled to Vertue*. Comus, 'ye god of cheer or ye belly', has some physical traits of Falstaff and is brought in with a randy song.

[22] This does not mean that such discussions may not lead to interesting reflections by the way. But to use a fixed (although highly ambiguous) term such as cowardice is to defeat his peculiar mode of living, which is by the technique of evasion.

[23] The comparison was made by Empson, loc. cit. Hal has something in common with Bassanio.

[24] 2 *Henry IV*, 1. 2. 6–32, 3. 2. 324–369, 4. 3. 92–136.

[25] See note 21 above.

[26] In real life war has brought together all sorts of people who became very good friends in the mess, or the office, or the factory, but who found when they tried to renew the acquaintance outside that they really had had nothing in common except what the very special circumstances had provided.

[27] Cf. *Richard III*, where there is a pathetic effect in the titles given to the boy king by his little brother: 'Richard of York! how fares Our loving brother?' 'Well, my dread lord: so must I call you now' (3. 1. 96–97). The effect is heightened by the mock respectfulness of Richard Gloucester and Buckingham towards the boy, but it is a reminder that even within his own family the king was set apart. Hence the sense of distance between Prince Hal and his own father.

[28] *Seeming* is a word which had an evil colouring for Shakespeare: it is used of Angelo, in *Measure for Measure;* by Hamlet, 'Seems! madam, nay it is', by Othello, 'Certain, men should be what they seem': and by Claudio in *Much Ado* and Posthumus in *Cymbeline* when they are convinced of their ladies' disloyalty. See above, chapter x.

[29] In his remorse and guilt, the usurper's portion.

[30] See his own words to the king (1 *Henry IV*, 3. 2. 132–152), which may be coloured by the memory of the practical joke in the earlier play (it comes from Stow originally).

[31] For Sir Charles Percy, see *Shakespeare Allusion Book*, vol. i. pp. 86–87.

[32] Mainly expressive of mortality, e.g., Mrs. Quickly's words at the end

of the second Boar's Head scene (2 *Henry IV*, 2. 4. 219–222), and in Justice Shallow's epitaph on old Double (3. 2. 47–58).

[33] *Henry V* (4. 1. 309–311).

[34] *Henry V* (5. 2. 342–356).

[35] Loc. cit., p. 313.

[36] Reprinted in the *Shakespeare Apocrypha*. It was first printed in 1596. The most remarkable parallel with Shakespeare is the line 'lilies that fester smell far worse than weeds' (2. 2. 451, cf. Sonnet xciv). There are however many other parallels.

[37] The wooing of the Countess of Salisbury was also handled by Drayton in his *Heroical Epistles*.

[38] *Edward III*, 3. 4., 3. 9.: *Henry V*, 4. 3., 4. 7.

[39] *Henry V*, 1. 2. 103–110, 156–164, 2. 4. 48–64, 4. 7. 96–100.

Chapter XII

[1] See F. Yates, *A Study of Love's Labour's Lost* (Cambridge 1936).

[2] Miss K. M. Lea, *Italian Popular Comedy* (Oxford 1934, 2 vols.), does not consider that the influence of the *Commedia dell' Arte* is so marked as in *The Comedy of Errors* and *The Merry Wives of Windsor* which she singles out as the most Italianate of the canon in this respect. But Armado and Holofernes are constantly referred to as 'Braggart' and 'Pedant' in the speech-headings. In the *commedia dell' arte*, the comic group of characters wore masks.

[3] See below, pp. 227–8.

[4] Sonnet cxiii. See above, chapter I, p. 16.

[5] This song was inserted into *As You Like It* when the play was revived in 1740.

[6] O. J. Campbell, *Shakespeare's Satire* (Oxford 1943), chapter iii.

[7] See above, chapter iii, for a set of wit between these pages and a waiting maid.

[8] Sidney, *Apology for Poetry*, ed. cit,. pp. 176–177.

[9] In this of course they are a development of the lovers of *Much Ado About Nothing*, which is usually considered an immediate predecessor of *As You Like It*. But in Benedick and Beatrice the comic and the heroic alternate, and the audience's feelings vary. Rosalind and Orlando are never called upon for such serious business as the church scene demands: nor are the jests which Rosalind plays on Orlando as significant as those played on the earlier lovers.

[10] Lodge's *Rosalynde* belongs to the pastoral tradition, where such figures as William and Corin would be quite out of place: its decorum is simple and consistent, and the story was designed, according to Professor Sisson in *Thomas Lodge and some other Elizabethans* (Harvard 1933), in part as a

'shadowing' of Lodge's position as disinherited younger brother. Certainly the early scenes at the home of the two brothers are written in a vigorous, natural prose style, but the wooing scenes in the Forest of Arden are written in the high courtly style.

[11] For an exhaustive account of the sources and analogues of this speech see S. C. Chew, 'This strange eventful History' (*A.M.S.*, pp. 157–182).

[12] Jaques's moralizing upon the deer—parodied by Touchstone's moralizing upon Time—has all the features of an emblem: such for example as that which Camillo finds thrown in at his window in *The White Divel* (2. 1.) and which plays on the inevitable horn-joke with which Jaques later plays—in forgetfulness of his emblem—as he meets the foresters after they have actually killed a buck. The only purpose of this scene (4. 2.) is to introduce by the song a contrast to the earlier occasion. Compare the use of the horse and hare in *Venus and Adonis*. Touchstone's nearest approach to an oration is his speech on the Horn (3. 3. 50–67), which perhaps converts Jaques from his original serious moralizing to a more frivolous view of the woes of the deer.

[13] *Vincentio Saviolo his practise*, (1595) by the famous London fencing master, was a highly popular book, which gave the Italian code for ordering duels and may be the cause also of Mercutio's hard words about those who fight by the book.

[24] Compare Chapman's *Humourous Day's Mirth* (1599) where the play concludes with a lottery, in which Fortune tells the future of all the characters. The melancholy man of this play, Dowsecar, has at first some resemblance to Jaques, but is cured of his melancholy by love at first sight.

[15] See 4. 1. 1–31 which Professor Campbell reads in the light of the Duke's previous taxation of Jaques (2. 7. 64–69) for his libertine practices.

[16] See above, chapter xi. There is a good deal of Robin Hood's ingenuity in fighting and defiance of the law in the early part of Lodge's *Rosalynde*, and Adam Spencer as he is there presented is almost like the Adam of the old ballad, a stout man at his weapon.

[17] The point is made by Q in his preface to the Cambridge *New Shakespeare* (p. ix).

[18] See note 10 above.

[19] There is one significant exception: Malvolio's day-dream includes 'having come from a day-bed where I left Olivia sleeping' (2. 5. 54–56) and when Olivia, in concern at his madness, says, 'Wilt thou go to bed, Malvolio?' he replies rapturously, 'To bed! ay, sweetheart and I'll come to thee' (3. 4. 33–34). Just a touch of lechery behind the mask of the well-trained upper-servant.

[20] As played by the Marlowe Society in the summer of 1949, an eighteenth-century Sir Toby, attended by a spaniel-wigged Sir Andrew, was most convincing. As for modern Sir Tobys, they are to be found in the pages of Somerville and Ross, in plenty.

[21] Chapman's plays are full of extremely biting jests: but indeed Portia's trick of the ring, played on her newly-married husband, is somewhat outrageous by modern standards.

[22] Keats, *Letters*, ed. cit., vol. i, p. 245.

Appendix

See Joan Evans, *History of English Jewels* (London 1921) for a detailed description of the Darnley Jewel.

[2] Reprinted in Norman Ault's *Elizabethan Lyrics* (London 1925), p. 389.

[3] *The Arcadia*, ed. cit., p. 57.

[4] Chapman, *Poems*, ed. Phyllis Bartlett (Oxford 1941), pp. 70–71.

[5] S. Daniel, *Poems*, ll. 372–413 (ed. A. C. Sprague, Harvard 1930), pp. 51–52.

[6] See R. Freeman, *The English Emblem Book* (London 1948), pp. 94–95, for discussion and illustration of an embroidered jacket, said to have belonged to Queen Elizabeth and now in the Victoria and Albert Museum, which is decorated with designs taken from Whitney's *Choice of Emblems*. Cf. the portrait of Elizabeth by Zucchero at Hatfield where she is shown in a dress painted with emblems. Puttenham in his *Arte of English Poesie* (1589) talks of emblems, 'a Deuise, such as man may put into letters of gold and send to his mistresses for a token or cause to be embroidered in scutcheons of arms, or in any bordure of a rich garment to giue by his noueltie maruell to the beholder' (*Elizabethan Critical Essays*, ed. G. Gregory Smith, Oxford, 1906, vol. ii, p. 106).

[7] Or Walton's *Thealma and Clearchus*, if we are to believe H. J. Oliver (*Review of English Studies*, vol. 25, 1949). The poem is reprinted by Saintsbury in his *Minor Caroline Poets* (Oxford 1906, vol. 2).

[8] *Early English Prose Romances*, ed. W. J. Thoms (Routledge, n.d.), pp. 658–659.

[9] A. H. Gilbert, *The Symbolic Persons in the Masques of Ben Jonson* (Durham, North Carolina, 1948), gives a detailed account of these figures and reproduces a large number of illustrations from Cesare Ripa's *Iconologia*, which codified the appearance of allegorical virtues and vices.

INDEX

A. SHAKESPEARE'S WORKS

B. GENERAL